Screens and Veils

T0326742

NEW DIRECTIONS IN NATIONAL CINEMAS

Jacqueline Reich, editor

Screens and Veils

Maghrebi Women's Cinema

Florence Martin

INDIANA UNIVERSITY PRESS *Bloomington & Indianapolis*

This book is a publication of

INDIANA UNIVERSITY PRESS
601 North Morton Street
Bloomington, IN 47404–3797 USA

iupress.indiana.edu

Telephone orders 800–842–6796
Fax orders 812–855–7931

*Manufactured in the
United States of America*

*Library of Congress
Cataloging-in-Publication Data*

Martin, Florence, [date]
    Screens and veils : Maghrebi women's
cinema / Florence Martin.
        p. cm. – (New directions in national
cinemas)
    Includes bibliographical references and
index.
    ISBN 978-0-253-35668-0 (cloth :
alk. paper) – ISBN 978-0-253-22341-8
(pbk. : alk. paper) 1. Motion pictures
– Africa, North – History – 20th
century. 2. Motion pictures – Africa,
North – History – 21st century. 3.
Women motion picture producers and
directors – Africa, North. 4. Motion
pictures – Social aspects – Africa, North.
5. Women in motion pictures. 6. Africa,
North – In motion pictures. I. Title.
    PN1993.5.A35M37 2011
    791.430961 – dc22

                            2011006527

1 2 3 4 5   16 15 14 13 12 11

To the brave men and women of Tunisia who dare speak their minds

To Robin

Contents

Acknowledgments

"Gratefulness" shares with "grace" the generous Latin root of *gratia*, whose variegated sphere of meanings includes thanks, charm, even pleasure. What a delight it is to share gratefulness with all of you, who have been so giving of your stories, articles, ideas, laughter, love, companionship, films, enthusiasm, patience, meals, even your homes with me all the way to the end of this book. The book took several years in the making, during which I lost two of my dearest, wittiest conversationalists: my father, Roger-Marc Martin, and my mentor, Michel Fabre. Both of these losses have left my world askew and strangely muted, and I wish to honor their missed smiles and fatherly voices here.

For his careful, smart editing and deep friendship, my thanks go first and foremost to John Boughton, an extraordinary reader and interlocutor without whose patience and brains this book would be a pale and awkward shadow of its present form. For their friendship, readings, encouragement, and careful comments, I wish to thank from the bottom of my heart Susan Hayward, Isabelle Favre, and Maryse Fauvel, as well as "the reading group" – Mark Ingram, Dan Marcus, Antje Rauwerda, John Turner – and, of course, Mifa Martin. For their generosity in sharing films, insights, laughter, meals, coffee, and friendship, I wish to warmly thank Selma Baccar, Farida Benlyazid, Sonia Chamkhi, Nadia El Fani, and Naceur Sardi. For their unfailing help in everything in Tunis and their *chaleur humaine* in the dead of winter, I wish to thank my Tunisian family: Lotfi, Amel, Firasse, and Ward Mallek. For his amazing resources and knowledge, my gratitude goes to Taoufik Thamri, without whom large parts of the history of Tunisian cinema would remain a mystery to me.

This book would not have been possible without several summer grants from Goucher College, or without my dear student Anndal Narayanan's help on the appendix. I am also indebted to the editors of *Studies in French Cinema Journal,* who gave me permission to use and revise an article published in their journal ("Transvergence and Cultural Detours: Nadia El Fani's *Bedwin Hacker* (2002)," vol. 7, no. 2, 2007: 119–129) and to Yoram Allom, who authorized the use of extensive passages from a chapter I contributed to Gönül Dönmez-Colin's anthology *The Cinema of North Africa and the Middle-East* ("*Bab al-samah Maftouh /A Door to the Sky,* Farida Benlyazid, Morocco/Tunisia/France, 1988," London: Wallflower Press, 2007, 123–132).

Finally, this book, at long last in your language, is dedicated to you, Robin, you who opened your arms wide so I could fly away for months at a time to do research overseas, and who closed them back on me at the end of each journey.

Screens and Veils

Maghrebi Women's Transvergent Cinema

For over three decades now, women from the Maghreb (i.e., Algeria, Morocco, and Tunisia) have directed unique films, full of cultural revelations and allusions. The purpose of this book is to show, through the close analysis of seven specific films as exemplars of Maghrebi women's production (two Algerian, two Moroccan, and three Tunisian), how these directors have developed original, innovative filmic languages. The study of two pioneering works, Assia Djebar's *Nuba nisa al djebel Shnua/La Nouba des Femmes du Mont Chénoua/The Nuba of the Women of Mount Chenoua* (Algeria, 1978) and Farida Benlyazid's *Bab al-sama maftouh/Une Porte sur le ciel/A Door to the Sky* (Morocco, 1998), opens the way to the study of five much more recent films: Yamina Bachir-Chouikh's *Rachida* (Algeria, 2002), Raja Amari's *As Sitaar al Ahmar/Satin rouge/Red Satin* (Tunisia, 2002), Nadia El Fani's *Bedwin Hacker* (Tunisia, 2002), Yasmine Kassari's *L'Enfant endormi/The Sleeping Child* (Morocco, 2004), and Selma Baccar's *Khochkhach/Fleur d'oubli/Flower of Oblivion* (Tunisia, 2006).

Most Maghrebi women directors have been trained in France and reside at the intersection of various cultural groups to which they can claim affiliation: for example, their gender, their ethnicity, their class, their education (perhaps in France, perhaps elsewhere), their language(s) (Arabic, French, Tamazight, or other), their citizenship of a nation in the northern part of Africa, their affiliation to a region, history, and Muslim culture. Their transcultural position and agility allow them to craft unique images of their own despite two oppressive, patriarchal systems of representation of women: a global one derived from Hollywood and the traditional regional male one.

This project answers three needs: the first is to study Maghrebi women's films as a cohesive yet diverse body of work emanating from particular cultural confluences; the second, to learn from their practice/ praxis – rather than examining these films through a ready-made, at times ill-fitting, Western theoretical framework; the third, to give visibility to Maghrebi cinema (and in particular to Maghrebi women's cinema), often absent from studies in "African cinema"[1] (usually sub-Saharan) or treated as a mere footnote in "Arabic cinema" (usually "Middle Eastern"),[2] and, recently, a subset of Mediterranean women's cinema.[3]

This study frames its object in what is commonly called the Maghrebi "postcolonial" era and locus. This first chapter lays out the main entries into the topic, by mapping its territory, by critically evaluating the various theoretical tools at our disposal, and by envisioning how this regional cinema can constitute a "cinema of transvergence," that is, a cinema that traverses various cultures and both borrows from and resists the discourse that each of these cultures proposes. Finally, this overture traces regional cultural traditions and their influences on women's narrative and discursive strategies. In the wake of the latter I hope to show how today's filmmakers use the screen to project women-made images of women and play with the polysemy of the hijab.

MAPPING THE MAGHREB

The Maghreb as Locus

1. *al maghrib:* literally, "where the sun sets," "the West," or "Morocco," the westernmost country in North Africa.
2. "The Union of the Arab Maghreb": North Africa minus Egypt (Mauritania, Morocco, Algeria, Tunisia, and Libya, united by a treaty ratified in Marrakech in 1989).
3. "Maghreb": another term for "North Africa" (the former colonizers' name for the region) that comprises Morocco, Algeria,

and Tunisia united by a common official language, Arabic, and a still widely used second one, French (not forgetting the indigenous Berber languages spoken by various groups throughout the region).

Geographically, let alone geopolitically, the name "Maghreb" is thus fraught with ambiguity. For some (as Dönmez-Colin points out[4]), it comprises Morocco, Algeria, Tunisia, and Libya. In my study, the Maghreb will designate the region comprising Tunisia, Algeria, and Morocco, a region under Berber, Arabic, and French cultural influence, on the *western* margins of the Muslim world centered on Mecca. Away from *al mashreq*, the sacred East of Mecca, and the Gulf (which we call the "Middle East"), it might be considered the outlying post of the "Arabo-Muslim" world – a term that is relentlessly used (and abused) as a vague and monolithic construct to encompass a large diverse and complicated region.[5] Beyond languages (neighboring Arabic dialects, Tamazight – Berber languages – and French), history (in which French colonial occupation played a crucial role), and religion (illustrated by the soundscape of the muezzin's call five times a day), these three Maghrebi nations also share a similar visual landscape (the lush, green shores to the north, and the Sahara desert to the south), ways of life, economic circumstances, and authoritarian political regimes. Furthermore, as we shall see, they share a history of filmmaking that attempted to give each newly independent nation its *grand récit* (something that Mauretania or Libya, for instance, do not share).

Tunisian film professor and critic Tahar Chikhaoui sees in the name "Maghreb" a significant clue to the identity malaise of the entire region. For if it is the West in the eyes of most of the Arabs from the (Middle) East, it is most certainly South of another "West": Europe. It is a region with a plural affiliation: to Muslim practices and cultural customs inherited from an Arabic past on the one hand, and to mostly French-inflected secular values on the other. While the name "Maghreb" spells out the Arabic cultural affiliation of the region, it also asserts the latter's will to deny or transcend its recent French, colonized history:

> The problem with "Maghrebi cinema" also has to do with the adjective. It supposes an identity that this cinema (still) does not have, the adjective, like the

substantive from which it derives, expressing a wish more than designating a reality. In reality, the Maghreb is constructed on the denial of the colonial expression "Northern Africa." The North (of Africa) became the West (of the Arab world), and, in a *soft* form of retaliation on the part of history, what had hitherto belonged to the Third World now became part of the South. This semantic puzzle tells a lot about the situation. The frenetic force of the Arab identity claim highlights, *a contrario,* the influence of the French and more generally speaking Western culture. It does not erase it.[6]

Hence the very site of "Maghrebi cinema," steeped in a complex interplay of denials, desires, and identity quests, while puzzling to the onlooker, might also reflect the bias of that onlooker's own origin: a French person will understand it one way, an Egyptian another. Yet there is something undeniably common in the three countries of the Maghreb: their cinema has been the political battleground (even before independence) between – to use a shorthand – Arab and French influences. Before independence, in the 1940s and 1950s, the French were trying to promote, as a last resort, a local cinema to succeed their own colonial one and counter that of Egypt. "By seeking to create a Maghrebi cinema, they were trying to preserve the countries of the Maghreb from the influence of the Arabo-Muslim nationalism and its independentist goals."[7]

One further complication emerges with its other locator: the Mediterranean. With its feet in the sea of Odysseus, Queen Elissa (Dido), and Caesar, the Maghreb has hosted numerous guests and invaders from various cultures. As Woodhull notes, "Conquests by Romans, Arabs, Ottoman Turks, French and Italians make of the Maghreb . . . a veritable mosaic of cultures,"[8] inscribed in the texture of its landscape dotted with the architectural remains of previous occupiers. The Maghreb does not erase the traces of its past: it leaves them exposed or recycles them, as the masons of Carthage did, building some of their houses with the old stones of previous temples and abodes. Rather than removing these traces, it either changes them to fit its own needs or integrates them into its cities and countryside, as well as into the gestures of contemporary rituals inherited from ancestral traditions. It is against the nurturing backdrop of this long-established custom of constant cultural recycling that filmmakers create their own narratives and images. The plural culture of the Maghreb, as we shall see, distinctly inflects cinema in its aesthetics, narrative, rhythm, and discourse.

Finally, the Maghreb hosts other very significant groups: the Ima-zighen (the masculine, plural form of "Amazigh": "the free men" – Berbers), who have lived there since pre-Islamic times (in "Barbary" long before the latter became the Maghreb), and who still have distinct languages and cultures, especially in Morocco and, to a lesser degree, in Algeria; their presence has dwindled in Tunisia so that only a few Amazigh languages survive today on the island of Jerba and in the vil-lages of the Matmata.[9] After independence, the states of Algeria and Morocco wanted to arabicize the population, thereby marginalizing the various Amazigh languages.[10] Moroccan and Algerian Imazighen num-ber in the millions and have resisted these state-driven linguistic and cultural policies. In Algeria, after several severely repressed Imazighen revolts starting in 1980, the constitution was amended on April 10, 2002, in order to declare Tamazight a national language. In Morocco, the lan-guage was introduced in primary education, and Amazigh film festivals such as the ones in Casablanca and in Agadir now pepper the landscape. Several filmmakers in the Maghreb have been making films in Berber languages, for instance, Abderrahmane Bouguermouh, *La Colline Ou-bliée/The Forgotten Hill* (Algeria, 1997), and Azzedine Meddour, *La Mon-tagne de Baya*/Baya's Mountain (Algeria, 1997). While the survival of the Amazigh languages is still in question, Maghrebi cinema has given a new impulse and recognition to the Berber cultures and contributed to an acknowledgment of a Berber, transnational, plural culture that expresses itself in songs and films in and outside the Maghreb.

Interestingly enough, today's Moroccan women filmmakers in par-ticular seem to be taking up the Amazigh cause by shooting their films in the local Berber language – fighting for a double recognition as women and Berbers. Hence 80 percent of the dialogues in Narjiss Nejjar's film, *Les Yeux Secs/Cry No More* (Morocco, 2003), for instance, are in Berber. We shall analyze one such film, in Arabic and Berber, in this study: Yas-mine Kassari's *The Sleeping Child* (Morocco, 2004 – see chapter 6).

Finally, let's not forget the presence of an old and vibrant Jewish community and its contribution to the multiethnic fabric of the Maghreb over centuries – in the wake of two main waves of immigration, one dating back to the foundation of Carthage (800 BC) and the second to the Reconquista (i.e., the expulsion of Muslims and Jews from Spain in

1492), before the more recent waves of European Jewish immigrants to North Africa at the turn of the twentieth century. In the 1940s, Constantine in Algeria and Fez in Morocco had such thriving Jewish districts that both cities were (independently) dubbed "Maghreb's Little Jerusalem."[11] However, the creation of Israel, the independence of the three countries, and most recently the second intifada and 9/11 caused the departure of many Jews from the Maghreb.[12]

Over time, some elements of the Berber and the Sephardic Jewish cultures, ranging from cooking to religious practices, fused (as they did throughout the Arab world). Certain beliefs peripheral to the central religious institutions are strikingly similar: devotions around rabbis' tombs mirror the devotions to Muslim *marabouts* ("holy" men endowed with magic powers) and recourse to talismans and magic is shared by both Muslim and Jewish segments of the population (e.g., the Hamza, or Hand of Fatma, to ward off the evil eye). Two filmmakers who reside in France have documented such an integration of cultures and given visibility to the Sephardic Maghrebi culture: Karin Albou, a filmmaker of Algerian origin who shoots fictions around Jewish Sephardic identities in the Maghreb,[13] and Moroccan director Izza Génini (see appendix B, Primary Filmography), whose oeuvre is entirely devoted to documenting Maghrebi Jewish culture.

The site of our inquiry – Maghrebi women's cinema – is thus replete with strata of meaning to be decoded, histories to be unearthed, personal and collective longings and cultural postures to be identified. Furthermore, its initial layered complexity echoes in the modes, funding, and processes of Maghrebi women directors' production, as we shall see below.

Mapping Women's Cinema(s) in the Maghreb

Where does cinema take place in the Maghreb? Where is it produced? Where is it shown? Where is it discussed? Who funds it? When did it start? These questions receive answers that are regional and national. The territory of Maghrebi women's cinema is both spatial and temporal: the directors started to make films shortly after the independence of their respective countries, often in the margins of national production,[14] yet women's film production has grown by leaps and bounds only over the past two decades or so. This territory is clearly illustrated in appendixes A and B at the end of this book, which offer a chronology of Maghrebi women's cinema alongside a political one (which includes the dates of the main laws pertaining to women's rights in each country) and a detailed primary filmography.

Originally, immediately after independence, the main source of funding and the main locus of production for each of the Maghrebi national cinemas (those made by both male and female directors) was the state in each country, but not equally so. While Tunisia (independent in 1956) and Algeria (independent in 1962) became republics that used cinema to fashion and broadcast a new *grand récit* of their nation against the recent French colonial one, Morocco (independent in 1956) was a monarchy whose national narrative was already solidly anchored. In the first years of independence, women filmmakers were a tiny minority who competed with a large majority of male directors for film production funding in a Third-World economy. "As is the case with First World cinema, women's participation within Third World cinema has hardly been central, although their growing production since the 1980s corresponds to a worldwide burgeoning movement of independent work by women made possible by the new, low-cost technology of video communication."[15] The first Maghrebi feature films by women are Selma Baccar's *Fatma 75* (Tunisia, 1976 – see chapter 7), Assia Djebar's *Nuba of the Women of Mount Chenoua* (Algeria, 1978 – see chapter 1), and Farida Bourquia's *Al jamra/La Braise/The Ember* (Morocco, 1982).[16] As will be more fully discussed in each case study, the sources of funding for films are diverse, and have changed over the years since independence. In each of the three countries, the government originally controlled the shaping and funding of film production as well as its distribution.

> In each of the three countries a state monopoly within the ministry of information and culture was established after independence: ONCIC [Office National du Commerce et de l'Industrie Cinématographiques/National Bureau of Film Industry and Trade] in Algeria, CCM [Centre Cinématographique Marocain/Moroccan Cinema Center] in Morocco, and SATPEC [Société Anonyme Tunisienne de Production et d'Expansion Cinématographiques/Non-Profit Tunisian Production and Cinema Development Company] in Tunisia. These organizations controlled the import, distribution, and exhibition of films, as

well as production. They were the censorship bodies, controlled access to the profession, and, when and where state funding was available, they distributed this too.[17]

Over the past fifty years or so, the shape of the governmental control has changed in each country, however: the CAAIC (a more recent incarnation of ONCIC) no longer exists, while private production companies have multiplied in Algeria;[18] and the SATPEC has been abolished in Tunisia, but the government still aids and controls cinema via the Ministry of Culture.[19] In each country, the state TV channels have also played a crucial part in coproducing and, of course, airing the films made in the Maghreb. However, films are expensive, and the financial aid given by these institutions at home cannot cover the full cost of the production (and postproduction). Filmmakers also appeal to governmental funding agencies abroad such as the Fonds Sud (Funds for the South) in France – in turn funded by, among others, the French Ministry of Foreign Affairs, the French Ministry of Cooperation and Culture, and the CNC – Centre National Cinématographique/National Cinematographical Center; the French Ministry of Culture; the Belgian Ministry of Culture; and TV channels such as Belgian, German, and French state TV channels, as well as Arte or Canal +. They also apply to private European foundations such as the Fondation Gan pour le cinéma (Gan Cinema Foundation) or the Fondation Beaumarchais in France, the Hubert Balls Fund in the Netherlands, and Montecinemaverita or Stanley Thomas Johnson in Switzerland.[20] Debates have been raging in Maghrebi cinema circles opposing directors who believe they have to please Europe – and France in particular[21] – and hence conform to the latter's orientalist views of the Maghreb in order to get funding from the North – and those who have a "universalist" view of cinema that ignores borders.[22] Although the members of the European commissions change over time, the same funding criteria seem to apply to both men and women directors today. However, such was not always the case and may still not necessarily be the case in Maghrebi governmental commissions, from which women are often glaringly absent, causing women filmmakers from the Maghreb to believe they are still fighting against an old boys' network that discriminates against them.

The distribution circuits have also evolved significantly since the 1960s, both regionally and globally. Gone are most of the *ciné* clubs that used to dot the Maghrebi landscape in the 1960s: these venues for film screenings followed by discussions that became more and more heated and politically charged were closed down for economic as well as political reasons. The number of movie theaters has also drastically decreased in the three countries: from 304 in Algeria in 1977 to 30 in 2009; from 90 in Tunisia in 1985 to 17 in 2010; from 280 in Morocco in 1980 to 37 in 2010.[23] Pirated copies on DVDs are available sometimes on the very day of a film première, and it is possible to stream the same film online only a couple of days later. Movie theaters have become refuges for lovers with nowhere else to meet, and have thus acquired a terrible reputation. Furthermore, the popular and profitable films that are advertised (and have an advertising budget – a privilege local productions do not enjoy) and screened in the theaters are imported: either big Hollywood block-busters (e.g., James Cameron's *Avatar* sold 20,000 tickets over a six-week period at the CinemAfricArt movie theater in Tunis in the spring of 2010, when such volume of sales usually takes six months), Bollywood musicals, or Egyptian films.

Another totally different distribution circuit is available (besides airing on TV, which may or may not happen depending on the propriety of the film content): the festival circuit. The most famous one is the JCC (Journées Cinématographiques de Carthage/The International Film Festival of Carthage), an Arab and African film festival promoting a pan-African and pan-Arabic agenda created in 1966 that takes place in Tunis every two years, alternating with the FESPACO (Festival Panafricain du Cinéma de Ouagadougou/Ouagadougou Panafrican Film Festival) in Ouagadougou (Burkina Faso). These two longstanding Arabo-African international film festivals have been complemented recently by new Arab film festivals in the Gulf region, such as the Doha Tribeca Film Festival, created in Qatar in 2004, and in the UAE, the Dubaï International Film Festival (DIFF), created in 2004, and the Abu Dhabi Film Festival (ADFF – formerly known as the Middle Eastern International Film Festival), created in 2007. Each Maghrebi country has also created its own set of film festivals that are more regional or national in scope (e.g., the longstanding Festival du Cinéma Amateur de Kélibia/Amateur Cinema Festival of Kelibia, created in 1964 in Tunisia). Morocco alone counts sixty different film festivals, with distinctive themes (e.g., Amazigh, Mediterranean, Arab, Maghrebi),[24] and these remain probably the easiest way to get one's film seen (and noticed by critics) in a variety of places throughout the Maghreb. These festivals also have a regional dimension that allows directors to meet and highlight shared identity politics (e.g., Amazigh cinema, women's cinema). This is particularly important for women directors who often hesitate to identify themselves as Maghrebi *women* directors, caught as they are between allegiances (as film director, Maghrebi, woman, Arab, Amazigh, for example) that they sometimes feel pressured to prioritize.

Finally, Maghrebi women's cinema is not only diverse but also authored transnationally. Although our corpus consists of films made by women in the Maghreb, a number of their directors reside in the North, thus posing at times the question of which label of national identity should be applied.[25] (Interestingly enough, Morocco, for one, does not differentiate between the cinema of its directors living abroad and the cinema of its directors at home: they both receive the Moroccan label.) For women directors, being appropriated by one nation or another may not necessarily constitute a central issue, but it may affect the construction of their film reception. Furthermore, from the very beginning, their films have differed from the nationalist discourse of their male colleagues in the Maghreb. This is not to say that they do not have national or regional concerns, but their aim is clearly to talk to a multitude of audiences, not merely a discrete Algerian, Moroccan, or Tunisian one. Occasionally (very occasionally, given the geopolitical landscape of the Maghreb), Maghrebi women have worked in Maghrebi collaborations, pointing the way to a possible transnational regional cinema: for example, Tunisian Moufida Tlatli edited Moroccan Farida Benlyazid's *A Door to the Sky*; Selma Baccar used a Moroccan studio to develop her film *Flower of Oblivion*; Algerian Nadia Cherabi is the producer of Tunisian Abdellatif Ben Ammar's *L'Avenue des palmiers blessés*/The Avenue of the Wounded Palms (Algeria and Tunisia, 2010).

Hence, mapping women's cinema(s) in the Maghreb becomes a dynamic exercise in tracing their transnational and transregional meanders

on a variety of levels (e.g, production, distribution, culture). The transnational dimension of the women filmmakers' practices and spaces does
not negate the construction of their work as "Maghrebi" either at home
or abroad.[26] Yet in the end, the fertile, transnational, interdiscursive,
and financial montages that produce their films underline one constant
in the construction of their audience: as early as the initial stage of their
making, each of their films has to "talk" to people from all sorts of places
at home – in a changing region that is replete with complex sociocultural
strata and minority enclaves – and abroad.

CRITICAL CARTOGRAPHY

The analysis of Maghrebi women's cinema also requires mapping the
existing critical terrain so as to devise appropriate critical routes to approach the topic while avoiding potential minefields along the way (in
particular the possible misrepresentations that derive from my own
Northern, female perspective, caught in a transatlantic French-U.S. academic tension). Hence my first task is to review and question the relevant
postcolonial and postmodern critical apparatus at my disposal before I
navigate my way from it to more contemporary approaches. Among the
latter, two emerge as useful routes to the deciphering of the cinematic
texts: transnational feminism and the critique of transvergence as applied to cinema.

A good look at the critical tools of "poco" and "pomo" to decode
today's "postcolonial" films from North Africa reveals a number of problems. Concocted by the university thinkers of the North, postcolonialism has served a double Northern academic critical function: that of
categorizing texts from the South after having assessed them along the
criteria of a variegated global canon, and that of "de-colonizing" (i.e.,
undoing the colonizing posture of) the minds of Northerners in the
process. Its labeling approach, however, often subsumes texts that emanate from a variety of cultures into a larger corpus sharing one Southern
"postcolonial condition," even if the conditions of the latter vary greatly
between, say, Algeria and India. There is a tendency therefore to flatten
out all nuances within both the various postcolonial situations and the
various postcolonial texts.

Hence, for instance, it may be reductive to read today's Maghrebi women's films as solely "postcolonial" expressions of an "indigenous feminism" in what the U.S. academy – and French politics – call "francophone countries" after two generations of independence, in a global visual media landscape both saturated by a generously disseminated hegemonic, U.S. visual culture and bristling with satellite dishes relaying the agenda of a variety of countercultures. Meanwhile, as Anglo-Saxon postcolonial studies multiply attempts to distance the descendent of the colonized subject from the former colonizer through discursive strategies of resistance (Spivak) or mimicry (Bhabha), French academia still codifies the contemporary cultural "indigenous" production of a multiethnic Maghreb (e.g., Berber, Arabic) as "francophone" – a unifying term meant to encompass a powerfully diverse yet coherent, colonialist heritage.[27] Both approaches wedge the critic in an unsustainable discursive practice that revolves, seemingly interminably, around a persistent "colonial" ghost.

Leaving the "Post" Route

In my attempt to stay away from this apparent one-way street back to the North, I need to devise itineraries beyond the main thoroughfares. Mine will be a necessarily meandering critical path. Along the way, I shall retain some elements of poco, pomo, and poststructuralism that are useful to the project of reading Maghrebi women's films as steppingstones, given our present transmodern condition, to the more fluid and adaptive concepts of transvergence and transnational feminism.

FROM THE POCO CIRCLE As a theory, postcolonialism tries to give a voice to the "subaltern" – or affirms, as Spivak did, that there is no possibility for the subaltern to speak – and acknowledges the former colonizers' cultural rape of the formerly colonized. It also analyzes the various historical, economic, and social elements that have maintained the shocking disparities between wealthy countries and destitute ones. It remains, however, a gyrating notion (imagine a roundabout or a circle), mostly because it embraces a variety of phenomena under a single term: a condition (the condition of independent countries with a recent colonial

past), a time (roughly, from the 1960s onward), an imperfect state of becoming (the transition time and space between reaching independence
and the next stage), and, last but not least, a multifold theoretical project
(e.g., literary, cultural, political).

The latter, the brainchild of a variety of academic stars in the North,
including some who migrated from the South or the East (e.g., Bhabha,
Spivak), is part of a rich intellectual debate that takes place in the luxury
of neat faculty lounges and conference halls far away from the jumble of
the actual site upon which they theorize. Although the aim of the double-
edged term is to establish a clear distance from the former colonial state,
the "colonial" in "postcolonial" still reverts to the time of colonies, as if
any evaluation of the cultural products of most of Africa, for instance,
could be weighed only in contradistinction to the former colony – and
the colonial master.

The first part of the word is also problematic, for the "post" in postcolonialism points to a temporality that may obfuscate the very present
traces of colonialism (and neocolonialism) today, and mask the need for
an investigation of the precolonial space, time, and culture.[28] As a theory
used in cinema studies, it has been indicted on the following counts:

> Postcolonial theory has been critiqued for 1) its elision of class; 2) its psycholo-
> gism (the tendency to reduce large-scale political struggles to intrapsychic ten-
> sions); 3) its elision of questions of political economy in an age where economic
> neo-liberalism is the driving force behind the globalized cultural changes
> registered by postcolonial theory; 4) its ahistoricity (its tendency to speak in
> the abstract without specifying historical period of geographical location); 5) its
> denial of the precolonial past of non-European societies; 6) its ambiguous rela-
> tion, in academe, to ethnic studies, where postcolonial theory is seen as militant
> and crude; and 7) its ambiguous relation to indigenous or "first" peoples. While
> postcolonial thought stresses deterritorialization, the artificial, constructed na-
> ture of nationalism and national borders, and the obsolescence of anticolonialist
> discourse, Fourth World indigenous peoples emphasize a discourse of territorial
> claims, symbiotic links to nature, and active resistance to colonial incursions.[29]

From this picture emerges a sense of intense cacophony in postcolonial
discourse: academics in the North use it for one purpose, academics
elsewhere for another. Even the term "deterritorialization" seems to acquire different meanings depending on where the postcolonial theoreti-
cian talking head is from. And yet, even in this messy state, the debates

postcolonial critique has engendered (on, for instance, hybrid identities and cultures or the status of the subaltern; on claiming, embracing, and describing difference[s] in cultures, belief systems, values, traditions, systems of knowledge; on Third-World feminism or womanism) are still fecund and relevant today, especially to Maghrebi women filmmakers who have been immersed in both Northern and Southern Mediterranean culture and thought, their creative process at the confluence of both.

In my quest for a way out of hierarchies of discourse (European, Northern American, religious, political, or otherwise) I shall turn, for instance, to Homi Bhabha's concept of "liminality" in postcolonial culture. Appearing as a space of discursive negotiation (located in between different identities, ethnicities, languages, political communities, and so on), the "liminal" or interstitial offers an aperture out of unmovable, preestablished different and differing elements and a channel of negotiations flowing back and forth between them. Illustrating his concept with the example of a postmodern staircase that both separates and joins the two floors of a museum exhibit, he describes the latter as the "liminal space, in between the designations of identity, [that] becomes the process of symbolic interaction, the connective tissue that constructs the difference between upper and lower, black and white."[30] In our study, the screen becomes that postcolonial liminal space on which Maghrebi women directors negotiate and represent their own mobile cultural hybridity in becoming.

VIA THE FOUCAULDIAN DETOUR In his Collège de France inaugural lecture, Foucault's reflections on the restricted conditions that govern the production of discourse point to both its power and the limits imposed on it, meant to quash that power: "In every society the production of discourse is at once controlled, selected, organized and redistributed according to a certain number of procedures, whose role is to avert its power and its dangers, to cope with chance events, to evade its ponderous, awesome materiality."[31] Discourse is controlled by "rules of exclusion," Foucault adds, intended to narrowly define the following: the object of the discourse (its topic, what one may discuss); its "ritual" (where and how one may speak); the exclusive privilege to participate in the discourse (who has the authority and the license to speak). These rules of exclusion are significant in the context of female film production in the Maghreb, given the scars left by its recent past on the one hand and its current strong political regimes and patriarchal social hierarchies on the other. The redistribution of discourse after independence, for instance, had to both renegotiate residual discourse of the colonialists and residual discourse of the freedom-fighters (in Algeria especially) and revive and revise indigenous forms of discourse. Furthermore, rules of exclusion in today's context seek to marginalize the politically charged discourse of some Islamic fundamentalist factions. Forceful governments, buttressed by various patriarchal systems, have delineated discursive rules and devised a censoring apparatus that is difficult for women filmmakers to circumvent. Foucault is useful in that he illuminates with crystal-clear lucidity how the crisscrossing currents of power intersect at various levels. His theory, as applied to Maghrebi women's films, will help us delineate the liminal spaces in which the directors operate and the deftness with which they negotiate the latter in order to formulate their own images and discourse. In that respect, Foucault can lead to a fertile reading of Baccar's *Flower of Oblivion,* for instance (see chapter 7).

My analysis of Maghrebi women's cinema will therefore integrate some concepts brought to us by postcolonial and poststructuralist thought that extend to the "beyond" of poco, and that are poised to transcend their original "post" conditions – but it will also refrain from seeing and using these theories as total, or even totalitarian, systems of explication. That critical stage that lies "beyond" (beyond the *post*modern, *post*colonial condition and project) takes into account the virtual global dimension of cultural production today.

TO THE TRANSMODERN Marcos Novak describes our cultural era as that of "transmodernity," a term whose prefix invites the notion of movement, of boundaries being constantly crossed, or even being irrelevant; in short, the recognition "that ours is a global *transmodern* culture directed toward the condition of *virtuality,* in both a technological and a philosophical sense."[32] The "trans" in *trans*modern condition signals its lack of fixity and points to its ceaseless motion: the global condition of today (as opposed to the various states and forms of globalization through prior human history), is also a virtual one in which physical distance has been reconfigured. What is known here can be *transmit*-ted with the click of a mouse to the other end of the human world. Our globe has no end! In fact, it has transformed itself, outdone itself: in order to navigate or to spy on our neighbors, we even use satellites orbiting around the globe, beyond it. In a philosophical sense, our perceptions of time and space have completely shifted under the weight – or rather the lightness – of this new condition. Hence, the transmodern subject is constantly in becoming, refashioning him- or herself, and projecting images of him- or herself, that are but virtual emanations of subjectivity (ranging from Facebook pages to Iranian activist women's blogs). This transmodern condition, which seems to erase known borders, does not necessarily reconfigure geopolitics, but it does reshape the concept of otherness. "Neither for men in general nor for women in particular is now the time of 'post.' It is rather the time of 'trans.' Transhistory, transvanguard, transpolitics, transsexuality . . . basically, transmodernity. What can today be taken from postmodernism in order to reply, however paradoxical it may seem, to the questions posed by modernity is, rather than Otherness or difference, what is light, simulated, simulation."[33] Rodríguez thus sees transmodernity as the paradigm for various narratives (e.g., the narratives of globalization, of history, of feminism) that *trans*cend the terms of the questions previously asked by postmodernism, and negate previous distances (e.g., between the self and the other). And, of course, it is in the currents of this transmodernity that the films of Maghrebi women directors were created, with narratives that also reshuffle notions of time and space and that also blur the line between the self and the other, as we shall see in the film studies below.

For the "Trans(national)" Route

The term "transnational" has been applied to diasporic and postcolonial cinemas to indicate a variety of phenomena associated with the filmic object and its production: for instance, it often designates its international funding schemes, its alliances of technical teams from various countries, its mode of production (the making of the film proper). It has also been the site of critical inquiry (as illustrated by the birth of the

British film studies journal *Transnational Cinemas* this year) recently brilliantly explored by Higbee and Lim to help "interpret more productively the interface between global and local, national and transnational, as well as moving away from a binary approach to national/transnational and from a Eurocentric tendency of how such films might be read."[34] It is within this movement that extends beyond national boundaries that I wish to review the possible contributions of a transnational feminist cinematic critique.

TRANSNATIONAL FEMINISM Just as the "post" prefix signals a constant opposition/return to the Western, the various theories of feminism elaborated in the academic circles of the North with an eye toward the South might also signal an unintentional similar opposition/return. First of all, Northern, bourgeois feminism often proposes representations of "Arab women," "Muslim women," or even "Middle Eastern women," reified as monolithic objects of study outside history, often without a nuanced examination of each particular region's socioeconomic and cultural conditions. Postcolonial feminists, Algerian feminist Marnia Lazreg argues, look at the models of English colonialism and Indian postcolonialism and draw conclusions that they then apply indiscriminately to the study of the condition of women elsewhere. This "sanskritisation of knowledge," she writes, "is perhaps a welcome change in centuries of Eurocentric knowledge, but it does not transform it."[35] Taking into account Lazreg's admonitions, I propose to enroll the help of Maghrebi feminists (e.g., Lazreg herself, Fatima Mernissi from Morocco, Emna Ben Miled from Tunisia) to see how regional forms of feminist discourse might challenge and help redefine women's positions in their cultural context and gender history. At the same time, I am aware that the very notion of Maghrebi feminism implies a crossing of multiple borders, a form of transnationalism akin to Lebanese Evelyne Accad's "huma-feminist" stance, that is, a form of feminism applied to a solidarity with the oppressed that extends beyond gender to embrace all victims of oppression anywhere on the globe.

The very intersection of gender and nation creates a rather complicated outline. For when a young nation institutes its own discourse (in the Foucauldian sense mentioned above), it reconfigures the representation of its perceived characteristics in order to fashion a timeless master-narrative of national identity (e.g., in our Lake Wobegon nation, "all the women are strong, all the men are good-looking, and all the children are above average"). Hence, as Kaplan writes, it is

> through racialization, sexualization, and genderization that the nation is able to transcend modernities and become a timeless and homogenized entity. In this sense, woman as a monolithic category – represented either in the particularistic discourses of nationalism or in the universalizing discourse of "global feminism" – is problematized and put in crisis not only because of their inability to bring into view the instability of a national or international order that transcends itself to the level of "essence," but also because they guarantee agency to some while at the same time turning others into a spectacle.[36]

Kaplan, Alarcòn, and Moallem go on to object to the center-periphery positioning of both man (as central agent and decision maker) and woman (as marginal to power), and the North (an economic, political, "discursive" center) and the postcolonial Third World (still neocolonized and therefore dependent), for these two oppositions maintain the representation of power untouched. Just as the Third World needs to come to a self-definition outside the purview of the North, similarly women need to circulate across national borders and class hierarchies in order to escape all forms of essentialism concocted by old patriarchal systems, and the more recent power structures to which they have been subject engendered by global capitalism. The latter are pervasive and have also taken various guises. Hence homogeneous, hegemonic, "hard" cultures (e.g., Hollywood cinema) might well push heterogeneous, "fluid" cultures from the South (e.g., Maghrebi women's cinema) to the side. "At the same time, discernible patterns of domination channel the 'fluidities' even of a 'multipolar' world; the same hegemony that unifies the world through global networks of circulating goods and information also distributes them according to hierarchical structures of power, even if those hegemonies are now more subtle and dispersed."[37] In order to empower Third-World women, Chandra Mohanty paraphrases Anderson[38] to propose a transnational form of feminism that unites "imagined communities of women" with "divergent histories and social locations, woven together by the *political* threads of opposition to forms of domination that are not only pervasive but also systemic."[39] In a way, their argument is consonant with the one above on postcolonialism: in order to leave old structures of power and leave former authorities in the dust, so to speak, one needs to invent, or cobble together in a bricolage form, other instruments.

The second gift from the theory of transnational feminism is that it further opens the way toward what Mineke Schipper calls a "culture of interdiscursivity," among individuals from not only diverse national groups, but also diverse ethnicities and classes and different genders – a form of global culture beneficial to all, for "interdiscursivity as a dialogical intercultural encounter is by its nature mutually enriching."[40] Such a practice also circumvents the predetermined rules of exclusion, and looks down on patriarchal and Northern seats of power. One cinematic example of such transnational, interdiscursive practices can be seen in the collective *Beyond Borders: Arab Feminists Talk about Their Lives East and West.*[41]

It is this interdiscursive, transnational fluidity that nurtures the films made by Maghrebi women directors at each stage of their film production: the screen play and its languages, the transnational bricolage of funds, the making of the filmic object itself, its aesthetics, its narrative, its cinematic inventiveness.

ACCENTED CINEMA Hamid Naficy's coinage "accented cinema," although it mainly – but not exclusively – points to exilic or diasporic cinema by directors of both genders, is attractive for our purpose because it mirrors the interstitial and mobile positioning of Maghrebi women filmmakers in between cultures and nations, in between cinema-making practices and movements, and because it is negotiated in a transnational space of cultural creation. These filmmakers, who are at least bicultural and at least bilingual, who often commute between Europe and North Africa, and whose work is performed in the interlocking margins of these cultural spaces, are part of this varied, transnational group. They could constitute one branch of Naficy's global family of accented filmmakers and their cinema: "Unlike most film movements and styles of the past, the accented cinema is not monolithic, cohesive, centralized, or hierarchized. Rather, it is simultaneously global and local, and it exists in *chaotic,* semiautonomous pockets in symbiosis with the dominant

and other alternative cinemas."[42] The notion of an accented cinema, of
a cinema bearing traces of "otherness" in its very expression, reflects a
duality (comparable to the diglossia experienced by its bilingual cre-
ators) in the very act of filmic creation. It also presupposes its accents
as value-laden in contrast to a "value-free,"[43] dominant cinema (Hollywood, for instance).

> By that definition, all alternative cinemas are accented, but each is accented in
> certain specific ways that distinguish it. The cinema discussed here derives its
> accent from its artisanal and collective production modes and from the filmmak-
> ers' and audiences' deterritorialized locations. Consequently, not all accented
> films are exilic or diasporic, but all exilic and diasporic films are accented. If in
> linguistics, accent pertains only to pronunciation, leaving grammar and vocabu-
> lary intact, exilic and diasporic accent permeates the film's deep structure: its
> narrative, visual style, characters, subject matter, theme, and plot. In that sense,
> the accented style in film functions as both accent and dialect in linguistics.[44]

We are not to understand accented cinema as *superficially* different (as,
say, the sound of an English sentence spoken with a foreign accent) but
as deeply inflected by the director's culture(s) and language(s), which
work their way throughout the entire film (similar in scope to the way in
which the foreign speaker thinks through her statements before uttering
them). Accented cinema thus derives its unique language – rather than
mere accent – from the confluence of various cultural modes of expression transmogrified into the creation of film.

Naficy further describes how deeply "accented style" affects films
in their very structures (e.g., narrative, visuals, music, language) as well
as by its twist on Third Cinema aesthetics and ideology (e.g., standing
against oppression and authoritarianism but in the name of the individual, not in the name of a class or the people). In this regard, Maghrebi
women's cinema is accented: the narrative is often framed and the visual
is often haptic, that is, of a tactile nature (see chapter 4 in particular).
Furthermore, the filmmakers tend to negotiate their filmic narratives
along a serpentine path around the various strictures of a patriarchal
and heavy-handed political regime. Their "accent" is Maghrebi and female, which means several things: (a) their representation of gender is
different from the male Maghrebi one (a tempting body needing to be
hidden) and from the Northern one (a tempting body needing to be

exposed and fetishized); (b) their narrative techniques are steeped in traditional womanspeak (see the section on Echo and Shahrazad later in this chapter). With that, they take a stand against a system of oppression (in society and at home) in precise, effective ways, as the study of their films demonstrates. They also share themes with accented cinema: crossing borders, voyages, returns (or the impossibility thereof), and an "exilic acousticity" similar to the one noted in accented cinema:[45] the sonic background of their film includes modern variations on traditional melodies or songs from North Africa or even samples and mixes of music reminiscent of what goes on in the global hip-hop culture (see chapter 5 in particular). Finally, the language is most often the local Arabic dialect, sometimes Tamazight and occasionally French. As a result, viewers from the North experience a feeling of simultaneous cultural estrangement and initiation, the latter all the more blatantly since the film is subtitled.[46]

The notion of accented cinema might also apply to describe some of the cultural sharing and movements that contribute to the creation of Maghrebi directors' cinematic language and modes. Paradoxically, the themes of dislocation, of nostalgia for the home left behind, and the feeling of uneasiness verging on claustrophobia in the new cultures that Naficy describes as staples of exilic accented cinema are the negatives (in the photographic sense of the term) of those found in Maghrebi women's films. In these, characters often feel claustrophobic at home and dream of a space elsewhere while simultaneously feeling nostalgic for a lost paradise, a lost mother figure, or previous dreams abandoned. This difference echoes the one Carrie Tarr describes when she compares "*beur* cinema*" (i.e., made by French people of Maghrebi descent) and Algerian immigrant cinema in the 1990s and 2000s. The former seems intent on "representing Algeria through the filter of the imagined and remembered experiences of their parents as first-generation immigrants" and depicts feelings of conflicted identity loyalties, while the latter is "also concerned with questions of belonging and identity in multi-ethnic postcolonial France, but is more concerned with, and represents with more despair and longing, the situation of the homeland."[47] In both cases, films dream of a space elsewhere, filtered either by an idealized parental nostalgia or by a personal aching memory. However, in Maghrebi women's films, the longing for elsewhere is configured differently, as we shall see in the subsequent chapters.

As has been noted recently, Naficy's work locates "diasporic and postcolonial cinemas firmly on the margins of national/transnational cinema production in both artistic and economic terms."[48] Hence, although I wish to retain the concept of "accented cinema" as a useful tool, I also wish to stay clear of its potential contribution to marginalization. In short, Maghrebi women's films do share some of the characteristics Naficy attributes to accented cinema, but not exclusively so. Their films also use the scattered manifestations of the various cultures to which they relate in order to form a narrative and a worldview of their own. In that, they follow their own "transcultural" vision, in the sense defined by Fethi Triki:

> Culture is the possibility afforded to an individual or a group of individuals to create, judge, critique, think, and communicate. The transcultural retrieves the critical aspect of each culture to determine both transversally and transcendentally what can be universal in it, and constitute thereby a corpus of values shared by mankind that is at once critical and always renewable.... Cultures do not enter a dialogue, thus looking for and finding a dialogical order among cultures is pointless. Rather, there is an "encounter" of cultures, an encounter that can take place in the realm of hospitality, estrangement, exteriority, but also in the realm of hostility and a desire for "consumption" and destruction.[49]

This concept of the transcultural that insists on the critical aspect of cultures helps us envision the various moments of thinking that permeate the creation of the films in our study. Some films project the cultural critique of another culture (e.g., a Moroccan critique of French social mores in *A Door to the Sky*) but do not stop there in their critical quest (the same film critiques Moroccan Muslim gender segregation). Suddenly, these films stage lines of flight away from the initial critical stance and transcend it. Maghrebi women directors thus seem to set off on one prescribed trail, but then deviate from it and pick up another track. In that, they share common attributes with the cinema of *transvergence*.

CINEMA OF TRANSVERGENCE   The notion of cinema of *transvergence* was first explored at a conference in Studies in French Cinema in London in 2006, before it became the topic of 2007 issue of *Studies in*

French Cinema.[50] Inspired by the notion of transvergence described in
his field by postmodern architect Marcos Novak, the notion of a cinema
of transvergence provides one of the clearer lenses with which to look
at our films because of its shifting positioning. Marcos uses the term
"transvergence" to describe

> the clusters of cultural impacts and creative conditions brought about by accel-
> erating technological change. This work articulates and explores the realization
> that we are not only witnessing the "convergence" and "divergence" of media,
> disciplines, institutions, and so on, but a much more radical "transvergence"
> leading to widespread epistemic speciation in practically all areas of knowledge
> and expression, and to the continuous emergence of entirely new fields. On
> a global scale, the projects we are most captivated by, and often most highly
> invested in, are projects that no longer progress along expected lines of develop-
> ment, but that are instead jumping across diverse and initially mutually alien
> territories.[51]

Will Higbee sees it as transcending the conceptual frontiers of national and even transnational cinema, and allowing the filming subject
to be connected – via a Deleuzian rhizomic network[52] – to the local and
the global via ceaselessly shifting positionings.

> The concept of a cinema of transvergence views the exchange between the global
> and the local not as taking place within some abstract or undefined "global
> framework." Instead it proposes a clear understanding of the discontinuity, dif-
> ference, and imbalances of power that exist between various film-makers, film
> cultures and film industries as well as the elements of interconnectedness that
> may bind a film-maker to a given film culture or national identity at a given time.
> Because of the open-ended possibilities of both transvergence and the rhizome,
> the identity and the positioning of the film-maker within any given national or
> transcultural cinematic "network" is never fixed, it is always under negotiation,
> always in a process of becoming.[53]

This negotiation in progress is not only what creates a film as a (multi)
cultural object, but also what is at work in the matter of the film itself,
for the director keeps juggling disparate realities while making the film.
Hence, the director of a transvergent film starts shooting a film (Raja
Amari, say, directing *Red Satin*), with funds obtained on the basis of
its script written in French from the Ministry of Culture in Tunis and
Fonds Sud in Paris. The dialogues, however, are spoken in Tunisian Arabic, even if the leading actress is actually Palestinian (Hiam Abbas) and

needs to be coached in order to "sound" Tunisian. The narrative refers to both a Tunisian *Zeitgeist* and a French film staple (*Red Satin* could be seen as a new variation on a love triangle of sorts) and borrows its musical spectacular aesthetics from Egyptian classic cinema. Signifiers throughout the film are turned on their heads, in sync with the exhilarating rhythm of the *darbouka* (drum) to which women dance for a male audience, behind the door of a cabaret. The love story swaps characters; the happy end is not happy for everyone. In short, it is a transvergent narrative that follows a couple of prescribed paths at first, to better veer from them later and launch into unpredictable escapades.

This specific quality of open-ended negotiation is one of the trademarks of the cinema of Maghrebi women, as they never follow a model doggedly, but create detours, or what Novak calls "lines of flight," between divergence and convergence. In other words, this transvergent cinema does not subscribe to any totalitarian regime of certainties. "While convergence and divergence contain the hidden assumption that the true, in either a cultural or an objective sense, is a continuous landmass, transvergence recognizes true statements to be islands in an alien archipelago, sometimes only accessible by leaps, flights and voyages on vessels of artifice."[54] As I have said elsewhere,[55] cinema of transvergence enables the director to initiate dissident detours away from hegemonic regimes of truths (whether political, religious, or social, for instance), while still feeling free to borrow an element or two from the latter. The director, empowered by her own transvergent moves, subscribes to no fixed, established discourse but instead weaves her way in and out of them, away from all possible hierarchical order.

Finally, transvergence creates a dynamic of *allo*genesis (creation/production of the other) that is consonant with the transmodern condition of transnational filmmaking. For, through the various virtual connections that we establish across previously unassailable physical distances, we have reached a state of "disembodied proximity" that makes us align ourselves (here and now) with other selves (there and then).[56] Gradually, we produce other selves, *allo*-selves that grow out of our consciousness. The production of the *allo*-self has implications in identity politics (especially at the intersection of gender and geopolitics) and ontology (the subject is in constant becoming, the same and the other at the same time). This has all sorts of implications in the movie theater itself: if I apply the concept of "disembodied proximity" to my viewing of a film, then the screen is a site that mirrors the production of an *allo*self that is both other and my own. Hence, a critique of cinematic transvergence will also pose the question of reception, as will become clear in the following chapters.

While looking at films by Maghrebi women directors, I propose to examine some of the many ramifications that the concept of transvergence yields in their cinema. This notion, while it highlights the various energies and currents intertwined in the making of a cinematic text, does not reduce the final film to a mere icon of, for instance, a "female Mediterranean cinema," but helps interpret the complications and idiosyncrasies – or arabesques – in each work. Each film has its own design, much like the intricate architectural designs on the walls of the old palaces and mosques, which require the help of an optic from the South to be fully illuminated.

CULTURAL SUBTEXTS: INHERITED STORYTELLING PRACTICES

The Maghreb is an ancient place, as we have seen, deeply haunted by its past histories as well as by the narratives that have been imported, performed, and adapted on its Mediterranean shores. It is impossible to ignore the rhizomic connections between this region and the history of the larger Mediterranean region with its tri-continental coastline, and impossible to ignore its entanglements in the *longue durée* (panoramic, extensive duration) as Fernand Braudel put it, in particular with the Phoenicians, Carthage, Ancient Rome, or Ancient Persia;[57] later with the Arabs from the Peninsula, then the Andalus, and later still the Italians, the Spanish, the French. The Mediterranean, with its multiple crisscrossing of cultures, constitutes a fertile, multiaccented, open market for the exchange of multiple narratives and storytellers. Several mythical female figures, such as Cassandra, Dido, and Medea, have been invoked in hypotheses about the status of Mediterranean women in general.[58] My aim is different here; I wish to explore how narrative traditions have helped shape specific cultural narrative practices and expectations, and how they apply to Mediterranean women's storytelling processes, in particular. Two avid female speakers stand out, then: Echo (the nymph immortalized by Ovid) and Shahrazad (the storyteller par excellence).

Echo

In Ovid's rendering of the myth of Echo and Narcissus, the male figure sits at the center of the stage, talkative and absorbed in his self-reflection, while the female figure, previously reduced by Juno to "the briefest use of speech,"[59] pines away. Yet, Echo, rather than simply reiterating the end of Narcissus's sentences, carefully selects what she repeats in order to express her eternal love to Narcissus.

> Amazed, he looks around in all directions, and with loud voice cries "Come!"; and "Come!" she calls him calling. He looks behind him and, seeing no one coming, calls again: "Why do you run from me?" and hears in answer his own words again. He stands still, deceived by the answering voice, and "Here let us meet," he cries. Echo, never to answer other sound more gladly, cries: "Let us meet."[60]

Hence, as she sits, less and less visible, on the periphery of an elusive and rejecting center, she nonetheless appropriates the discourse of the latter and inserts her own meaning therein. Unsurprisingly, the (male-centered) myth gradually erases Echo from the masculine landscape: "Only her voice and her bones remain: then, only voice; for they say her bones turned to stone. She hides in the woods and is seen no more upon the mountain-sides; but all may hear her, for voice, and voice alone, still lives in her."[61]

And yet, from her *invisible* location, Echo endures and keeps engineering her own utterances in between the male words spoken from the center. In a rare coup, the female figure inverts the usual cliché of oral powerlessness: *vox manet* – her (haunting) "voice remains" thus contradicting the adage that only written words remain; *vox manet*, her female voice endures. Meanwhile, Narcissus, when he finally disappears from the core of the tale, turns into a beautiful, yet obviously mute, flower. (Here, the myth operates a second reversal in traditional gender roles: the male character has turned into a silent object of the gaze while the unseen female character is the thieving talker, who by now has appropriated speech from the now speechless male!)

This myth constitutes almost a textbook illustration of Derridian *différance,* as it shows how discourse originating from a central site of power can be *differed* (that is, uttered and eliciting a delayed, reconfigured response) in time and space by, here, a far-away "subaltern" (to echo Gayatri Spivak[62]) with no right or no position from which to speak. Echo can manipulate Narcissus's discourse because her own (female) cultural distance allows her to hijack his discourse to suit her own transvergent needs. Hence, if one listens closely to Echo's entreaties, one might hear beneath them how Echo becomes a figure of resistance within the limited sphere of action she has been granted. She starts to literally "talk back" to power, across time and space. Her words also reverberate for women listeners and storytellers long after the initial (male) word, now invested with a new entirely female meaning, has been uttered. Hence, out of the original word of the desired male, woman weaves her own discourse. Clairvoyant Tiresias, in his wildest dreams, could never have foreseen Echo as an Ovidian proto-feminist *raconteuse.*

Her story further highlights how oral traditions work – in particular, how stories are told and transmitted along generations of storytellers. Echo listens, records, and then – after a while, a time she alone determines – delivers her narrative. After she has made the original narrative her own (and thus tailored it to fit her own narrative needs), she relays and adapts a tale of the past to her contemporary audience. In other words, she *differs* the tale, that is, (re)tells it in her own voice (differently from the original story) and (re)produces it across time and possibly in a different space of performance. Her performance follows the jazz trope of improvisation, in which a theme is repeated yet always newly iterated, different, and familiar.

Shahrazad

Echo's strategies of narrative recycling and differing are replicated from storyteller to storyteller. Among the latter, women have performed inherited oral stories for centuries around the Mediterranean, at least as often as men, either in public spaces or, more often, more systematically, in the private sphere, as shown in *One Thousand and One Nights.* Using Echo's stratagem, Shahrazad chooses wisely the tales she tells the Sultan, for she will survive till morning only if the tale is good enough for him to forget about killing her that night. The story must seduce in the etymological sense of the term: it must lead away from under (*sub-ducere*) the Sultan's death project. Survival depends on Shahrazad's charm – as does the reproduction of tales and children (those of the Sultan, as we find out at the end of the *Nights*), and of the written word (the collected oral works, now translated and transcribed, have become a pillar of world literature).

The "reproduction" theme infects the structure of the tales themselves. Shahrazad's tales keep differing their ending from one tale to the next. In a magisterial *mise en abyme,* each tale contains another tale, which, in turn, contains another one; each narrative voice frames another narrative voice, and so on. This overarching structure inflects the (necessarily *pluri*vocal) delivery as well as the reception of the tale. The story, sometimes left open-ended, finds closure much later, in another episode, thus keeping the audience hanging on to the teller's every word. Loquacious Persian Shahrazad (at the other end of the spectrum from Greek Echo) thus prolongs her life by postponing closure, in a form of seductive and narrative filibuster.

The framing of the narrative voice is not alien to Muslim culture, as Omri explains. In order to report and hand down hadiths (the anecdotes narrated by the Prophet's entourage about his life and sayings), there needed to be some serious form of corroboration to establish who said what. Hence, what started as oral transmission to be written down later needed to be traced back to the origin in order to validate this or that hadith, reported first by X, then by Y, and so on, with each narrator/transmitter duly stamped with approval along established criteria:

> In addition to being an adult Muslim, they had to meet stringent criteria; both moral, such as decency and honesty, and intellectual, such as good memory. A chain (*silsila*) of transmitters where every link had to be reliable had to be proven uninterrupted . . . Each narrator or transmitter had to have heard the account personally from his or her predecessor, all the way back to the primary link and on to the Prophet.[63]

One could say that plurivocal tales constitute one of the staples of Muslim cultural transmission, whether within the religious context of Islam or in the entertaining tradition of storytelling (both traditions converging at times into the weaving of legends around the Prophet and his disciples). However, what interests me here is that a woman's voice is heeded and that Shahrazad's embedded narratives find a trusting audience in the Sultan, the (male) figure of power.[64]

The conflation of woman's survival and her urge to speak has deep repercussions in narrative strategies, reminiscent of the African American "signifying" trope:[65] the storyteller is a powerful trickster inside the Sultan's palace. Once again the female character talks (and talks) back. At first one can see her as a master of the game of micropolitics: she escapes the wrath of the Sultan even within the confines of his own palace. However, she does more than that: under the guise of weaving beautiful, vivid representations of other characters endowed with a whole array of powers (that the Sultan does not necessarily have), not only does she save her own life and that of the other women, thus becoming a literary proto-huma-feminist, but she also injects in the tales her own views on how to rule more fairly, and gradually gathers enormous political power (thus insinuating herself, in a protofeminist move, into the hitherto male power game).

There is more: Shahrazad defines her own audience. For when she takes it upon herself to tell stories and thereby save her life and that of all the young virgins whom Shahryar, the Sultan, plans to marry, deflower, and then kill, she asks the Sultan to grant her one last wish: that her sister Dunyazad be brought to the chamber. Dunyazad then requests a story "to while away the waking hours of our latter night."[66] And this is how Shahrazad actually starts to "frame" the framer! She defines all the terms of her storytelling strategy. She is the teller, she chooses the stories, and even her audience, which is double: female and known (her sister) and male, unfamiliar, and powerful (the Sultan). Dunyazad's presence receives at least two meanings: (1) it is a ploy, a dramatic posture on the part of Shahrazad – she is posing as a sister telling her sibling a story while actively resisting the Sultan and trying to survive; (2) it is a political act: she is addressing a multiple audience at once.

Similarly, a Maghrebi woman director tells a story to an audience in the know at home, and another one abroad. Meanwhile, she also has to work within a given structure of power: the censorship she faces at home is political – enforced by her nation's overbearing leadership – and cultural. As a result, the filmmaker's cinematic discourse has to escape the censor's vigilant radar while still sharing secrets with the local viewers *and* telling a story whose interest transcends the frontiers of her nation. Fortunately, cinema enables one to say one thing by showing something else through a semantic montage of off-screen and on-screen images.[67] Just as Shahrazad could refer, unbeknownst to the Sultan, to familiar tales and hints understood by her sister Dunyazad, today's director can play with an off-screen shared reality and an on-screen fictitious narrative.

In the wake of Echo and Shahrazad, today's women filmmakers negotiate and assert their own spaces and visions, as they maneuver their way out of two patriarchal systems of representation: the traditional, Muslim-inflected one in the Maghreb (which hides women's bodies) and the Hollywood projection of women (which reveals and fetishizes their bodies). Although these systems can be seen as mirror images of each other, they raise issues around the representation of women and the freedom of women to express themselves in very divergent ways. However, as we know from Mernissi's history of *nushuz* (female disobedience),[68] for instance, women filmmakers have many examples of strategies from which to choose in Muslim women's long-standing history of resistance to male hegemony. It is this tradition of a disobedience that never quite says its name aloud that women employ in their filmic texts: to those who listen carefully, the chaos of disobedience, of dissidence, rumbles beneath the surface of the organized narrative.

THE HIJAB INSIDE OUT: SCREENS AND VEILS

In order to understand what is at stake in the projection of a woman's film in an Islam-inflected region such as the Maghreb, we need to look at issues of representation. To that end, I propose we examine the Sufi tradition of *théâtre des ombres* (shadow theater), the hijab from inside and out, and forms of tactile visualization some of these films employ.

The Shadow Theater

In the Musée du Cinéma in Tunis, a permanent exhibit traces the history of cinema in Tunisia from its roots in Maghrebi culture to its modern incarnation. Thus constructed as a Maghrebi cultural object, cinema can claim aesthetics in, for instance, the *théâtre des ombres*, or shadow puppet theater, in which the silhouettes of characters were projected onto a screen. Hence cinema's visual mode of representation can be linked to the old Sufi tradition of itinerant performance (*khayal al-zil*) that brought its signature character, Karakouz, to the Maghreb all the way from Turkey. (The Turkish name of this character – "black eye" – probably actually derives from the Arabic *Qaraqush*, the name of Saladin's comrade-in-arms,[69] another illustration of the busy circulation of narratives in the Mediterranean basin.)

In the shadow theater, the old Islamic prohibition on constructing three-dimensional images "representing living beings endowed with vital breath (*rûh*), hence human beings and animals" (with the notable exception of dolls that play a useful role in the education of little girls) is circumvented by projecting the shadow of puppets (one-dimensional, articulated cutouts made out of cardboard or dried pelts) on a backlit screen.[70] Although the Qur'an condemns the worship of deities represented in the form of statues, idols, or stones, it does not mention images. (The word *sura*/image appears once in the Qur'an: "He fashioned you in the image He wanted" [82:8]. It is in a hadith that the first proscriptions appear, as images are thought by some of the Prophet's disciples to be impure.) Hence, the shadow theater seems to breach no Muslim rules.

This form of itinerant show served a double purpose: a didactic, spiritual one (the Sufis used it to impart their tales of wisdom) and an entertaining one now inscribed in folklore (especially during the Ramadan nights). Yet the farces of Karakouz, or Karagöz, also often contained obscene language. As the puppeteers were free to improvise their own shows around the very virile character of Karakouz, "each performance was accompanied by obscene lines, bawdy retorts, risqué proverbs and the mixed audience – men, women, children – would burst out laughing."[71] From bawdy, the shows became highly subversive in Tunisia, a fact that was not lost on the authorities. "In Tunisia, political protest insinuated itself behind this character who, in memorable performances, attacked the bust of beautiful Marianne [the female allegory of the French Republic] and a stylized map representing France. René Millet, General Resident of France in Tunisia at the time, outlawed him. But Karakuz is still alive and well in the Orient."[72] In fact, the seditious performances of the puppet were not limited to Tunisia in the nineteenth century. They were banned in Algeria as well by the French colonial authorities.[73]

Indeed, the character could be seen as powerful, given its popularity and fame. In Tunisia, for instance, Karakouz was well known from Halfaouine (a working class area of Tunis) all the way to remote villages, deep in the country. Bearing this tradition in mind, it seems logical to infer that, by the time the Lumière brothers' invention reached the region (as early as 1897), viewing a film on-screen was not that alien an experience, and that some of the aesthetics of the shadow theater – as well as some of its insubordinate language – might have transferred into the cinematic practice.

The image of a character thus produced, since it is projected onto a two-dimensional plane, consists in a necessarily reductive silhouette of the original character. Even if cinema brought along depth of field and perspective and tended to convey a more realistic simulacrum than the shadow theater, it still projected a two-dimensional illusion onto the same type of screen. This detour from the ancient Muslim interdiction could still function, to the joy of the assembled viewers gathered for a film screening at a *ciné* club.

The Hijab, Inside Out

Filmmaking can be seen as one logical expression of the politics of the gaze, an intense affair in the Maghreb. As Gönül Dönmez-Colin explains: "The gaze, which is the core of cinema and an integral part of North African and Middle Eastern traditions, is a very important aspect of the films from the two regions manifesting cultural restrictions of modesty, especially when applied to women, who cannot voice their concerns. However, no matter how restricted it may be, the gaze – of a veiled woman or the lens of a camera – always finds a way of independence from the authorities."[74] In the Maghreb, any discussion of the veil entails an entire debate in which there are variations from country to country – a point to which I shall come back later in this study. First and most importantly, I do not intend to reduce gender issues to the wearing of the veil for various reasons: (1) it has a myriad distinct connotations and meanings, and it has been legislated differently from one country to the next, as we shall see; (2) it has been the obsessive focus of outsiders, especially the French during the colonial period[75] and most recently in postcolonial France (see the March 15, 2004, French law that bans the wearing of ostentatious signs of religion affiliation and the May 19, 2010, bill banning Muslim full-face veil – *burqa* or *niqab* – from public spaces on the territory of the French Republic). Nevertheless, the veil stands as an important signifier in the region – even if differently from its counterpart in the Mashreq – and I simply wish to look, from the standpoint of women, at its function in the politics of the gaze.

The Arabic noun حِجَاب (hijab) does not simply indicate the generic "veil" worn by Muslim women (called by different names depending on the Muslim region – *abaya* in the Gulf, *chador* in Iran, *haïk* or *safsari* in the Maghreb, for instance), but also means the curtain (cover) that separates a room in two, usually to mark gender segregation. It is then a screen, a place behind which something is going on.

What interests me here is that with women's cinema comes a reversal of both space and modes of representation: women hitherto supposed to be hidden by the hijab in the public sphere (outside the house or the *hammam* [baths]), now find themselves exposed onto the other "side" of the hijab, or "screen."

Hence, the hijab can be seen as the point of both contact and separation – indeed, as the embodiment of the gazing paradox, for the eye needs distance in order to apprehend (be in contact with) its visual object. Women can project onto its surface representations of that which its flowing surface usually conceals. The hijab reveals the contours of the hidden, which attract the attention of the frustrated, desiring gaze. As Chebel points out, "Garments, far from assuming their social function of 'modesty,' exacerbate the tensions between what they mask, the body, and the voyeur. What is or pretends to be 'modest' in a garment thus creates its own 'viewer,' while the garment draws from its own dialectics: eroticism."[76] The dynamics of desire thus inscribed in the veil produce their logical paradox for the viewer: that which is hidden from view and desire actually fuels desire and activates fantasy. The latter does not escape Chebel in his portrayal of the politics of seduction in the region: "The entire veil paradox derives from the principal impossibility in rejecting the erogeneity that it enshrines . . . in a genuine 'denied offer' which is the essence of seduction in the Maghreb."[77] This, of course, is seen from the perspective of heterosexual male viewers located outside, that is, on this side of the screen; but what about women's gaze, to which Dönmez-Colin alluded? The veil also gives women the possibility – indeed the privilege – of seeing without being seen, to observe others (male others, for instance) from a nonreciprocal vantage point. Chebel notes that "the veil is to be considered as this garment essentially meant to prevent women from being seen, and, at the same time, giving them the possibility to gaze at others."[78] (Hence the importance of the figure of the blind man – the one who cannot see, in front of whom a woman can unveil – in the love mythology of ancient Arabia).[79]

But how, then, can women be on display *on* a film screen for all to *see*? Actually, not everything will be exposed on the porous screen from the inside world of women. The apparent transgression is possible only because it is not a real one: it is only a *re*-presentation, a proposed image, a ghost or double of the woman as sudden object of gaze, a Hegelian *Vorstellung* (i.e., not a replica of woman, but an image of woman that stands in front of, and separate from, the original subject). Hence we end up not with a woman's presence (in spite of the confusion between actress and character in early cinema and the identity politics of stardom) but with a backlit shadow, a silhouette of the real thing, a visual manifestation of Echo.

This imaging of woman is defined by women (not by men) and by aesthetics and social norms that are not Western. Although women's interiors are shown, made public, they remain "interiors-in-performance," and do not necessarily betray women's secrets[80] – although they might publicize men's dirty secrets (e.g., how they abuse their wives and others at home; how they abuse power). Here, woman is not fetishized, as in a Western patriarchal film. Her (clad) shadow is projected from the inside, and is not the construction of a voyeuristic look, always condemned to remain outside.

Finally, I need to consider the issue of audience and film reception: who is the constructed spectator in these films about women on the other side of the hijab? The screen that used to conceal from the gaze (while also pointing to the forbidden) now reveals, and attracts the gaze of the spectator to, a projected replica, a ghost of the object, a *re*-presentation of the subject distinct from the subject herself. This is no "real" revelation, as we have seen; it is an artistic one. It posits the spectator in an ambiguous position that is not voyeuristic – as filming a woman's interior might suggest – but rather entails a new viewing pleasure: pleasure at recognizing the elements of home, or the inside, the private sphere, as opposed to the spectacular, for instance.

The Haptic

In her work on intercultural cinema and haptic cinema, Laura Marks analyzes contemporary films (that we could loosely call "accented") as nostalgic pieces evocative of the homeland (e.g., Stephen Frears's *My Beautiful Laundrette*, UK, 1985; Mira Nair's *Mississippi Masala*, U.S. and Uganda, 1992; Julie Dash's *Daughters of the Dust*, U.S., 1992; Haile Gerima's *Sankofa*, Burkina Faso, Ghana, Germany, UK, U.S., 1993) as well as noncommercial, experimental video work. The images of what was – and of what the narrator has lost in her exile – tremble under the weight of memory and emotions. In order to re-create the landscape now out of reach, the director, in a search comparable to Proust's, conjures up various senses and attempts to render, on film, the sights, sounds, smells, and tactile feelings that belong to the lost land. The title of her study, "The Skin of the Film," is meant to convey the image of a viewer touching a film with her eyes, in what Marks calls "haptic visuality." This tactile dimension of film is one intrinsically linked to the emotional aura of film, beyond its audiovisual dimension. "Cinema itself appeals to contact – to embodied knowledge, and to the sense of touch in particular – in order to recreate memories."[81] In other words, the audiovisual creation is constructed to evoke senses other than merely hearing and sight.

Paraphrasing Marks, I would like to trace the haptic dimension of Maghrebi women's cinema as expressed through not the skin of the film, but the thin, evocative veil of the film. The dynamics of representation in their constant dichotomy of contact and separation seem to both awaken vivid memories or images and then blur them behind the shroud of the past or the unspeakable. (I am thinking here, for instance, of Tlatli's *Silences of the Palace,* and its wonderful close-up of the protagonist uttering an inaudible scream, her hands wrapped tightly around the wrought iron bars of the gate to the palace; or of Amari's *Red Satin,* in which the protagonist fingers a red satin slip in a shop with an incredulous smile at the softness of it). Each film seems to *suggest* rather than show, in a revelation-and-concealment dialectical movement. The screen, then, gives out a glimpse but then stops in mid-revelation, allowing the viewer to imagine and feel the signified and prolong it even as it safely retreats to the other, indistinct side of the hijab.

BOOK STRUCTURE

To examine Maghrebi women's cinematic texts does not mean to reduce each creative piece to a part of a regional uniform entity, as the close viewing of each film reveals. For each film is inflected with its own "accent" and its own mode of transvergence. And yet, while original, each film by these directors also illuminates confluences among the women from the western region of North Africa.

My approach to Maghrebi women's films is transvergent on several levels as it incorporates in the reading of films several theoretical elements without subscribing to an entire theoretical regime. It also follows the twists and turns followed by each director in and out of various cultures, and looks at how these directors propose new modes of filmmaking in the process.

Through a close viewing of seven different films as exemplars of Maghrebi women's cinema, it is my hope to make clear how a transvergent critique of each director's work illuminates the novelty of her cinema. I propose to highlight particular aspects of transvergence in each case study so as to offer as precise an understanding of this new cinema as possible.

The selection of these particular films as exemplars was carefully considered with certain criteria in mind: (1) Films are meant to be seen, not just read about! That goes for the films analyzed here as well. Hence availability was a factor in my selection, and, with the exception of one film (*Flower of Oblivion*), all films are available on DVD or VHS in the United States and in Europe. It is my hope that *Flower of Oblivion* will also be distributed in DVD form soon. (2) Maghrebi women come from three different nations, and I wished to have a balanced, if not perfectly equal, representation of the cinematic work of each country: hence my choice of two Moroccan, two Algerian, and three Tunisian films.

The aim of this book is also to cast a light on a cinema that has not been widely distributed, and therefore is not widely visible. As appendix B shows, Maghrebi women have made numerous films, some more famous than others, from which to choose. The films by Tunisian director Moufida Tlatli, for instance, have enjoyed international success and critical praise. Academics (myself included) have written and theorized about her, and information about her work is so readily available that she has at times become a symbol of Tunisian Women's Cinema.[82] I made a conscious decision to stay away from such reifying schema and chose to give visibility to other women directors from Tunisia, hoping to provide a more plural image of Tunisian women's oeuvres.

Another conscious decision of mine was to include two pioneers (even if Assia Djebar is a writer rather than a filmmaker) in order to look at the different ways in which women began their filmmaking careers in the Maghreb. Hence my choice of Assia Djebar and her film *The Nuba of the Women of Mount Chenoua*, and Farida Benlyazid and her film *A Door to the Sky* as starting points.

This study is one entry among many other possible ones into the cinema of women in the Maghreb, and follows a loose chronological line; it also tags along the meanders of a transvergent critique. Hence the three "acts" of the book, each of them underscoring the various strategies used by Maghrebi women directors to compose and project films of their own, using Shahrazad as a guiding metaphor along a transvergent arc of interpretation.

Act I. Transnational Feminist Storytellers:
Echo, Shahrazad, Assia, and Farida

Both Assia Djebar and Farida Benlyazid returned to the Maghreb to direct their first films in a cinematic landscape from which women directors were mostly absent. These film pioneers take after the two Mediterranean storytelling figures of Echo and Shahrazad: Assia Djebar turned Echo retells the history of the Algerian independence struggle and the role of women in it from the margins to the center; Farida Benlyazid turned Shahrazad tells a story that opens up onto a series of embedded narratives.

Chapter 1 proposes an analysis of a transvergent narrative in Djebar's *The Nuba of the Women of Mount Chenoua* (Algeria, 1978). In it, Djebar provides a series of female narratives of the Algerian Revolution in the Kabyle region, which are then broadcast on Algerian TV. Djebar as Echo is here refracting what happened, and projecting it fifteen years or so after the fact for the benefit of, first and foremost, an Algerian audience. Women finally see themselves on-screen. This chapter also describes and analyzes the transvergent quality of the film's narrative and musical structure.

In chapter 2, Farida Benlyazid's *Door to the Sky* (Morocco, 1988) images the return from France of a young binational woman to her Moroccan roots and her initiation to Sufism. The film clearly addresses two distinct audiences – one that is French or francophone and secular, another that is Moroccan and Sufi – as we follow the spiritual journey of Nadia, initially secularly minded and rebellious, to Sufism. Benlyazid here initiates extra-diegetic viewers into a woman-friendly form of Muslim mysticism. The initiation takes the form of embedded references that are gradually revealed to the alert viewer. At the same time, the film proposes a new form of culturally grounded Maghrebi feminism and maps out a possible itinerary toward self-actualization and individual spiritual fulfillment, independent of the diktats of both Islam and Western feminism.

Act II. Transvergent Screens

This act examines the concept, in three different films, of the hijab as a polysemic surface on which new and reversed cinematic images of women are projected in a novel fashion.

Chapter 3 explores how Bachir-Chouikh's film *Rachida* (Algeria, 2002) seems to return to one of Shahrazad's stories, already revisited by Assia Djebar, evoking a long tradition of violence against women. However, rather than allowing the embedded tale in her film to be told by another narrative voice (e.g., the media, the government, the Islamic

Front), she chooses to tell the story from the point of view of Rachida – thus recycling Shahrazad's tale while, at the same time, overturning Shahrazad's narrating *mise en abyme*. In the end, the filmmaker is projecting in one story the current and ancient narrative of violence done to speaking women of her group.

Chapter 4 reads Raja Amari's *Red Satin* (Tunisia, 2002) as the story of the personal liberation of a widow whose sensual perception of the world is rendered through a haptic visuality on-screen. The latter then helps define a new concept of the term "screen" as no longer a two-dimensional flat surface but, rather, as an interface with a woman's world hitherto perceived as enclosed and remote.

Chapter 5 offers Nadia El Fani's *Bedwin Hacker* (Tunisia, 2002), the first Tunisian spy thriller, as the exemplar of yet another interpretation of screens: the cinematic screen contains a computer screen, which contains a television screen, each of them containing snippets of narrative that both conceal and yet complement one another. This journey across various planes of representation establishes a model for a transvergent form of dissidence challenging both French and Tunisian authorities and cultures.

Act III. From Dunyazad to Transvergent Audiences

The third act focuses on the construction of a transvergent transnational audience in the cinema of Maghrebi women directors. The guiding metaphor of Shahrazad's performance helps us understand how Maghrebi women directors construct their audience, with the storyteller talking to both the Sultan and sister Dunyazad at the same time. Each film then simultaneously addresses a "global" audience (or at least an unfamiliar audience outside the borders of the Maghreb, reminiscent of the Sultan) and one that is regional and as familiar as Dunyazad.

Chapter 6 examines the way in which Yasmine Kassari embeds video screens in *The Sleeping Child* (Morocco, 2004) to provide a backlit view of transnational migration from the women's perspective in rural Morocco. The men's initial "burning" (illegal crossing of borders) reverberates in all sorts of multiplied, unpredictable ways: the men's transgression triggers women's transgressions; the men's exodus from Morocco corresponds to the inner exile of women at home. In this film, Kassari speaks both to a Moroccan, rural audience and to a transnational one.

Finally, chapter 7 studies Selma Baccar's *Flower of Oblivion* (Tunisia, 2006) as a political allegory structured along a multilayered narrative whose meanings can be decoded by distinct groups sharing particular sets of references off-screen. In it, the director frames her audience in several ways. The film proposes two competing perspectives to tell the emotional (as well as political and historical) journey of a Tunisian woman from addiction (or dependence) to independence. Making sense of the various semantic layers of the film also requires some elements of transvergent critique from its alert extra-diegetic audience.

Transnational Feminist Storytellers:
Shahrazad, Assia, and Farida

Assia Djebar's Transvergent *Nuba: The Nuba of the Women of Mount Chenoua* (Algeria, 1978)

PRELUDE

Shahrazad's tales included other tales in a *mise en abyme* that deepened as the *Nights* unfolded. Contemporary Maghrebi women's filmic narratives often follow a similar pattern. The resulting films offer a complex narrative web of embedded tales. In *Barakat,* for instance, the surface narrative of the quest for a disappeared woman soon reveals another narrative embedded within it: the story of a past *mujahida* (woman freedom fighter). Shahrazad also embedded political messages in her narratives: this Sultan whose story I am telling you, she whispered to the caliph prettily, is "fair," is "wise," and acts in a politically courageous way. Similarly, *Rachida,* for instance, tells a fictitious story focused on one female protagonist that embodies the plight of Algeria during the 1990s (see chapter 3); and *Bab al sama maftouh/Une Porte sur le ciel/A Door to the Sky* by Farida Benlyazid, for instance, tells a fictitious story focused on one female protagonist whose spiritual and feminist choices reach into the history of women in the Maghreb, and shows how to make significant personal/political choices.

Yet the narrative *mise en abyme* of Maghrebi women directors seems even more whimsical than Shahrazad's: it plays with the possibility of one narrative before skipping circuitously to another, peripheral, one and returning to the original one. Assia Djebar's *Nuba* points to sev-

eral other narratives that resonate in the Algerian landscape beside the
narrative of the *mujahidat's* (women freedom fighters') resistance to
the French occupier. She resurrects musical echoes of Bartok's Algerian pieces, but also places myths side by side with archival footage and
blurs the boundaries between history and legend. Yet at no point does
she remain fixed in one particular narrative genre. At no point does she
validate one narrative over the other. Rather, in a flowing motion, she
traverses the various possible narrative realms, alights here and there,
and weaves a meta-narrative, which is, in essence, "transvergent": it is
beholden to no specific regime of truths. In the end, both intertexts
and narrative genres end up contaminating the very format of her film.
The film's lack of resolution also adds to the fluidity of the transvergent
narrative enterprise: the film itself does not adhere to its own regime of
truths and awaits a pen or a camera to pick up the story line where it was
and keep on writing/filming.

Acclaimed novelist Assia Djebar's adventure with cinema yielded
two films: *Nuba nisa al djebel Shnua/La Nouba des Femmes du Mont Ché-
noua/The Nuba of the Women of Mount Chenoua* (1978) and *La Zerda ou
les Chants de l'oubli/The Zerda or Songs of Oblivion* (1982). Cinema is not
her customary mode of expression, and yet, in what may superficially
look like a Sembène-like move,[1] she one day decided to take up the camera instead of her French-writing pen to communicate with her "clan":
the women of Algeria – not the French-educated women (like herself)
but peasant women, most of them illiterate, most of whom have never set
foot in a cinema. "At the end of the 1970s, in Algerian cities, movie the-
atres were patronized by an audience that was almost exclusively male.
At the same time, most women of all ages, of all walks of life, would watch
television. This is why *The Nuba of the Women of Mount Chenoua* was
produced, originally, by Algerian television – when, in fact, it deserves to
be seen on a large screen."[2] If this film breaks the silence surrounding the
women's Algerian revolution fifteen years after the fact, while the government headed by the victorious FLN (Front de Libération Nationale/
National Liberation Front) is busy singing the exploits of its male heroes,
it does not monumentalize women as heroic subjects. (The Algerian war
of independence, 1954–1962, which ended the French occupation of the
country that had started in 1830, was headed by the FLN. The latter has

been ruling Algeria ever since.) It does not tell a straight story either. Rather, it builds a narrative as a succession of various echoes of the central narrative of the role of women in the liberation struggle. With its mix of fiction, documentary, reconstructions, and archival footage, along with its use of a female voice-over and of music as both structure and sign, the deeply experimental form of the film did not win praise among the established critics in Algiers, as was evident by the reviews after its airing as part of the *Téléciné Club* program on TV. It was so controversial that, after its first screening at the Journées Cinématographiques de Carthage (the International Film Festival of Carthage, Tunisia) that year, Algerian filmmakers had the film removed from the competition – to the vigorous outcry of foreign critics. Thereafter, *The Nuba* received the Critics' Prize in Venice.[3]

The film is often described as slow, not readily accessible, yet it is also a striking foray into *narrative transvergence* on the part of Djebar, who here undertakes not only her first film but also the first by a woman director in Algeria. The stylized narrative of the film is transvergent on several accounts: it traverses multiple layers of narrative and silences, without remaining solidly anchored in any of them for too long; it is fluid; it includes, in its various stages, diverse alien components, even obscure spots, without necessarily fully deploying them.

Finally, the film undeniably acquires added shades of meaning after the publication of *Vaste est la Prison* (*So Vast the Prison* – 1995) and *La Femme sans sépulture* (*The Woman without a Grave* – 2002), as followers of Djebar place it in her oeuvre and against the larger context of the Algerian experience.

ASSIA DJEBAR AS DOUBLE AGENT

Djebar, one of the most visible Algerian literary figures of the second half of the twentieth century, elected to the Académie Française in 2005, routinely rumored to figure on the list of finalists for the Nobel Prize, turned to the camera in 1977 after ten years during which she had written no novel. Over these ten years, she had wondered about writing again: the war of independence was over, Arabic was the language of the new nation, and yet the language she wrote in was French. During that hiatus, she felt attracted to the performing arts, to theater in particular. In 1969, she coauthored a play with her then-husband, Walid Carn, *Rouge l'aube/Red Dawn,* staged and directed at the time by Mustapha Katab and performed at the third Pan-African Cultural Festival held in Algiers that same year. The play attracted only 1,953 spectators. Its topic, the war of liberation, was treated on an individual scale, and the play insisted on the cruelty of war (rather than adhering to the contemporary state discourse that tended to focus mostly on the heroism of the National Liberation Front male veterans), as its conclusion underscores: "Like you, I cannot see anything, neither the executioner, nor the martyr. Only the sky and the purple of dawn; a red dawn above my brother's blood."[4]

She also acted as assistant director in a number of productions, and finally directed her own adaptation of American playwright Tom Eyen's 1971 play *The White Whore and the Bit Player* in 1973, in Paris. She was no stranger to cinema either – or at least its critical study, having taught French literature and cinema upon her return to Algiers, in the French Department of the university in 1974–1975 (fellow author Tahar Djaout even took her film seminar before he shot a documentary on the making of *The Nuba*).

Hence, when Assia Djebar took up directing, she apparently sought to speak to women (and men) in Algeria, a larger public than her usual francophone literary one. And as her film explored a new way of delivering a message to a larger audience, it also experimented with a range of media. Although she switched languages, and addressed her audience in Algerian Arabic (rather than in her customary written French), Djebar did not leave her literary art behind: the opening credits of the film (in Arabic lettering) metamorphose into a long text read by a voice-over in Arabic:

> This film, in the form of a *nuba,* is dedicated, posthumously to: Hungarian musician Béla Bartók, who had come to an almost silent Algeria to study its peasant music in 1913; Yaminai Oudai known as Zoulikha, who established a resistance network in the city of Cherchell and its mountains in 1955 and 1956. She was arrested in the mountains when she was in her forties. Her name was subsequently added to the list of the missing.
>
> Lila – the protagonist in this film – could be Zoulikha's daughter. The six other talking women of the Chenoua tell bits and pieces of their life stories.

The *Nuba* of the women is the moment when their turn comes to tell their stories. But the *nuba* also refers to the classical "Andalusian" musical form with its precise tempo.

Pointing here to what Aresu identified as Djebar's "creative continuum" between spoken and written text,[5] the words, both printed and read aloud by a female voice, open up the film to various interpretations: the construction of its meaning will be manifold, accessible via multiple tracks, the oral and the written ones constituting only two among others.

The fact that this film would allow the novelist to take up her pen again later on in order to explore the making of the film (in *Vaste est la prison/So Vast the Prison,* 1995, in particular), and thus prolong the film experience into the realm of the written, is in many ways crucial to the understanding of *The Nuba.* The latter is – literally – "inscribed" in an overarching oeuvre that contains and supersedes it. The film would also launch the writing of an entire novel, *La Femme sans sépulture (The Woman without a Grave,* 2002), centered on Zoulikha, the *mujahida* to whom the film is dedicated and whose story occupies 7 minutes of the 115 of the entire film. As a piece of the Djebarian "re-membering" of story/history (that is, piecing diverse stories to the main body of history), the film is a pivotal point in the author's work:[6] it builds on previous experiments with theater and also fuels future written textual production. It also marks a transition from what one might call "straight fiction" to "mixed media": Djebar now explores storytelling in radically different ways, far from, say, her storytelling in *La Soif (Thirst* – 1957) or *Les Alouettes Naïves (Naïve Larks* – 1967). In *The Nuba,* she mixes fiction with oral history, myth with history, and intersperses excerpts of documentary archival footage. She would write in a mix of narrative genres similar to these in several of her later books.

She acts as a double or triple agent as scriptwriter and filmmaker, as she draws from her formal training as historian (at the French École Normale Supérieure and the University of Algiers), from her talent as novelist and playwright, and then breaks both sets of formal rules as she edits her film in a striking nonlinear fashion in order to constantly reorient her collective, female history/storytelling. "Narrating must not tell the story, but interrupt it: i.e., suspend it, surprise it at all costs."[7] She also takes advantage of her outsider/insider position. For, if Djebar returns to Cherchell to shoot *The Nuba,* she also brings with her a vision of independent Algeria as a French-educated woman of Arabic and Berber ancestry, who does not, however, speak Tamazight, the Berber language of that region (just like her fictitious character Lila, who admits that much to the women she interviews); she is also a vocal, unveiled, and bicultural (French and Algerian) urbanite, removed from the women of the country she is filming. This film could be seen as Djebar's attempt to fill gaps (along lines of class, education, culture, language) in her representation of the peasant women of the Cherchell region. In it, Djebar wants to target, first and foremost, the women who have been the victims of French colonialism and then of independent patriarchal Algeria.[8]

While the film is for and by these strong women, these heroines of the war, it also reflects a formal quest on the part of author-turned-filmmaker Djebar. In that sense, because the film talks to several audiences at the same time (e.g., movie buffs and women of Algeria), it starts to remedy what historian Benjamin Stora described as one of the most dire shortcomings of the cinematic representation of the Algerian war: "Memories do not mix: when one makes a film, it is a film for oneself or for one's own 'community.' It creates a constant feeling of absence which comes from the non-encounter of memories."[9] Instead of targeting a specific audience (e.g., former colonists, Algerians, Harkis[10]) on either side of the Mediterranean, Djebar narrates history/herstory to both audiences: the first time, ostensibly to the women in Algeria, and the second time, when she publishes *La Femme sans sépulture,* to a francophone, literate audience in 2002. Hence, seeing her film in the larger context of her oeuvre, *The Nuba* constitutes the first panel of a diptych representing Zoulikha, the disappeared, forever mute Algerian woman fighter.

LA NOUBA BELOW THE SURFACE OF HISTORY: NARRATIVE TRANSVERGENCE AT WORK

The narrative format of the film is framed: a fictitious story leads to a documentary of sorts, spliced with a very few black-and-white frames of French archival footage (since the only available archival film of Algeria until its liberation is French). It is structured in the seven movements of a *nuba* as announced in the written text, a fact to which we shall return.

The narrative layers of the film function along various degrees of anamnesis (as thoroughly and brilliantly explained by Donadey).[11] The framing narrative opens up onto three distinct temporal subjective tracks, as the character of the framing fictitious story, Lila, puts together the memories of women (oral history), and through their accounts, uncovers an episode of history. The latter eventually reaches a mythic dimension, as she narrates the story of the local saint and his seventh wife, a story of blessed abundance and loss.

Film Synopsis

Framing fictitious narrative: Lila is a young woman, married to Ali and mother to Aïcha. The three of them live in a small house in the country outside Cherchell, near Mount Chenoua. Lila drives around to interview and collect the stories of women who have participated in the war of liberation.[12] Ali, a veterinarian, has fallen from a horse and, as a result, must use a wheelchair at the beginning of the film. This image of powerlessness is compounded by the fact that he barely speaks throughout the film. As the story unfolds, he starts to gradually walk again, with the help of crutches. Although we are shown that his initial paralysis will eventually end, he sits as the remote observer of his wife and child, in whose games he cannot participate. He appears in stark contrast to Lila, who is mobile (she is constantly walking, driving, and is even seen on a boat at the end of the film) and expressive: her inner monologue reaches the extra-diegetic spectator in an almost constant voice-over.

Framed collective narrative no. 1: the stories Lila hears are multiple and told by each woman "in turn" (in their *nuba*) *and* by Lila herself. The narrative voice is female and multiple yet also orchestrated by the supra-voice of Lila, the protagonist of the fictitious piece and the reporter of women's memories and stories of the war, who had been, herself, a prisoner during the war, as we learn later in the film.

Framed narrative no. 2: Lila's voicing of these narratives leads to other reminiscences that predate the war of liberation. Lila remembers her grandmother's tale of an episode of heroic resistance to the French invader in 1871. At the time, the Amazigh clan from which she descends, the Beni-Manacer of the Berkani tribe, had rebelled, and their leader,

Sidi Malek Saharaoui, had been killed by the French troops as he was riding his horse. The latter is shown on-screen returning without its rider to the Dahra grotto, where the women of Mount Chenoua had taken refuge.

Framed narrative no. 3: one of the women remembers the story of a mythological figure – that of the seventh wife of benevolent saint Abdel Rahman, whose curiosity led her to open the plentiful jars of oil, butter, and honey, to which the villagers would help themselves every night. As she did so, she released the magical doves that allowed the miracle of abundance, thus leaving the jars forever empty. The saint later informed the sad villagers: "That woman stripped you of my blessings."

Hence, already, the filmic narrative destabilizes the audience's expectations: far from leading to the reconstitution of a clearly defined episode of the past, with a framing narrative anchoring a moment in history – in documentary style, for instance – associated with a protagonist with whom we can identify, this film operates the reverse move: our framing narrative follows the meanderings of Lila, a fictitious narrator, and we witness her entering into the spaces and characters of history and of myth. The filmic narrative (the visual and aural one) is itself "framed," sandwiched between the written script in the beginning (at the conclusion of the credits) and a song performed by a man at the end of the film, whose Arabic text is translated into English or French subtitles (depending on the film version). The film seems to lead from the written text to the performed song via its three-tiered narrative structure, the latter constantly riding between fiction and history, mythology and memory. But there is more: it is further complicated by the overriding structure of the *nuba*.

The Nuba Structure

A *nuba* is a musical form derived from Andalusian music and now found with local specificities in the Maghreb. In Algeria, for instance, the Andalusian *nuba* is usually played by a band or orchestra of seven musicians, and comprises several pieces, which reflect seven different rhythms. "The *nuba* is a suite or concert program with several musical pieces that are performed one after the other, hence its literal meaning: your *nuba* =

your turn."[13] A democratic musical suite, it seems to not give precedence to any particular moment of the performance, but gives a voice to each loosely connected piece "in turn." In the film, each woman's voice will be heard "in turn," each memory will be given time to express itself "in turn." In that, the *nuba* presents, in Bensmaïa's words "a world in formation or gestation,"[14] that is, not a whole having achieved its final stage of construction, but some world caught in its own fluid polyphonic, serial becoming.

The film is presented in seven chapters or movements following the seven movements of the *nuba:* (1) *touchyia,* or overture; (2) *istikhbar,* or prelude; (3) *m'ssadar,* or adagio; (4) *b'tayhi,* or allegro; (5) *derj,* or lento; (6) *nessraf,* or moderato; (7) *khlass,* or finale. Yet even the musical *nuba* architectonics of the film are playful. Their relationship with the narrative "progression" visible on-screen is complicated by the fact that the musical text, rather than illustrating the topic – engaging in text painting in the musical sense of the phrase – has both a loosely structuring function and a highly symbolic one. The film is dedicated to two individuals: Zoulikha, a heroine of the Algerian resistance, and Belá Bartók (1881–1941), the Hungarian composer and proto-ethnomusicologist. The latter collected peasant songs and musical pieces not only in the Magyar, Slovakian, and Romanian regions but also in Algeria, where he resided briefly in 1913, gathering folk pieces in the Biskra area.[15] As avid collectors, the musician and the filmmaker share the same project: listening to and recording humble voices "in an almost silent Algeria" (as the opening text makes clear), and honoring them in their work (whether cinematic or musical). Djebar explained that her aim was to transmit the chronicle of women "as they narrated themselves in the ordeals they had known in the war. I also wanted them to be able to see themselves, their true presence, with the authentic beauty they had, yet never suspected."[16] As Lila, the narrator who speaks for Djebar in *The Nuba,* says: "I am not looking for anything but I am listening."

Similarly, Bartók described how a composer of modern music listens to folk music until he "has completely absorbed the idiom of peasant music which has become his musical mother tongue."[17] The Algerian journey of the Hungarian master to listen to peasant songs almost foreshadows Djebar's own careful mode of listening. Hence the entire *nuba*

resonates as a homage to both Bartók and the women in Mount Chenoua. But this is where the musical parallel stops, as the filmic *nuba*
diverges strongly from Bartók's ethno-musical preoccupation early on,
to signify something else, distinct from folklore. As Malkmus and Armes
have commented, Bartók's "Algerian pieces" are heard playing when the
women villagers are talking, or at least emanate from their tale-telling
locus, whereas the indigenous flute solo is heard when the camera turns
to Lila (the urbanite, the insider/outsider) and her world. This points
to two different meanings attached to music: music as folklore (the old
peasants do not need to rely on it to tell their stories in an authentic
voice); and music as gender marker (no music accompanies or responds
to Ali, the only male character in the film, who, furthermore, is mute).[18]

Moreover, if the use of the *nuba* as a structuring device in the film
constitutes a homage to Algerian music and culture, it is also almost
systematically derailed from its authentic settings and initial functions:

> These *nubas* have existed in a collective culture for four centuries.... This is a
> film on the rural, whereas the *nuba* is an urban form, an ancient court music! In
> the film, I used diverse types of music. Visually, the film is as region-specific as
> it can be, yet aurally, it includes musical pieces from all the regions of Algeria.
> There was a will to alternate them, and put them next to one another. There is a
> flute piece from the Sétif area, and I used some Tuareg music in the ancient sec-
> tion. I tried to have a soundtrack that would illustrate the Algerian aural reality,
> both in its past and in its space.[19]

Djebar's use of this particular form of composition can therefore be explained only in the context of Algerian post-independence, unity-build-
ing élan: the sound of the urban *nuba* can now resonate in villages because in the new state of Algeria, the city and the country, the rulers (the
court) and the peasantry, are busy constructing one national identity,
one (Algerian) music, perhaps.

Additionally, Djebar mentioned that she wanted the emotions in
her film (the part that results from human relationships) to be conveyed through music because, she remembers, "at a time when Algeria
was completely besieged, isolated people in forsaken places expressed
their helplessness with the sound of a flute."[20] It is hard, then, not to see
women's voices as being these "isolated people in forsaken places," who
remain to be heard. In that case, the use of the *nuba* configuration of the

film acts as metaphor for the coming into voice of a hitherto silenced womanspeak.

Yet the Djebarian *nuba* structure does not necessarily follow its pre-scribed path. As Bensmaïa points out in his analysis of the film as a work of fragmentation, there is no coincidence between the musical and the narrative series that constitute the film, whose very structure signals no organized, continuous whole.[21] On one level, then, the intensely frag-mented soundtrack illustrates the chaos of post-independence Algeria, whose construction was in progress in the 1970s, as Djebar was making this film. One could also look at the musical structure of the piece, in its very insistence on being open (somewhat like a jazz standard leaving room for call-and-response, solos, improvisations) and its mobility and malleability (a musical piece is in progress, a suite is being played, things are moving), as another sign that the form of the film espouses its central concern: the film is always in progress, just as the (re)telling of the years of *mujahidat*'s resistance is in progress, with no end in sight, as the final song closing the film intimates. In that, *The Nuba* contributes to several larger oeuvres that supersede its singularity: the telling of the war (his-tory and herstory), or the emergence from silence of Algerian women – or, perhaps more aptly, the listening to the "heretofore ignored words of women,"[22] and, of course, Djebar's own textual production both writ-ten and cinematographic. The film then echoes womanspeak within its diegesis and outside, as it fragments and unites the voices and whispers of women in the messages they convey. The apparent *nuba* structure of the film opens up the possibility for a transvergent narrative to bloom and branch out, in synch perhaps with the women's voices that are captured on tape, but never continuously, never along a given immutable path, but rather, in a mix of direct and indirect voices orchestrated by narrator Lila.

FILM ANALYSIS: TRANSVERGENCE
OF VOICE(S) AND SILENCE(S)

Lila as Transvergent Narrator

Telling and staging such an expansive narrative requires a narrator who can be both understanding of the voices (able to share their references) and slightly remote (an arm's or camera's length away) so as to capture the women's stories in an alternatively intimate and fresh, almost alien, way. Hence the gatherer of stories (who is also a generator of the story of these stories) engages in what we would call a form of "*allogenetic* narration." Adapted from Novak's understanding of *allogenesis*, this dynamic form of narrative signals a tension between the familiar and the alien within, as the narrator (re)produces the narratives of the women around her: "While *xenogenesis* implies a fertile encounter with an initially alien species, the *alien-from-without*, *allogenesis* suggests the production of an alien species from initially genetically compatible lineages, or the *alien-from-within*."[23] In the evolutionary process of allogenesis, the species has reached a point at which it has become alien to its origins. I would argue that *über*-narrator Lila, who once left the region of Mount Chenoua, and has recently returned in her quest for the *mujahidat*'s stories, has become the alien from within in the process: the outsider who has come back to claim her place inside the house (and collective narrative) of women. As she is prodding the memory and words of the women, she is also interrogating her own memory. She thus ends up weaving a narrative, the very making of which is caught in an allogenetic tension: on the one hand, it springs from a shared, known origin (e.g., the shared ancestry and geography of the women of Mount Chenoua); on the other hand, it also points to a deeply alien element (e.g., Lila is a reporter equipped with cameras, driving a Mehari Citroën; and Lila is a former prisoner). The cultural sharing and common need to remember and vocalize the repressed stories open up the possibility of disinterring a silenced story within – a story therefore as yet unknown, unclear, alien. While Lila is herself engaged in her own anamnesis, she is also engaging others in the same kind of memory quest (as has been amply described by Donadey, Bensmaïa, and Mortimer):[24] somewhere in me lies a story in waiting, a story I cannot yet fathom but that I will make emerge. Similarly, history-making in Algeria needs to unearth and connect – re-member – the crucial roles played by women in it (Donadey, Khannous). So the allogenetic narrative "caught" in progress on-screen is both a writing/righting of history and a deeply individual and gendered quest.

What will be found is alien because repressed, and alien because newly acknowledged to the world. Women have not talked about their actions during the war. They have not appeared on-screen, and have not been decorated by the FLN authorities after the war. They simply returned to the home, and stayed indoors, as we are told at the sobering end of the film.

The role played by Lila the narrator is complicated by the fact that she never speaks directly: her voice has an acousmatic-like quality. Although we see whose voice it is, we are seldom given the opportunity to make the visual character coincide with the haunting inner voice we hear. As a result, the isolated voice has the ghostly quality that characterizes Michel Chion's notion of *acousmêtre*,[25] that shadowy presence of a disembodied voice on-screen. It also puts us, extra-diegetic viewers, in a skewed position: we are listening to an inner monologue to which the intra-diegetic characters have no access. Moreover, the other narratives are often filtered through it to the point of erasure of their original voices: Lila's voice at times covers and relates the stories of other women.

Her repeated professed desire to hear (e.g., "I could not speak. I am beginning to hear you: you, the women of Chenoua. Open a door, greet, say nothing, let them speak.") constitutes a necessary prelude not only to other women voicing their memories of the war, but to herself regaining her own memory, and then freeing herself from it (in a talking cure of sorts). Here, Lila remains mute to make room for the women's voices and listen to them. Yet, her generous initial listener's aphasia is only temporary: "I will speak of the death of Zoulikha and of my old days in prison. To be able to speak, I need to be free – free of these events that haunt my memory." In the end, then, Lila's narrative embeds others, becomes plural and deeply personal, historical, and emotional. It is a transvergent narrative in that it succeeds in traversing various storytelling genres without adhering to their individual strictures for too long. In fact, it only traverses each woman's story, as it flashes clips of each tale, never its full account. Furthermore, all these narrative fragments, although echoing one another, neither converge into a unidirectional meta-narrative, nor diverge from one another. In that way too, they are transvergent: they are simultaneously similar and different, familiar and alien. They also traverse several narrative modes, from first-person to third-person accounts, from factual tales to legends handed down at home by women from generation to generation. By giving her interviewees an intimate space in her film comparable to their home (metonymically illustrated by the shot of Lila and her grandmother sharing a bed in which the little girl is told stories of her ancestors' exploits), Djebar succeeds in transmuting private stories (and mute pauses) into public ones.

The Nuba with its "turns" and twists, can play with the "eloquent" silences of these women, including Lila's, and provides a space and time in which their tremulous voices can finally free themselves from repressed narratives that echo one another not only in their common themes (acts of resistance during the liberation war) but also across time (the resistance against the occupying forces in 1871 at Mount Chenoua). Here two phenomena are at play: on the formal narrative level, what Zimra has called the "'nestling' effect of the dream-recreated fiction of their pasts within the very real 'documentary' interviews that recreate their present"[26] (e.g., the episode of the women characters gathering and dancing in the Dahra grotto); and on a more symbolic level, the expression of women's deeply buried narratives in a film can be perceived as a loud act of resistance against the systematic erasure of women in Algerian official history in 1978.

Silence

The point of departure of the film lies in an initial rupture, then: the breaking away from silence for the Algerian *mujahidat,* their being filmed and recognized. Yet that very point is problematic, given the manifold, polysemic quality of a silence that refers to several local, cultural traits having to do with the specificities of Algerian history and gender politics.

Early in her beautiful analysis of Algerian women's silence from precolonial Algeria to the early 1990s, Marnia Lazreg demonstrates that throughout Algerian history women's silence, far from signaling passivity, either results from pressures exerted by various forces (e.g., social, political, economic) beyond the women's control, or conceals actions of resistance (louder than words or silence). Hence what is perceived as an absence (of words, of expression), a lack, may in fact signify a lot. But it is silence that has become one of the staples of representation of Algerian women. It has become a salient feature of a stereotypical portrayal of them, even in cinema.

TABLE 1.1. Trends in Enrollment Ratios in Algerian Schools
according to Census Data – Gender Population Aged 6–14 Years

	1948	1954	1966	1977	1987	1998
Male	13.4%	23.5%	56.80%	80.80%	87.75%	85.28%
Female	4.6%	9.5%	36.90%	59.60%	71.56%	80.73%
Both	9.1%	16.6%	47.20%	70.40%	79.86%	83.05%

Source: Kateb, "The Expansion of Access to Education and the Demography of Algeria."

> The first Algerian film to have featured women prominently as active agents in the history of their country, *The Battle of Algiers,* managed to provide no information about their biographies – as it did for Ali-la Pointe, a major male protagonist – or the process through which they became urban guerrillas. Their participation was presented as arising *ex nihilo,* and confined to taking orders. Typically, they spoke very little, thus highlighting women's silence at the very time that their actions spoke loudly.[27]

If the history of representation of women has muted them systematically for centuries, then Lila's professed intent to listen to them in the *nuba* constitutes a revolutionary gesture. The film finally gives them a space to record their voices, that is, to literally capture them and give them permanence. For in the landscape of Algeria in the 1970s where schooled children have learned to write in French and the proportion of illiterate girls and women is still huge (see table 1.1), filming them also preserves their voices. Here, cinema saves women's heritage, as it negates the danger of erasure (endemic to oral transmission) by recording it with the tools of a written, technological culture driven by its need to leave its traces.

Lazreg's point further underscores the necessity to decode each womanly silence as a signifier that produces meaning. Capturing the semantics of these silences is no easy task, and if the meaning of each silence is at stake in this film, the process of decoding it takes center stage. In the final analysis, Djebar tells several stories in one: she unfolds the hidden meaning of each silence, hints at the history that has led to each silence, and also tells the story of the unraveling of the women's previous muteness. The aim is not necessarily to fully divulge what the silence has been concealing, but rather to signal the existence of a secret, in a form of writing/filming that Calle-Gruber has called "narrative diffraction,"[28] which flashes intimations of the secret to be stitched together. In order to do that, she uses narrative detours and employs a filmic montage in which both the words and the silences of women will be heeded. Filming such a history of women requires a new system of narration, away from the previous schemes of tale-telling and history-writing. As Bensmaïa noted, "Here we are done exchanging stories, in order to start writing our complicated history. We have gone from the closed world of tales to the open and fragmented universe of History."[29] That openness necessitates a flexible narrative structure. This is what Djebar sets up with her framing tale (Lila's tale): it allows the fiction to interrupt or solicit memory (whether individual or collective). Thus, women's silence(s) can be broken, and their history claimed and projected publicly. Yet, it also allows a space in the film for silence. The latter produces meaning next to – and with – the uttered tales.

Silence: *The French Musical "Rest"*

The musical meaning of *silence* in French is "rest," as in the rest between two notes, two chords, between two rhythmic patterns, or within a rhythmic pattern. In some ways, the French musical term is more apt to describe one of the constituents of the musical piece, for it is not a "rest" but a momentary absence of sound that gives meaning metonymically to the sounds that surround it. It is an organic part of a composition, of a *nuba,* and of expression.

We have seen already that the narrator is mostly silent with the intra-diegetic characters but very talkative with the extra-diegetic spectator. If her silence on-screen is part of the pattern of communication with the women of Mount Chenoua, it is not part of the second phase of filmmaking – the postproduction phase. In the latter, Lila, who has witnessed and participated in the painful irruption of memories, now talks, insatiably. Her volubility, superimposed on the film, is double-edged: it both expresses the hitherto muted stories entrusted to her by the interviewed women and refashions them in one continuous narrative voice that becomes the narrating voice of a unified yet multiple Algerian female storyteller. A modern incarnation of Shahrazad, she follows her legendary model's narrative ploy, as the story she tells similarly contains other narratives. She also follows a similar goal: instead of saving women from the Sultan's death threats, she rescues them from oblivion and restores their agency. Now the *mujahidat*'s feats will be known, their stories recorded in a meta-narrative of female memory.

Meanwhile, the women in the film are coaxed out of their silence. But they, of course, do not tell everything. Here is how Zoulikha's daughter recounts the last time she saw her mother who had joined the freedom fighters: "Eight days before her arrest, my mother really wanted to see us. Wearing a veil, I took the bus alone to the station, then was led over the mountains. There I spent three days with my mother. All the *mujahidin* called her 'mother.'" The text reflects an inordinate degree of reserve. The woman evokes an intensely precious memory of herself as a young girl braving all sorts of dangers and fears in order to see her mother, from whom she has been separated. In telling the story, she does not describe her feelings (possibly the memory of the pain endured during separation), but, rather, is careful to defend her mother's honor after all these years: Zoulikha's comrades in arms saw her as a mother, not as a potential sexual partner.[30] She does not reflect on the choice her mother had made to join the resistance, which meant depriving her children of their mother. She does not comment on the fact that she too is a victim of Zoulikha's engagement with the *mujahidin*. What is left unsaid is as significant as what is said, and completes it (as a musical *silence* would).

Furthermore, Lila stitches the various stories together around some events that do remain silent. For instance, we know Lila has gone to prison and remains quiet about what happened there. The film resorts to an imaginary visual sequence (jailed women dressed in white) to signify it. That silence echoes the one that surrounds the death of Lila's brother and the disappearance of Zoulikha's body. These silences become the Barthian *puncta* of the film (i.e., the details in the representation that "point to me"[31]), the driving enigmas around which other narratives circle endlessly, unable as they are to provide any answers: "These stories remain forever juxtaposed, scattered fragments that constantly refer to two blind spots: Zoulikha's disappearance and the brother's death. But this is probably one of the great lessons of the film: history is impossible to achieve without a true anamnesis; and the condition for the latter is to suspend meaning, the short-term goal, in short, to go into fallow."[32]

By "going into fallow," an expression borrowed from psychoanalyst Ma-
sud Khan, Bensmaïa means putting oneself in a position of receptivity
to one's intimate self, to become still instead of busy in order to have
the space and freedom to be able to reconstruct oneself. Truly, these
mystifying "blind spots" whose elucidation never comes, deprive us,
the viewers, of a much desired resolution. In that, the narrative keeps on
its allogenetic trajectory: it contains a couple of elements identified as
alien, then circles around them, branches out of them, registers them as
blanks, and protects the layers of silence that surround them. There will
be no answer. There will be no closure. And yet, the story of Zoulikha,
for instance, remains at the core of the entire film.

CLOSE-VIEWING: THE ZOULIKHA NARRATIVE

This particular "visible blank" of a story will become an obsession for
Djebar, long after the time of her making the film. She will eventually
write a novel on Zoulikha for the latter's daughters, *La Femme sans sépulture,* published in 2002. As I have said elsewhere, her later rewriting and
re-membering of Zoulikha's story after the film merges with the telling
of a myth.[33] But in the film version, Zoulikha's absence is represented
in the aural and visual montage of her. It is the precise elements of this
"blind spot" in the film to which I now wish to turn, in an attempt to
further understand the precise workings of such an allogenetic, transvergent filmic narrative.

The sequence (53:00–60:00) has the voices of the women who knew
her tell her story off-screen. Even Lila, our official guide and narrator, has
disappeared from the screen and the soundtrack. Three female acousmatic voices are heard telling her story: Zoulikha's two daughters and
sister. Views of Cherchell by day accompany their aural narrative fragments: the sequence opens with a long shot of the city, followed by a
zoom that will take us all the way into the various streets, courtyards,
and enclosed patios of the medina, where the women and children live.
These shots are high-angle ones, as if an omniscient narrating camera was
looking for what the place had to say about the heroine of the Algerian
resistance who still has no tomb to her name. The entire sequence closes
on a symmetrical shot of Cherchell: this time, the camera zooms out.

In between these two points, however, the visual images both serve as counterpoints to the simultaneous aural narrative and retrospectively add meaning to a previous narrative segment. At some point, Zoulikha's sister relates the episode of joining the resistance network in the mountains and adds: "My sister took out her dentures to look older. Dressed as a peasant, she got arms, medicine, and ammunition and brought them to the mountains, hidden in a basket." While we hear this, we see, from behind, a woman veiled in white from head to toe crossing a street, and the screen, diagonally, from lower right to upper left.

This shot evokes the French black-and-white archival high-angle shot that is spliced in the emblematic opening sequence of the film, before the credits roll: a woman entirely veiled in white crosses a street – and the screen diagonally from upper left to lower right. Freeze. Retrospectively, we can now decode the possible meaning of the French archival footage: the phantom-like figure in white might be hiding food or weapons for the insurgents under her *haïk* (as the women are shown doing in *Battle of Algiers*). The anonymous ghostlike silhouette is an individual, a Zoulikha. Now we are given the narrative that goes with the muted white shadow. We are given access to her individuality. We see what the French military did not. Yet Djebar gives us the information close to an hour after she has shown us the French black-and-white frame.

Similarly, as the sister describes the last time Zoulikha was seen, the camera lingers on a fountain in Cherchell's square. "When they made her leave the forest, surrounded by jeeps and tanks, she yelled to the crowd of sobbing peasants: 'Why are you crying? Look! All of this arsenal for just one woman!'" Doves are then seen flitting about the top of a fountain in Cherchell and remind us of the shot of the doves that the local saint's seventh wife released (see figure 2 and figure 3). This reported scene around Zoulikha's impending death thus signals her power on several levels: the hyperbolic means used by the French to capture her reveal their inordinate fear of her, and forecast their defeat; she is able to comfort and inspire "sobbing peasants"; she chose to be free and fight for freedom (as the flight of the doves illustrates).

This is not the only instance in which Zoulikha is linked to the saint's wife. As Ramanathan notes, she "becomes the subject of a folk song, like the seventh wife of a folk tale, where neither is monumentalized."[34]

The story of Zoulikha is anchored both in the factual testimonies of the women from her family and in a mythical text that will close the film. It is exposed (in the photographic sense of the term) only via Djebar's film but will remain incomplete, with no closure. The transvergent narrative that takes on an incomplete mosaic form in the film will be prolonged in a written text over twenty years later, thus erasing the boundaries between written and audiovisual text. *The Nuba* constitutes but one fragment of an ambitious larger project: writing and righting the history of Algerian women. This is only its first step.

CONCLUSION

Examined here as the first manifestation of a transvergent form of narrative, Djebar's *Nuba* is nonformulaic in the largest sense of the term. Viewed as a stand-alone piece, this film steers away from linearity and successfully weaves together narrative disparate elements on various modes (it traverses genres: e.g., documentary, archival footage, fiction, history, legend), and knits the unknown into the known, and vice versa. Taken as a moment in Djebar's textual production, the film inscribes cinema in a literary oeuvre, and highlights in the process the author's daring experimentation with narrative techniques. Seen in its historical context, the narrative strikes as a crucial, urgent step toward the righting of Algerian history: orchestrating the voices of Algerian women also means giving back the *mujahidat* their agency. In the end, on all levels, *The Nuba of the Women of Mount Chenoua* is still a narration in progress, waiting to be heeded and augmented. Seeing this film today, after the unspeakable violence of the 1990s as well as more recent outbreaks in Algeria, reminds us that we still need to make known the plight of the "isolated people in forsaken places" and find the peasants' flutes and the images to articulate their suffering.

2

Farida Benlyazid's Initiation Narrative:
A Door to the Sky (Morocco, 1988)

As soon as Dunyazad enters the Sultan's chamber, Shahrazad's narration becomes clearly bifurcated: thanks to the presence of her sister, the storyteller addresses two audiences as the same time. Shahrazad, having placed Dunyazad (the familiar, powerless, female character) alongside the Sultan (the less familiar, powerful male figure), is thus able to play with the familiar and with power, and find the adequate terms to address both audiences at once, as she makes the alien and the strange familiar, so as to enthrall the Sultan with her tales.

Similarly, a Maghrebi woman director tells a story to an audience in the know at home, and another one abroad. This is where the notion of transvergent spectatorship arises as a descriptor of today's viewers of Shahrazad's cinema. Two films in our corpus give two widely different interpretations of such a phenomenon: Farida Benlyazid, in *Bab al-sama maftouh/ Une Porte sur le ciel/A Door to the Sky*, constructs her double audience and shifts from one to the other in the middle of the filmic narrative. Hence it addresses two distinct audiences one after the other. On the other hand, Selma Baccar, in *Khochkhach/Fleur d'oubli/Flower of Oblivion* (see chapter 7), keeps the extra-diegetic gaze in flux. *Flower of Oblivion* requires the extra-diegetic viewer to change perspectives throughout the film via an ingenious system of relays through the gaze of various intra-diegetic spectators.

A Door to the Sky, a unique film about Muslim spirituality in the Sufi tradition, talks to a transvergent audience (both Moroccan and French – or European) through the character of Nadia, the bicultural protagonist. The latter finds herself gradually exchanging one cultural identity for another, in a process comparable to Virginia Woolf's protagonist in *Orlando*, who changes from a woman into a man. In *A Door to the Sky*, Nadia, through her various stages of becoming, is able to initiate both cultural audiences into her narrative and the meaning of her spiritual and feminist journey.

The first film directed by Farida Benlyazid, *A Door* was also produced and written by her. "I wrote *A Door to the Sky* which, while not autobiographical, was inspired by my own spiritual quest. This experience was a great adventure."[1] The film received a number of awards (e.g., the bronze Tanit at the Tunis International Film Festival, the bronze Annab in Annaba, Algeria, the prize for best scenario in Meknes, Morocco), was selected in a number of international film festivals, and was shown on various television channels in Belgium, France, Germany, and Morocco.[2] Although it appealed to viewers within *and* outside Morocco, the film is squarely rooted in the old city of Fez and its history. It inaugurates Benlyazid's city trilogy: (1) *A Door to the Sky* (1988) on the holy Moroccan city of Fez; (2) *Casablanca, Casablanca* (2002) on the corrupt financial capital of Morocco; (3) *The Wretched Life of Juanita Narboni* (2005) on the cosmopolitan Moroccan city of Tangier.

OPENING DOORS

Farida Benlyazid's Free Spirit

Born in Tangier, where she resides today, Benlyazid grew up loving cinema from a tender age, a love that was connected to her mother from the start. When she was a child, her mother took her almost every day to see "American, Spanish, Italian, French, Egyptian and even Indian films," with an infectious enthusiasm that stood in stark contrast to her father's deprecating assessment of the illusory nature of film: "They take you for a ride, they tell you tall tales and take money from you."[3] When Benlyazid describes her "enchanted" childhood in cosmopolitan Tangier, she evokes the various cultures that made up the city with obvious pleasure:

> We heard flamenco. At Christmas, the Spanish would come out and everybody would party. At Purim, the Jewish kids would walk from house to house offering pastries. At school, we celebrated Muslim and Christian holidays, and taking the day off was allowed on Jewish holidays. It is this multiple identity, these different religions residing in convivial neighborhoods that I would like to find again in the world today."[4]

Her multicultural upbringing (she spoke Spanish with her mother, Arabic with her father) has not only shaped her outlook on life and her own brand of wisdom, but has also imbued every single one of her films: her first one, *A Door*, is, of course, no exception.

She left Morocco for Paris in 1971 to study, at first, French literature at the University of Paris VIII, then, from 1974 to 1976, cinema at the École Supérieure des Études Cinématographiques (ESEC). She directed her first film in France, *Identités de femmes* (Women's Identities), a short piece about women immigrants in France that aired on French television in 1979. She returned to Morocco in 1981 to find a rather weak cinema industry in her country: the impetus for local filmmaking after independence had died out during the repressive "Years of Lead" suffered under the rule of King Hassan II (1961–1999), marked, among other harsh measures, by unprecedented levels of censorship. She joined a group of enthusiastic filmmakers and started her career as a scriptwriter, before she also became a producer, a maker of documentaries and films for TV, an assistant director, and a production manager. She describes their shared commitment to cinema as both a cultural necessity and an intensely political act: "Day after day we tried to convince the authorities of the importance of cinema for our culture. Today, a country without images looks like a country whose culture is bound to disappear. Only the images fashioned by the Other have been imposed on our youth and have molded their identity unilaterally (hence their desire to emigrate)."[5] Such alienation in the representation of Moroccan subjects was prevalent in the films projected on the screens of Tangier in the early 1980s: the market was flooded with American, Egyptian, and Indian films. She remembers the rare local productions as almost foreign novelties to a Moroccan audience: "I remember that in the beginning, the Moroccan audience could not but laugh as they saw and heard characters speak in their language, in a décor with which they were familiar."[6] A very large part of Benlyazid's aim, whether in the scripts she wrote or the films she directed, became to engage a Moroccan audience in a conversation on shared terms. This meant she would (a) lead her viewers to a comfortable place of recognition of images of themselves on the screen and (b) speak their language(s).

Before her first feature film, she wrote several film scripts, most notably for two Moroccan directors whose films focus on women in Morocco: her second husband, Jillali Ferhati (*Charkhun fi-l Hâʿit/Une Brèche dans le mur/A Hole in the Wall* [1979], and *'Arâʿis min qaçab/Poupées de roseaux/Reed Dolls* [1981]) and Mohamed Abderrahman Tazi, with whom she coauthored the scenario of *Badis 1564* (1989) and for whom she wrote the screenplay of *Bahthan 'an zawj Imraʿatî/A la Recherche du mari de ma femme/Looking for My Wife's Husband* (1993). More recently, she wrote the script for *Qosat Warda/L'Histoire d'une rose cueillie trop tôt/A Story of a Rose* by Abdelmajid R'chich (2007). Meanwhile, her literary talents also expanded from script writing to journalism and criticism in journals and magazines such as *Kantara, Le Libéral, El Mundo,* and *Autrement.*

If her films and scripts bear the unmistakable mark of a woman of letters, they also raise political consciousness in Moroccan society. Her script for Ferhati's *Reed Dolls* can be seen as mapping a possible itinerary out of female subjugation, silence, and isolation in its call for women to "join forces and stand for each other" across generations.[7] Similarly, she adapted a courageous book[8] for her film *Casablanca, Casablanca* (2002), which denounced the corruption endemic in every stratum of society (in an especially abhorrent way in the privileged classes, in the political and financial milieus) and she insisted on inserting in her film a quotation from the book, which she regarded as a central statement by its author, Rida Lamrini: "There can be no democracy without true justice."

Her feature films and documentaries are animated by a similar desire for justice for women. After *A Door to the Sky,* she made *Keid Ensa/ Ruses de Femmes/ The Wiles of Women* (1999). "*Keid Ensa* which means, in Arabic, 'the wile of women' is a tale originally from Andalusia, whose trace can be found in Federico Garcia Lorca's puppet theater."[9] Lalla Aïcha, a very bright and vivacious merchant's daughter, marries a prince, who locks her in a cellar to teach her a lesson, only to be outwitted by her. If the tale has some of the trappings of *One Thousand and One Nights,* it also conveys a strong feminist message about female resistance to patriarchal constraints. Similarly, her documentaries take up women's issues at home and abroad, be it in the short film she shot in France about immigrant women, *Identités de Femme/Women's Identities* (1979) or in her study of a Senegalese woman, *Aminata Traoré une femme du Sahel/ Aminata Traoré, a Woman of the Sahel* (1993). Her last feature film, made in 2005, also focuses on the story of a Spanish woman who remains single her entire life in Tangier. It is the eponymous screen adaptation of the novel by Spanish author Angel Vásquez,[10] *La vida perra de Juanita Narboni/Juanita de Tanger/The Wretched Life of Juanita Narboni,* and it was coproduced in Spain and Morocco.

A true free spirit in politics and in life, she is also a fiercely independent filmmaker and created her own production company, Tingitania (from the ancient name of Tangier: Tingis), in order to make the films she wanted, without having "to worry about the market."[11] A versatile director, equally at ease with fiction and documentary, Benlyazid codirected with Abderrahim Mettour her most recent production, *Casanayda/Casa ça bouge/Casa Is Rocking,* 2007). This 52-minute-long documentary traces the ten-year history of a cultural youth movement (music, graphic arts, vernacular languages, poetry, dance, and fashion) from its first *L'boulevard* festival, which grew from its initial alternative, underground form into a vibrant, highly visible presence in Casablanca and, beyond that, into one of the most important urban movements in the Maghreb through the Internet and the print and broadcast media. Its adepts claim their right to speak and write in *darija,* the Moroccan Arabic dialect, instead of *fusha,* classical Arabic, and to adopt and mix hip-hop aesthetics and politics into their various art forms. Here again, Benlyazid initiates a conversation with a young, hip audience, and informs an older one about the positions of the younger. In that, I contend, she establishes transvergent links to a multiple audience. Some of its members are in the know, others out of the loop, but she creates a space of exchange in her film for all viewers. This is not the first time she has done so: her very first feature, *Bab al-sama maftouh/ Une Porte sur le ciel/A Door to the Sky* (1988), also establishes a conversation with a multiple audience off-screen, along a transvergent path that shifts in the course of the film between men and women as well as between secular, Westernized viewers and Sufi believers in Morocco.

Film Synopsis

The film follows the spiritual voyage of Nadia (played by actress, writer, director, producer Zakia Tahri, who most notably directed *Number One* in 2009), a young woman with a Franco-Moroccan identity, from Paris to Fez, and from a secular life to a Sufi order. It is both an individual tale and an emblematic one. While the narrative raises questions about gender politics, identity, and Muslim practices, the film also illuminates the issues at stake in relating to an extra-diegetic multicultural audience.

Nadia returns from Paris, where she has been living with French press photographer Jean-Philippe, to Fez, where her father lies dying. Nadia's mother, a French painter, died when she was a child. In contrast to her two siblings – Leyla, who lives in an affluent, modern suburb of Fez with her Moroccan husband and children, and Driss, who lives in France with his French wife and children, and has "chosen to be French" – Nadia claims her identity as both French and Moroccan.

Her father's death precipitates an intense form of depression that isolates Nadia. However, the voice of Kirana chanting a Qur'anic litany to honor the dead father seems to elicit buried emotions, imaged on-screen through flashbacks of Nadia's childhood. Kirana, a devout Muslim woman of great wisdom and tolerance, gently coaxes Nadia out of her melancholy and mourning, and teaches her a woman-centered interpretation of Islam. The latter boasts a long history of female leaders as empowering models whom Nadia reads about as she studies Sufi texts and is initiated into Muslim mysticism. Nadia, under Kirana's guidance, uncovers the parts of her Moroccan Muslim cultural and spiritual heritage that she had hitherto ignored, and distances herself from the French part of her identity. (She ends her intimate relationship with Jean-Philippe, who is now just a long-distance friend.) After she fights against the inheritance laws that privilege her brother in Morocco, she decides to turn the palatial family house into a *zawiya*, a shelter and spiritual center for women. Nadia is soon on the verge of bankruptcy. But the spirit of Ba Sassi, a family friend who died a long time ago and who has visited her in several visions, advises her to unearth some treasure buried in the garden.

Nadia's *zawiya* is successful, until the women start resenting the presence in their midst of the newly arrived and unconventional ex-convict Bahia, and refuse to admit Abdelkrim, a sick young man whom Nadia is trying to heal. In the end, Nadia's open spirit can no longer flourish there: she and Abdelkrim leave both the *zawiya* and the city of Fez.

The Door of Interpretation

The Arabic title of the film – *Bab sama maftouh*, literally "The door of the sky is open" – echoes a recurring phrase in the Qur'an in which the gates of heaven open up for the righteous and remain closed to liars.[12] It further resonates along various waves of meaning, depending on the set of references shared off-screen with particular sets of listeners/readers.

To Arabic viewers and feminists it might evoke the 1963 film by Henri Barakat, a screen adaptation of the novel by Egyptian feminist Latifa Al-Zayyat, *Al Bab al maftuh/The Open Door*, published in 1960. The latter traced the journey of a young woman freeing herself from patriarchal rules just as Egypt was also liberating itself from the shackles of neocolonialism in its battle against the British and the French over the nationalization of the Suez Canal. The similarity of the title highlights a parallel strong, public, female stand against patriarchal institutions: "The first novel by a woman to be recognized by the legitimate criticism, *The Open Door* was certainly admired at the time for its artistic qualities, but perhaps above all because it represented a break with traditional women's writing, which had concentrated in the main on the domestic sphere."[13] If Benlyazid's film shares a feminist bent with Al-Zayyat's novel, the authors differ on how to empower women: Nadia reinvests the domestic sphere, redefines it as a women-only haven away from patriarchal authority, and eventually attains an autonomy that transcends the walls of the *zawiya*. Benlyazid also defines woman's power in ancient, Muslim terms rather than new, possibly Western-inflected, ones. First of all, Nadia is a *sherifa*, a descendant of the Prophet, and, as such, endowed with inherited spiritual powers. And then, given the location of the story (Fez), Nadia also appears as a late-twentieth-century element of the potent Muslim matriarchal lineage that gave birth to such eminent figures as Fatima al-Fihriya, founder of al Qaraouine Mosque in Fez in the tenth century,[14] to whom the film is dedicated. The title would then hint at the role of women as scholars and interpreters of the sacred text, as well as at the act of interpreting itself – an issue constantly evoked in the exegeses of the Qur'an.

The difficulty in interpreting refers neither to the possible available glosses on the holy text by this or that branch of Islam, nor to the ways to understand, for instance, the role(s) the Qur'an ascribes to women. Rather, the title and its suggestion of openness shows how to interpret any situation through one's own independent critical evaluation of the principles revealed to Mohamed. The figure of the scholar, the judge, the interpreter is central to the practice of Islam.

> His work is to understand the *hadith,* the Qur'an. The good thing is that we have the door of interpretation (*bab al itjihad-maftuh*) open, so you can continue to develop, you keep reading, the world is progressing, religion didn't come to restrict you. . . . There are issues, worshiping issues that aren't set, so these are about interpretation. So on these issues, each believer looks to his own interpreter [*mutjahid*] for understanding . . . If there was going to be only one opinion, there wouldn't be a need for something called interpretation.[15]

This open door of, and to, interpretation leads to a more flexible vision of *shariah*, the Muslim law, as the latter becomes subject to the possibility of a plurality of meanings. According to some Sunni scholars, "current generations have not only a right but a duty to exercise *itjihad* or independent judgment, if they want Islam to be adapted to the modern world."[16] Benlyazid seems to illustrate that very point by giving visibility to her gender in that function: women too have the "right" and "duty" to practice *itjihad*. The latter is dynamic: opening the door of *itjihad* widens the liminal space between faith (and its duty of obedience) and critical thinking (judgment). And it shows the way to a daring, authentic form of liberation theology applied to Islam. In the end – almost literally – the sky is the limit!

This open door to *itjihad* guides the spiritual content of the filmic narrative, its structure as well as, literally, its visual language and its space. We see Nadia closing doors to the outside world once she has created her *zawiya,* as she feels she has reached certainty in understanding her role in life. We also see her sliding open the glass door of Jean-Philippe's hotel room to listen to the call to prayer, to show Jean-Philippe what she calls "the timelessness of Islam," as if that gesture alone might open up his mind and spirit to her quest. Later she opens up the door leading to Abdelkrim's chamber (against his will). Throughout the film, doors are filmed in fixed, lasting shots that punctuate the narrative with symbolic reflective pauses, as each opening or closing of a door marks a step toward this or that understanding.

Nadia has "interpreted" her father's house as a *zawiya.* Leonardo De Franceschi describes the new value of the space in almost sacred terms: "the house itself, organized around a patio is willed by the protagonist-subject to change functions from family temple to *zawiya,* i.e. refuge for women in trouble."[17] The blue door of the house thus changes values: from the door that opens to welcome back the returning father in the flashback scene at the beginning of the film, it becomes the symbolic entrance into a female world that is contained within. If Nadia wishes her *zawiya* to be open to battered, dispossessed, desperate women, she has to close it to their male abusers. However, when the women of the *zawiya* refuse to give sanctuary to Bahia (the rebellious young atheist woman recently released from jail) or Abdelkrim (the young man whom Nadia heals), then the door needs to be open again for Nadia. This time, the door opens out for her to leave a house that has by now acquired the repressive, segregationist quality that Nadia has never tolerated in her life.

As the door of interpretation opens wider and wider, the dynamics of spiritual growth move the narrative and its protagonist along a trajectory that leads her from a secular view of the world to a Sufi one. Nadia is both the agent and the locus of her own spiritual metamorphosis.

NADIA AS PIVOTAL CHARACTER

Nadia as Franco-Moroccan

When Nadia arrives in the pious city of Fez to be at her dying father's bedside, she comes straight from Paris, where she has been living for years with French press photographer Jean-Philippe. Her persona immediately clashes with her surroundings. Dressed in jeans and a black leather jacket, she has a punkish, two-tone hairdo, smokes cigarettes, and answers in French rather than Arabic (although she is bilingual). She asserts her double heritage (French by her mother and Moroccan by her father), stating at a family meal that she "wants it all" and refuses to choose one identity over the other. Yet, she still exhibits all the outward signs of Frenchness, and none of the Moroccan ones. For instance, she states that she feels like an alien in Fez. She also refuses to wear a *jellabah* (the traditional man's covering garb now worn by women over their garments to venture outside the house), and calls it a "masquerade." She seems to act out a deep refusal of an exclusive allegiance to her father's culture, and she adamantly refuses to have her French, secular identity translated into a Moroccan, Muslim one through the local dress code. At the beginning of the narrative, she appears as a hybridized postcolonial subject eager to claim and protect her own brand of hybridity, which is why she refuses to follow her siblings in electing one side of her identity over the other. However, after her father's passing, Nadia experiences her own perceived identity as such a source of painful tension that she falls into deep depression. In very short order, her once proudly heralded hybrid self starts to shatter into multiple shards, a process that the tried and tested French remedies of the past, chain smoking and hard liquor, fail to halt.

At this point in the narrative, she is enacting Western codes of behavior, and feels lost in a home that has now become unfamiliar to her. She suspects it has changed during her absence. "It is as if everything were smaller," she tells her sister on her way from the airport. She writes long letters in French to Jean-Philippe, in which she describes her sudden confrontation with what Novak calls her *alloself*: a self that has gestated unbeknownst to her while she lived in Paris, and that no longer conforms to the self that surfaces in Fez. She writes: "I have taken refuge in my mother's workshop to write to you. My father is dead and I have not even cried. I feel alien. I miss you. Everything is so absurd. My head feels wobbly. I feel guilty: what for? what about? I drink and it has no effect on me."[18] At the same time, she faces issues of identity and gender, and an emotional upheaval of great magnitude for which she is unprepared, for which she has no appropriate defense mechanism or tool at the ready. This letter sketches the various dimensions of her despair. It is no accident that she chooses to write it from her mother's space.

In fact, she is connected to her mother from the very first scene of the film, both in her father's mind and in her "Frenchness." The film starts with a flashback corresponding to the dying father's recollection of an episode in his life. He comes home to find his pregnant French wife and his mother together in the inner courtyard (see figure 4). The Moroccan mother gives blessings in Arabic to the unborn child and tries to have the mother repeat the *shahada* (the Muslim profession of faith and first pillar of Islam). The unwitting French speaker repeats phonetically what she is told without understanding either the meaning of the words or her mother-in-law's attempt at forcing a conversion upon her. This first scene shows a beautiful, brightly colored Moroccan interior garden, with lush plants, the walls tiled in arabesque designs, in golden sunlight, accompanied by bird chirps, and the prayer in Arabic. It also shows the return of the father, the ensuing short dialogue in French with his wife, and the soundtrack of Bach's *St. Matthew's Passion*. As I have said elsewhere, the particular aria is the last before Jesus asks his Father why he has abandoned him, and it foreshadows his death (just as this scene will foreshadow Nadia's father's death and her subsequent feeling of abandonment).[19] Her mother was a painter whose workshop still hosts her canvases, especially those of Ba Sassi, a figure of tremendous importance for Nadia and for her mother. At this point in the narrative, Nadia returns to the womblike workshop to mourn. In so doing, Nadia reconnects with a mother who died when she was a little girl.

The beginning of the film thus introduces the child-mother dyad before the child is born and then the child-father dyad as the father is dying. No wonder orphaned Nadia experiences such dizzying grief as to leave her mind unsteady. Both dyads show a tragic lack of synchronicity: Nadia has had to grow into adulthood motherless, and she is now going to go through the next stage of her life fatherless. Now deprived of all ties to her previous identities, she will need a third parental figure to lead her through her next rebirth. Enter Kirana, the next parental figure in the new, transient, initiator-initiate dyad.

However, the boundaries between the various guiding parents are not as fixed as the narrative structure of the film might imply. In that, *Door to the Sky* is almost a riff on the "feminist 'matrilineal' cinema" that Lucy Fischer describes, with its "daughters celebrating and speaking for their mothers, removing them from the realm of essentialism and locating them within the frames of race and history."[20] The mother always retains some presence, whether visually – through her paintings of Ba Sassi – or aurally: the music by Bach, a canonical piece of Western sacred music, bathes the first scene of the film, an extension of the maternal voice.

The cameo appearance of the mother as emblematic of France presents a complicated picture of the former colonizer, for it undercuts the clichés associated with it, and highlights what the former "protector" could have been for its protectorate. Hence, the French character is here feminine rather than masculine. Moreover, the mother is a painter who is not "orientalist" and does not objectify her models as Delacroix did, for instance. Instead, she interacts with her masculine model (Ba Sassi) and engages in long conversations with him before she paints him, after she has reached an understanding of him. Here the character of the mother is at least two-dimensional: as the idealized and feminized version of France that might have been, and as the particular mother who dies too young for Nadia to learn from her.

A little later in the film, she will come back to Nadia through a vivid reminiscence. In it, the mother asks: "What are you doing?" to which Nadia responds: "I am stopping time." Here, as Fischer would say, the daughter "ventriloquises"[21] the mother in her memory, a process that is also visible in other characteristics that she shares with her mother: not only the maternal French culture, but also her mother's openness to others, and a quest for meaning in which Ba Sassi plays a central role.

The presence/absence of Nadia's mother haunts the first part of the film, but not the second. It is as if Nadia were mourning both parents during the first movement of *A Door* and then moves on; as if she were growing out of the unresolved questions of her childhood before she moved into adult independence. However, her delayed coming of spiritual age is not easy: hurled into deep depression, she has a bout of anorexia, and needs Kirana to achieve some serenity. She is the figure of the initiate and is filmed as such.

Nadia as Initiate

Nadia isolates herself, and wishes to take no part in the family reunion and funeral ritual. Yet she finds herself drawn to Kirana's voice reciting the *surat* (chapters of the Qur'an) traditionally recited or chanted at funerals, "Ibrahim" and "Dawn." The latter describes the return of the appeased soul to God's embrace, to Paradise. Even though each *sura,* as Bourget demonstrates,[22] resonates with the surface narrative in its religious evocation of the departure of the dead to a better world, it can also be heard as the promise of a better world in the Muslim faith. Hence Nadia would understand both the comfort brought by the funeral chant that accompanies her father to a place of sheer happiness and an invitation to share in some of that happiness through faith. If this is suggested, it is only faintly: Nadia falls under the spell of Kirana's voice more than under the spell of the *sura* per se.

The singer is a beautiful, older woman, deeply grounded in her faith. Free and ready to travel anywhere to spread her faith and good words, she attracts Nadia as a Sufi figure exuding serenity and an iron faith. She opens the door to a womanly tradition of critical thinking in Islam and helps Nadia reconnect with her own lineage and responsibilities. Hence when Nadia decides to keep her father's house against her brother's will (he wants to sell it), she meets with a lawyer to plan how to fight the unjust law and keep the house in order to open it to women according to an old tradition:

> What hurts is that we're getting rid of the best in our culture to retain the shell, empty of its meaning. I'd like you to meet Kirana. She's an extraordinary woman. Through her I've discovered a world of which I had no idea. In Islam women are free to dispose of their fortune and of their time. The wealthiest financed *zawiyat,* that is, refuges for women in need. You've got to understand: this kind of a house has always had a particular function in our society. It should not be lost.[23]

Here, Nadia is trying to resist not only today's social norms but also the principle of a law that she denounces as blatantly unfair to women: under the Islamic law that has shaped the Moroccan one, she and her sister, as women, can inherit only half what their brother can. Accordingly, they each inherit a quarter of their father's house while he inherits half of it.

The theme of asymmetrical inheritance along gender lines was also explored more recently on-screen by Tunisian director Kalthoum Bornaz, in *Shtar m'haba/L'Autre moitié du ciel/The Other Half of the Sky* (2008), to denounce its unfairness as well as to show the rift the law created between twin brother and sister. In *A Door to the Sky*, the rule is used to show what happens once it is subjected to Nadia's practice of *itjihad*: she is not blindly accepting the wholesale version of the Qur'an that has subsequently been erected into law, but denouncing it as inequitable. Here, Nadia first follows her initiator, Kirana. Already at this early stage of her initiation, she rebels against the unfairness of the *shariah* that informs the codes of her country. Her initiation follows the structure of a Sufi spiritual initiation, which then develops into the creation of a Sufi prayer center much in the way it used to in the beginning of Islam. As Renard notes: "The term *Sufi* came to be applied to some of these individuals, perhaps in connection with their wearing rough garments of wool (*suf* in Arabic). Initially, the circles used the humble dwellings of their spiritual leaders as their meeting places, but some groups soon grew to need larger facilities."[24] Sufis gradually came to meet in *zawiyat*, spaces outside the mosque for teaching and communal praying that were peripheral to the mosque. *Zawiya* literally means "corner" in Arabic and originally referred to a portion of the mosque used by a Sufi spiritual leader, or *shaykh*, for his teaching and communal prayers. Gradually, it became synonymous with the communes that were established by Sufis around a *shaykh*. Yet the very architectural origin of the term also underscored the position of a *zawiya* in relation to the religious institution: it stands at the periphery, almost independent of it, as it actively engages in *itjihad*, and may not always agree with the authorized interpretations of Islam. Over the course of history, Sufi communes have sometimes served as havens for both religious and political dissidents (especially in colonized North Africa, for instance). Hence a Sufi community is known in the Maghreb for both its mysticism and its independence.

In each *zawiya*, the *shaykh* has had to establish his authority via his lineage. Just as each hadith is transmitted via a chain of vetted, authenticated speakers, a *shaykh* needs to demonstrate a link all the way back to the Prophet, according to Renard:

Another important structural aspect of Sufi orders that relates directly to authority has been a concern over proper lineage (*silsila*, "chain" or *shajara*, "tree"). Indices of legitimacy have been as important to religious institutions as to political ones. Founders and successors of the various confraternities invariably locate themselves on a family tree traceable back to Muhammad and his earliest companions. A *shaykh* would pass along his authority to a successor, thus insuring the continuity of spiritual power and authority. . . . The spiritual trees of some orders became very complex.[25]

Hence the discovery that Nadia is a *sherifa*, that is, a noble woman, is crucial to her being able to lead the *zawiya*. It unquestionably supports her authority as *shaykha*. And it is as *shaykha*, both spiritually and politically, that she resists the Establishment. In fact, signs of resistance abound in the film: Nadia successfully takes over her father's house despite the inheritance law mentioned above; as I have pointed out elsewhere, Abdelkrim (literally, the servant of the Generous One), the young man with whom she ends up leaving, bears the name of a famous warrior, Mohamed Ben Abdelkrim (1883–1962),[26] whose resistance to the invading forces was so powerful that Spain and France had to ally to defeat him in the nineteenth century; the very location, Fez, is replete with women resisters, from Fatima al-Fihriya, who founded al Qaraouine Mosque and university in the tenth century (a century before the Sorbonne in Paris, two centuries before Oxford in the United Kingdom) to famous feminist Fatima Mernissi. Finally, the way Nadia never conforms to expected social rules (as we see in the beginning of the film) suggests that she might keep on following her own path after her initiation by Kirana. It is fitting that she founds her own *zawiya* for women: she positions herself (and her female companions) on the periphery of social norms, on the brink of what is accepted. The community hosted in the house constitutes a group of rejected women: the very first one is the maid who finds herself pregnant and is about to be dismissed from the family house by Leyla; she is joined by a little girl who has been abused, a woman artist whose mind and spirit need a haven, a married woman whose jealous husband torments her with his suspicions and who needs to find a space outside her painful marriage. At the *zawiya*, Kirana teaches the Qur'an while Nadia studies. Even here, the traditional role of *shaykha* is contested. Nadia seems to delegate some of it to Kirana, as we see in a scene when the latter listens to the little girl's memorization of a few *surat.*

Yet, Nadia remains the central force in the community and its care-taker. Hence, when she admits Bahia into the house, she is the one to whom other women go to complain. Nadia's lawyer friend brings Bahia to the *zawiya* right after she gets out of prison. Her look is somewhat reminiscent of Nadia's at the beginning of the film: she has short hair, wears jeans, speaks French, smokes cigarettes, drinks, reads Rimbaud (she even finds the poem she wants to read to Nadia from Nadia's copy of *Le Bateau ivre*), and expresses herself in a direct way: she needs a man, and hates nuns. Bahia appears as the other face of Nadia, the person she might have become. Here, Benlyazid opposes two possible versions of a subject: the good Nadia, *shaykha,* and an ex-con, Bahia. Nadia could be Bahia, and Bahia, Nadia. It is up to us to follow our own path lead-ing us in this or that direction, the director seems to say. The point of convergence between the two women is highlighted by the quote from Rimbaud: "As for an established form of happiness, domestic or not, I cannot embrace it. I am too dissipated, too weak. . . . My life is not weighty enough. It flies away and floats above all actions." Both individu-als rebel against the prescribed path to the conventional way of life of the Establishment: Bahia through illegal means, we suppose, since she was imprisoned, and Nadia through a spiritual quest. The meeting of the two characters highlights both the change in Nadia since the beginning of the story and a nonjudgmental appraisal of individual choices in life.

Nadia's transformation from a secular being into a believer in an idiosyncratic faith is translated on-screen visually and aurally for distinct extra-diegetic audiences as the film takes on the initiating function for a secular (French) audience and a Sufi (Moroccan) one.

FOCUS: SHOWING THE WAY TO TRANSVERGENT AUDIENCES

Switching between the Allo *and the Self*

Space in this film is represented along two axes: a vertical one, Fez, bris-tling with tall minarets, and a horizontal one, the house, with its traditional architecture around a central, open patio. The image of the house as womanly space is frequent in Maghrebi cinema, but what is unique here is the fluid visual representation of passages from one room to the next, of liminal spaces that Nadia crosses or in which she lingers. It suggests that the house is not strictly partitioned, that doors will open for Nadia, seen against a wall, a window, next to a door, looking through a door, a window, a *musharabieh* (an ornate wooden or stone lattice screen on windows and balconies, which allows women to see out of the house without being seen), passing from one room to the next, from one space to the next. Similarly, thresholds are highlighted throughout the film by numerous shots of windows, doorways, glass surfaces reflecting the outside landscape.

The outside spaces that are shot in or from the house, for example, low-angle shots toward the sky, shots filtered by the light let in through a window, suggest both a clear border between the inner sanctum of the house and its exterior, but also, as we see the blue gate open to let in women, an openness to the outer world – albeit a selective one. Such is not the case, however, when Jean-Philippe flies in to Fez to visit Nadia. The aural and visual montage and the shots of this sequence show how impassable the divide has grown between Nadia's receding French identity and her Moroccan one.

They meet in the lobby of a modern hotel. The camera is behind Jean-Philippe, who is seated, reading a newspaper. Nadia enters through glass doors, clad in white from head to toe (which means she is in mourning and "should" not be out and about, but mourning at home). She comes to him to the sound of syrupy Musak. She leads him to the hotel café outside: a medium close-up of Nadia against the landscape of Fez cuts to a counter medium shot of Jean-Philippe against the cold, modern building of the hotel. Their dialogue mixes with the sounds of the city, dominated by the calls to prayer emanating from the various mosques.

The camera then cuts to Jean-Philippe's bedroom: the latter is shot from the balcony, through closed windows that reflect the cityscape. The echoes of Fez and the muezzins' calls outside mute the couple's dialogue inside. Finally, Nadia comes toward the camera, slides the glass door open, and pauses there, in the same interstitial space she has occupied, symbolically, since the beginning of the film. He professes his desire to understand her; she accuses him of being a tourist. She walks out of his room (his Western space) onto the balcony (see figure 5) – the camera rotates, and shoots her from behind in a medium shot. He joins her – the camera remains in Nadia's previous vantage point, at the threshold of the bedroom and the balcony, and frames both characters side by side, against the backdrop of the old city: she faces the camera; his back is turned to it. "Listen to the timelessness of Islam," she tells him, referring to the muezzins' calls.

In this short sequence, each character is framed with a signifying backdrop: she belongs to Fez; he belongs to the modern Western hotel. The soundtrack also emphasizes, through the loud muezzin calls overshadowing their dialogue, the complete breakdown in their ability to communicate. Neither belongs to the other's landscape or "soundscape." Although the liminal spaces here – windowpanes – are transparent, it is as if an iron curtain of separation – a heavy hijab – had been drawn shut between both worlds. This scene is the site of one of the most disturbing value reversals of the entire film: Nadia's ease with secular France – a shortcut to "the West" – is forever a thing of the past. The "West" does not hear her, cannot hear her.

Meanwhile the positioning of the camera and the audiovisual montage underline the construction of a dual extra-diegetic audience. They establish three moments in the scene: a Western one in the hotel lobby as we follow Nadia; a second moment in which we are excluded from the characters' dialogue as we are left outside Jean-Philippe's bedroom, out of earshot; and finally, as the camera describes a 360-degree angle, we resume our position behind Nadia and now face and hear Muslim Fez. The scene clearly addresses two sets of viewers as the perspective shifts from the French secular (Jean-Philippe) to the Moroccan Sufi (Nadia). Yet the two audiences have one common origin: Nadia, the bicultural protagonist who is finally reacquainted with her former duality after having been only one part of herself for all her years in France.

The montage here signifies her becoming aware of her own transvergence, her own ability to acknowledge the *alloself* that she was repressing at the beginning of the film (through her behavior and apparent refusal to fit in the Fez landscape), and that was masked by her French self (the one known to Jean-Philippe). Nadia's 360-degree turn in this scene symbolically stages her opening up to her Muslim paternal side. However, it does not signify that she is necessarily denying her maternal cultural side. She is simply entering a new phase in becoming that escapes all "centrisms," all immutable belongings to defined states of being, to eurocentrism or islamo-centrism, a phase of becoming that Novak might identify as *allocentrism:*

> There is justifiable suspicion of totalizing centrisms and the abuses they can be put to. A safeguard against these abuses is already implied with the idea of the *alien.* Even at its most reflexive, the prefix *allo-,* like *trans-,* is restless and always pointing away from itself. *Allocentrism* is a centrifugal notion, one in which the centre is an absence only implied by the dynamics of tangential and transvergent vectors. It is totalising only in that it escapes all totalisations.[27]

In this scene, Nadia appears as the *allo* for the French/francophone, secular extra-diegetic viewers, and for the first time as a potentially identifiable *self* for the Muslim Moroccan extra-diegetic audience. Yet that position is unstable, and the film ends up addressing both audiences in a constantly shifting transvergent pattern that moves them away from their initial rigid positioning. Hence both audiences are initiated not so much to one another as to a transnational culture, Nadia's, through a deft use of intertextual, cultural references. Benlyazid plays with this dual address constantly throughout her film, which then becomes the audiovisual representation of a Sufi initiation journey.

Initiated Transvergent Audiences

The film's numerous intertextual links to two cultures further illustrate the dynamic movement from one audience to the other and back as it caters to both French and Moroccan audiences, much like Assia Djebar in her *Nuba* (see chapter 1), and proposes a transvergent process of identification with, and alienation from, the screen akin to the one we can see in *Bedwin Hacker* (see chapter 5). Each set of viewers is given solid anchors into the culture of origin via the musical, filmic, literary, and religious references that stud the film from beginning to end, but as one set of viewers decodes each reference, the other one is initiated to it. In that, the film proposes a cinematic form of Sufi initiation. Let's take, for instance, Nadia's allusion to Angela Davis glossing the words of her own sacred prophet: Karl Marx. She does not simply repeat the famous, oft misquoted, sentence "religion is the opium of the masses" in its usual truncated form, out of context. No, she reads the entire passage and applies her own interpretation to it – practicing her own *itjihad*: "*Religious* suffering is, at one and the same time, the *expression* of real suffering and a *protest* against real suffering. Religion is the sigh of the oppressed creature, the heart of a heartless world and the soul of soulless conditions. It is the *opium* of the people."[28] By evoking the entire passage, Nadia then speaks to both the secular and the faithful – to both, if we simplify, the North and the South. The one same overused quotation opens up to various meanings. Here, as the Marxist discourse on religion is corrected, the divide between the two sets of viewers – and, of course, both identities of Nadia – starts to shrink. Nadia's schizoid self becomes unified as she is shown borrowing from two distinct systems of thought to articulate her wholesome identity for herself and her viewers from both sides of the spectrum.

Nadia, steeped in her Western education, also quotes from the Enlightenment as she repeats Lavoisier's axiom "Nothing is created, nothing is lost, all is transformed." Yet, she also interprets Lavoisier in a spiritual sense as she adds: "I am speaking about the end of the world. We could see the world explode. All has been given in another dimension." Here, as she evokes an evolving, transformative universe as envisioned by Lavoisier and an explosive end of the world, she is also interpreting the Western Scientific Revolution as coming to terms with, or joining, what she has understood as a divine truth that predates human cognition. Lavoisier's Law of the Conservation of Mass, which played with permanence of matter (nothing is destroyed) and impermanence of form (under chemical reactions), then leads to: "Nothing is permanent. Only Allah is eternal."

As I have said elsewhere, the references to Arabic mystics' texts also abound.[29] The citations are translated and provide the same type of initiation to both audiences. Here, I wish to pay special attention to Ibn 'Arabî (1165–1240), the quotation in French of whose essay, *The One Alone,* adorns one of the walls of Nadia's bedroom. The fact that we, extra-diegetic viewers, come to see its translation in French instead of in

Arabic has a twofold significance: (1) it highlights the global relevance of Sufism; (2) it is already "talking" to a French or francophone audience – it already appears literally on their terms. As such it prepares the next intertext with Ibn 'Arabî, which will be translated in cinematic visual terms. According to his writings, the Sufi mystic came to the holy city of Fez, where he attained, for the second time in his life, the "abode of light," which he described as "more visible than what was in front of me. Also, when I saw this light the status of the direction 'behind' ceased for me. I no longer had a back or nape of a neck, and while the vision lasted I could no longer distinguish between different sides of myself."[30] This theophany (i.e., divine revelation) of light, through which the divine presence is revealed, occurs in "another dimension": the praying human is now engulfed in a union with the divine. Hence the loss of one's sense of direction and of human, bodily limits. Nadia experiences her own attainment of the abode of light on the Night of Destiny (the night on which the Prophet's birthday is celebrated during Ramadan). She loses consciousness and has a vision during which she finds herself in the garden in the middle of the night, when a glaring white light from above suddenly shines down on her (here, the camera is facing her from a high angle, not sharing her gaze as in the previous sequence): Ba Sassi then appears to her off-screen to reveal the secret of the buried treasure. It is through her filmic visual rendition of the white light that Benlyazid suggests that Nadia too, like Ibn 'Arabî, attains her "abode of light," her moment of revelation – and in the same city, no less.

Here the camera visually translates a thirteenth-century written text. The act of *itjihad* is cinematic and speaks to Sufis – whether Moroccan or not. Yet the process of translation (film) is not alien to the formulation of Sufi thought. As Ibn 'Arabî himself noted in "The One Alone":

> So if someone says, "I am the Truth!" do not hear it from any other than from the Truth Himself, for it is not a man who says it, it is the word of Allah. That man who utters these words is nothing but an image reflected in an empty mirror, one of the infinite attributes of Allah. The reflection is the same as that which is being reflected, and the words of the image are the reflected words of the Real One.[31]

The mystic's text can be read as a beautiful metaphor for cinematic creation and projection: the creator crafts her creation onto one plane, and the film (as creation) reflects back the image of the filmmaker – or the divine! In the wake of such an image, the old-fashioned leap of faith asked from a cinematic audience (to believe in the narrative projection facing it) takes on a new, spiritual dimension.

As we has seen, both the Western, secular and the Moroccan, spiritual extra-diegetic viewers are addressed on-screen, either one group after the other, or, as the initiation becomes complete, simultaneously. Hence the film, taking some of its clues from a Sufi text, proposes a transvergent mode of viewing on two levels: (1) I, the extra-diegetic viewer, glimpse images of the self (I recognize my own perspective, I identify with the familiar) and then of the *allo* (I see the perspective of the other, I am confronted with difference); (2) I learn about the other and, once confronted with the images of the self, I derive from both sets of images a sense of continuum. Benlyazid's film does not try to convert anyone to Sufism or Islam (the scene in the beginning denouncing a forced and ineffective *shahada* clearly dismisses the very idea of conversion), but aligns the self and the *allo* as creations on an equal and dynamic plane. In the end, her film speaks to a dual audience that becomes united. Such a union is represented visually by the very last camera shot, which pans in a smooth vertical movement from the embrace of Nadia and Abdelkrim to the blue expanse of the sky, away from the city. At the very end, then, instead of being reminded of our differences yet again, we are given a rare spiritual and filmic lesson about a possible way (among others) to grow together as men and women (and perhaps, as believer and secular).

Yet, this spiritual dimension should not obscure the political feminist message of the film: Nadia finds her way around not one but two patriarchal systems to assert her own independence. She reaffirms women's agency and its long history. It is up to women to seize it even at the risk of going against the grain of authorities, men, other women. Here, just as Djebar did in *The Nuba*, Benlyazid (see figure 6) honors Maghrebi women and tells their history through Nadia. Assia Djebar, Farida Benlyazid, and Selma Baccar (in her documentary *Fatma 75*) cleared the path to project empowering narratives and images of women in the Maghreb. In their wake, new narratives would emerge, brave and bold, from their sisters in the three countries.

1. The Mount Chenoua Women. (*Nuba nisa al djebel Shnua/
La Nouba des Femmes du Mont Chénoua/The Nuba of the Women
of Mount Chenoua*. Dir. Assia Djebar. Algeria, 1978).

2. The saint's wife releases the doves. (*Nuba nisa al djebel Shnua/
La Nouba des Femmes du Mont Chénoua/The Nuba of the Women
of Mount Chenoua*. Dir. Assia Djebar. Algeria, 1978).

3. Doves around the fountain in Cherchell. (*Nuba nisa al djebel Shnua/La Nouba des Femmes du Mont Chénoua/The Nuba of the Women of Mount Chenoua*. Dir. Assia Djebar. Algeria, 1978).

4. Nadia's French mother and Moroccan grandmother. (*Bab al-sama maftouh/ Une Porte sur le ciel/A Door to the Sky*. Dir. Farida Benlyazid. Morocco, 1988).

5. Nadia on the threshold of Philippe's bedroom. (*Bab al-sama maftouh/ Une Porte sur le ciel/A Door to the Sky*. Dir. Farida Benlyazid. Morocco, 1988).

6. Farida Benlyazid, Paris, April 2010.

Act II

Transvergent Screens

Yamina Bachir-Chouikh's Transvergent Echoes: *Rachida* (Algeria, 2002)

PRELUDE

Watching *Rachida* in the wake of Djebar's *Nuba* further illuminates the twists and turns of a commonly shared larger narrative in the Shahrazad tradition, as if Bachir-Chouikh had picked up her camera where Djebar had left her pen and camera. The transvergent quality of the narrative strategies that had started in *The Nuba* (with its active *mise en abyme* of women's narratives) shines forth again here, along an intertextual arc that joins the two films in unexpected ways over the twenty-four years that separate them. Furthermore, with the making of *Rachida* with its multiple intertextual detours, the director becomes the avatar of old storyteller Shahrazad. Hence a lineage is established that unites Shahrazad, Assia Djebar, and Yamina Bachir-Chouikh in their narration of an egregious violence committed by men against young women (one unnamed, Atyka, and finally Rachida).

The study of *Rachida* also opens this second section of the book, which examines the dual notion of screen and veil in a cinematic context. In this chapter, we shall see how unveiling and veiling by women becomes a powerful statement at a time of great chaos in Algeria in the 1990s, and how filming such scenes and screening them might also indicate a mode of transvergent resistance to the forces of oppression within Algeria.

YAMINA BACHIR-CHOUIKH'S TRIALS
AND TRIBULATIONS: 1996–2002

Rachida is Yamina Bachir-Chouikh's first feature film: she wrote its script, directed it, and edited it herself. Her multidimensional control over the film reflects her thirty-plus years in cinema as editor and scriptwriter of numerous feature films and documentaries.

She belongs to the generation of Algerian filmmakers who learned and applied their trade, in her case film editing, at home, at the Centre National du Cinéma Algérien (National Center for Algerian Cinema) opened by the Algerian Ministry of Information and Culture in 1964. After her graduation in 1973, she started immediately to work as editor on a long list of Algerian films, with directors such as Okacha Touita (e.g., *Le Cri des hommes/The Cry of Men,* 1990), Abdelkader Lagtaa, Mouredine Mefti, Ahmed Rachedi, and Mohamed Chouikh (e.g., *El Kalaa/La Citadelle/The Fort,* 1988), who also became her husband. Furthermore, she wrote the scripts of films that have since become Algerian classics, such as *Omar Gatlato,* directed by Merzak Allouache (1976), Mohamed Lakhdar-Lamina's *Rih al Raml/Vent de sable/Sand Storm* (1982), and more recently, *Douar n'ssa/Douar de femmes/Village of Women,* directed by Mohamed Chouikh (2005). Finally, she has turned to documentaries on women, with a short titled *Louisa Sid Ammi* (2003, 26 min), on the eponymous photojournalist who was twenty when the 1990s wave of terrorism started in Algeria, and a full-length piece titled *Hier . . . Aujourd'hui et demain/Yesterday . . . Today and Tomorrow* (2010), in which she interviews *mujahidat* about their roles and lives from the 1940s to independence.

It took her five years to produce *Rachida:* a long, arduous process, symptomatic of the conditions of film production in Algeria during the "bloody years" of the 1990s.

The "Faceless War"

Yamina Bachir-Chouikh, who then lived in France, wanted to represent the overwhelming violence during the 1990s and its effects on the psyche of women. Over that decade, Algeria was ravaged by a terror campaign and a bloody civil war, its population caught between, on the one hand, the armed wing of the FIS (Front Islamique du Salut/Islamic Salvation Front, a political movement created in 1989), called GIA (Groupe Islamique Armé/Armed Islamic Group), and on the other, the government controlled by the FLN and/or the army. Although various forms of unrest had started earlier (in particular in 1988), it was the government's reaction to the first round of voting in the elections of December 1991 that sparked the fire. When the results showed that the FIS was certain to win a majority of parliamentary seats, the National Assembly was dissolved. Then President Chadli, pressured by the military, resigned, and was replaced by a council led by the army. A state of emergency was declared, and the FIS was outlawed as a political party. Protests started immediately, and violence escalated. In 1992, the GIA (and at times the AIS, Armée Islamique du Salut/Salvation Islamic Army, another militant Islamist group) was held to be the main group responsible for the numerous assassinations, hijackings, bombings in airports and cities, massacres in villages, and abduction and rape of many women. Over one hundred thousand people were killed between 1992 and 1999 (there is no statistic on rapes). According to an official Algerian report, another six thousand civilians disappeared and are still unaccounted for. It is unclear who was behind these disappearances. Most of the hostilities stopped in 1999 with an attempt at national reconciliation and various amnesties.

The *Rachida* project started in the thick of the "war without a name" that ravaged Algeria: nothing was working in the country; the list of victims grew longer every day. Terror had spread from the cities to the country, and women and children, the most vulnerable and traditionally the most protected, were very much at risk. A large number of Algerian intellectuals, artists, and journalists received death threats. In the wake of the 1993 murder of journalist Tahar Djaout, who had famously said: "If you are silent, you die. If you speak, you die. So, speak and die!" others did speak and die, such as playwright Adelkader Alloula (1994), popular raï singer Cheb Hasni (1994), and National Theatre director Azeddine Medjoubi (1995). Numerous targeted victims in the intelligentsia (e.g., novelist and professor Rachid Mimouni, who dedicated his novel *La Malédiction/Doom*, 1993, "To the memory of my friend, writer Tahar Djaout, assassinated by a candy seller on the order of a former inmate") were forced into exile abroad. As a result of the dramatic, ensuing slowdown of Algeria's intellectual and artistic production, only a handful of films came out of Algeria between 1995 and 1999.

Algerian Film Production

The paucity of Algerian film production in the 1990s had other structural causes as well. In the 1980s, various reforms had chipped away at the state control of film production in place since independence, yet Algerian film directors were still basically considered civil servants and, as such, on the state payroll. When the government privatized the film sector in 1993, they received three years' worth of salary and started their own production companies. The state still supported cinema through the CAAIC (Centre Algérien pour l'Art et l'Industrie Cinématographiques/Algerian Center for Cinematic Art and Industry, created in 1987) that dispensed aid to the production of specific projects based on scripts selected by a commission.

The real blow came in 1998, in the middle of social and political instability, when the CAAIC, the ENPA (Entreprise Nationale de Productions Audiovisuelles/National Organization for Audiovisual Production, which was the television production organization), and the newsreel agency, Agence Nationale des Actualités Filmées (ANAF) were closed, and most people in the film industry became unemployed.[1] To add insult to injury, according to Roy Armes, "cinema audiences had declined from nine million in 1980 to just half a million in 1992, while the number of cinemas (now mostly converted to video halls) had declined from 458 at the time of independence to a bare dozen in 1999."[2] Indeed, although many had been transformed into cultural centers, reception halls, or video projection rooms to respond to local needs, the coup de grâce came in the 1990s, Hillauer writes, when they became "targets for attacks by fundamentalists who considered films shown there to be immoral."[3]

By then, going to the movies had become a hazardous pursuit. Similarly, for a film director, to stay in Algeria was an act of defiance that put his or her life at risk: "After 1992, Algerian cinema faced a double peril: the mighty weight of the Islamist hammer on film scripts, threatening and intimidating actors and technicians, attempting to murder directors (Djamel Fezzazz was critically wounded on February 6, 1995); and the anvil of the state, of governments that did not support the release of films they disliked during these hellish years."[4] In short, participating in cinema, whether as viewer or as director had turned into a risky, possibly lethal, proposition. Death threats forced people into exile (e.g., Merzak Allouache, a director living in France[5]). After the first few years of the FIS insurgency, even Yamina Bachir-Chouikh and her family moved from Algiers to Paris.

No wonder, then, that it took Bachir-Chouikh five long years to collect the €900,000 needed to make *Rachida*. No aid could come from the Algerian government. Her first support came from the Amiens Film Festival (in France) in 1998, where she was given €8,000 to revise her script. She was then able to apply and receive funds from the French Ministry of Culture as well as from two television channels (Arte and Canal +) and a private foundation (Gan). She also remembers fondly the "Franco-Algerian human chain" of goodwill that contributed to the making of the film: "the manuscript brought by a steward from Algiers to Paris to save time on snail mail, cash given by a detergent brand or a car-maker, Titra's free subtitles."[6]

Funded mostly by French sources, the film nevertheless was made in Algeria and retained its Algerian identity, as indicated by the publicity upon its release in three theaters in Algiers in 2002 ("the national TV channel broadcast the film preview all day long; all the walls of Algiers were covered with posters"[7]) and its warm reception ("On the night of the premiere in Algiers on December 20, part of the audience cried. Several recognized moments of their own experience – especially the funeral scenes"[8]). The director had reached her main goal: to film a chronicle of Algerian survival in *Rachida* to which viewers in her country could relate.

RACHIDA: AN EMBLEMATIC EPISODE OF VIOLENCE IN THE 1990S

Film Synopsis

Rachida was inspired by the factual story of a young teacher named Zekia Guessab, who was killed by terrorists in the 1990s. (The fact that fictitious, on-screen Rachida survives simply highlights that, in the history of human violence, fiction is often less cruel than life). Written in white against a black background reminiscent of a blackboard, the film's dedication reads: "To my brother Mohamed, to Zekia Guessab, and to all the others, . . ." referring to Bachir-Chouikh's own brother Mohamed, who was also killed during the years of terror in Algeria,[9] joined by thousands of anonymous victims.

The eponymous film tells the story of a young teacher in Algiers, Rachida, who is accosted on her way to work by Sofiane, a former student of hers turned Islamist. He hands her a bag carrying a bomb, asking her to simply take it to her school. Rachida refuses. Sofiane's accomplice shoots her. She survives, however, and, traumatized, moves out of the city with her mother to a house lent by a friend, in a village in the country. But the violence spills beyond the walls of cities and spreads to the countryside. The boundaries of the village have now become porous, and a unit of the GIA, located outside the village (literally "in the wild"), raids the community, damaging property and abducting women. When a woman comes back from her terrible ordeal with the FIS men (who, under a devious, self-serving interpretation of the Qur'an, temporarily marry, then rape and repudiate their victims), she is shunned by her father and denied entry to what used to be her home. The former cocoon provided by the family home and by the village has now become a place of estrangement and rejection. Throughout the film, several levels of violence are shown: the physical brutality of the Islamists but also structural violence in the form of unemployment reducing young men to "holding up the walls" (as the Algerian slang calls the resulting specific brand of frustrated idleness), malevolent gossip, antiquated patriarchal principles and societal hierarchies.

Filmic, Transvergent Intertextuality

The topic of violence is, of course, not new to Algerian cinema. Here, it is treated in a singular way, turning a collective narrative into an individual, emblematic one, while occasionally referring to another canonical film, *Battle of Algiers* (1966), and media reports in the 1990s. In that, it also follows a transvergent path, as it quotes these other sources to better use them as springboards and show visually and aurally the distinctive character of that decade, and of its filmic representation or lack thereof. In this way, the film establishes intertextual (interfilmic) links in a novel way: although she also inserts cameos of other films as other directors routinely do in their films (e.g., an excerpt of archival footage in *The Nuba of the Women at Mount Chenoua* – see chapter 1, and in *Bedwin Hacker* – see chapter 5), Yamina Bachir-Chouikh practices a new type of intertextuality by approximations that allude to a previous text/film but without repeating it. By so doing, she is staying away from the straight quotation and the wholesale acceptance of the previously established text, subscribing, once again, to no "prescribed regime of truth," but rather playing with its nuances. Hence, for instance, when she refers to *Battle of Algiers,* it is mostly to the form and intent of the film, not to the matter of the film itself.

Identifying reminders of *Battle of Algiers* in no way equates to reading the representation of the 1990s upheaval as a return to the former war of liberation, as has been suggested too readily by several commentators.[10] The parallels that were drawn between the war of liberation and the civil war situation of the 1990s are more revealing about the authors of such parallels than about the films of the 1990s. True, a similar bafflement blurs the very naming of both conflicts: each has been called a war "without a name," "without a front," and in both a "faithful" population was at stake – but faithful to whom? The "enemy" is invisible, indistinguishable because it blends in with the crowd, uses disguises, and because the demarcation between the Islamists and the army is rarely clear. However, as historian Benjamin Stora points out, these apparently shared traits mostly point not to a repetition but rather to an "intense *circulation* of images, ideas, representations, words all detectable in a memory exchange system."[11] It is this *circulation* of representations that interests me here: the various images of the war of liberation may have delineated an Algerian horizon of expectations in the representations of war at home. Furthermore, state censorship paradoxically contributed to the "circulation of images" of the 1990s: the Algerian government issued a decree on June 7, 1994, on the "security treatment of information," which basically censored images of the war. The only visual representation of the war was either filtered by a government the population no longer trusted or avidly watched on the French TV channel news via satellite dishes (accessible to the population since 1989). In either case, viewers lacked the necessary historian's distance to put events in context and analyze each report, writes Stora, while their emotions around the hellish, almost hallucinatory nature of each event (e.g., murdered infants, mutilated and raped women) ran wild.

Stora describes the fiction films made between 1993 and 1999 as sharing a common tendency to flash back to the first war.[12] The latter then serves as an interpretation grid or a magnetic point of return for the later war. His reading of the films is somewhat echoed or extended by Ratiba Hadj-Moussa, who believes that Algerian films have not "disengaged from the colonial past, but that the rapid evacuation thereof has rather led to a questioning of what it means to be Algerian and to live in Algeria today."[13] If so, then *Rachida* makes a clear break from this cinematic series: the FLN is basically absent from the film; there is no reference to any character involved with the liberation struggle, no flashback to the previous war. The only past shared on-screen is that of Aïcha (Rachida's mother), who tells her daughter about her divorce. What is evoked or narrated is not history on the national scale, but the history/story of individuals. And yet, the way the story of individuals experiencing a war is told does refer to representations of the previous war on Algerian soil.

This is how *Battle of Algiers* can be evoked as a fertile visual intertext in *Rachida*. Bachir-Chouikh uses its system of representations and by now mythical images to dramatize the events experienced by Rachida and inscribe them in national history. The intertextual link works here, I would argue, in a "transvergent" way. Instead of giving homage to Pontecorvo as the modernist would, or parodying him, as the postmodernist would, Bachir-Chouikh uses the earlier representation of the liberation war as a species of representational springboard. Instead of highlighting the first war as *the* topical reference, she points to the *filming* of that war as *a* reference – a reference among others, as the latter part of this chapter will make clear. One can see *Rachida* as a fictitious tale that reflects the recent, Algerian, collectively experienced fear of an *"alien-from-within"*[14] (as Novak would say): an extreme "other" that the community itself produced and has a hard time recognizing at all sorts of levels (e.g., are the soldiers fake or real at the roadblock? And also: are these brutes our sons, our neighbors? Do they belong to our community? How so?). It takes a specific filmic language to represent the affect of that fear. Here, Bachir-Chouikh incorporates recognizable images taken from the now canonical expression of a former collective experience of fear triggered by the massacres and tortures committed by the French army particularly between 1954 and 1962 as her canvas.

Furthermore, Bachir-Chouikh's inter-filmic language of representations is in and of itself a form of *alien* representation adopted from *within*, since Italian director Gillo Pontecorvo's masterpiece has become an Algerian classic embraced by the Algerian. Hence, she films the fear of the *alien-from-within* by framing some of her images in formats that have now become appropriated – and therefore recognizable – by the community (Algeria) when the latter was still confronting (and experiencing the fear of) a past, known alien turned *alien-from-within*: the French *colon*. Her formal intertexts thus point to a deft, transvergent manipulation of previous systems of representation, as she uses the images of Gillo Pontecorvo's film on the Battle of Algiers to let today's audience recognize the fear of the current *alien-from-within* and identify with that fear. In that, she experiments bravely with intertext in the etymological sense of the term, which shares its root with "peril," as Novak underscores: "Thus, to experiment means to purposefully engage in finite but potentially dangerous and frightening attempts, to initiate investigations that involve risk and confront fear. Obversely, to investigate without an engagement of risk and confrontation of fear is not to experiment at all."[15] Her experiment with expressing fear through such visual reminders poses the risk of being misunderstood: her viewers might believe she is equating the Islamists with the French *colons,* or that she cannot tell a story without referring to a colonial past as the unavoidable reference. And yet, her aim is to project identifiable images of the psychological affect of the war "without a name" (hence a war whose effects can reverberate with other wars).

For this reason, violence is never filmed frontally: it lurks in the shadow, in the off-screen space, while some of its effects are visible, or rather audible, on-screen. "When I started to write, I thought in images, movements, sound-track. And I told myself that without necessarily showing a state of siege or terror, I could suggest it through sounds:

ambulances, hails of bullets . . ."[16] Viewers are then left to probe the depth
of its devastating consequences on their own.

Bachir-Chouikh also wished to give faces to the Algerian tragedy,
as she repeats in interview after interview.[17] In that, she echoes Gillo
Pontecorvo, who wanted to give individual features to the anonymous
agents of the Battle of Algiers in his 1966 film.[18] Both directors chose
"faces" over professional actors. Hence, only a few actors in *Rachida*
are professional: for instance, Ibtissem Djouadi (a young student in her
third year at a drama school in Algiers), who plays the role of Rachida;
Bahia Rachedi (who was awarded a Tanit for best supporting actress at
the Journées Cinématographiques de Carthage, in Tunis), who plays the
part of Aïcha; Abdelkader Belmokadem (a veteran actor in Algeria), in
the role of Mokhtar. Most of the other actors are untrained, and yet it is
their faces on which the camera lingers, just as Pontecorvo's had done
on Ali's and others', thus effacing namelessness from mass victimhood.
Similarly, although we never learn their names, Bachir-Chouikh lets us
see – albeit briefly – the faces of the terrorists: young and handsome. She
explains her choice as realistic: "Recently, the young people who opened
fire on people at a beach were dressed in Bermuda shorts and carrying
beach towels. That's the terrorist system – they have to blend in with the
crowd. Those people are beautiful, and why shouldn't they be? They're
our children!"[19] As a result, we see young men who neither sport traditional beards nor exhibit any sign of piety; we never see them pray. In
giving faces to the Islamists, the director corrects the images aired by the
media: she erases the common, physical clichés associated with them.
Her "giving faces" to victims and perpetrators has two consequences: the
former are "viewed" as no longer anonymous, while the latter are "seen"
as more anonymous.

The filmic narrative, while following the trials and tribulations of Rachida and the small community in the village where she and her mother
have moved, is also intertextually linked to the media. Here, the director
has embedded a journalistic voice relaying a dry April 1996 news broadcast on the home TV set:

> The bodies of eleven Tibeherin monks, kidnapped by terrorists, have been found
> at the entrance of the city of Medea. The assassination of these monks by the
> terrorists adds to the brutal murder of eighty muftis, imams and muezzin. The

> Christian community and the inhabitants of the region followed the funeral
> procession to the monastery.... A new massacre in Mitidja: twenty-two people
> had their throats cut and four girls were kidnapped.

Men are killed, regardless of their religious affiliations; girls (of whom
we know nothing) are "kidnapped," a phrase used repeatedly to avoid
saying the unutterable (raped, mutilated, sometimes beheaded).

Another intertextual link is established aurally: Rachida often listens to music on her Walkman, and is once heard finding solace in a song
by Cheb Hasni, the much-loved singer killed in 1994. The entire aural
landscape resonates with signs of violence: the crackle of weapons, ambulance sirens, somber journalistic reports, a song by a murdered artist.

While these audiovisual intertexts help Bachir-Chouikh depict a
fictional episode set against the collective experience of brutality, she
also focuses on violence done to women. In that, she inscribes her tale
in a series that goes beyond the Algerian tragedy of the 1990s, and goes
all the way back to Shahrazad's *Nights*.

The Three Apples and The Woman in Pieces

It is almost impossible not to view Rachida as a sister of Atyka, the young
protagonist in Assia Djebar's "La Femme coupée en morceaux/The
Woman in Pieces," from her collection *Oran, langue morte/The Tongue's
Blood Does Not Run Dry: Algerian Stories*.[20] As I have said elsewhere,
Djebar's short story points to a narrative *mise en abyme* that links present-
day literature by Maghrebi women authors to the tales of *One Thousand
and One Nights*.[21] Here, *Rachida* adds a cinematic text to the long chain
of women's narratives (from written or oral literature) that link twenty-
first-century women's voices to legendary Shahrazad's.

In Djebar's short story, Atyka teaches French in a high school in the
city of Algiers. The time is 1994. Atyka is engrossed in her class on the
French translation of the "Tale of the Three Apples" from *A Thousand
and One Nights*. She is reading the tale in installments over several days.

The embedded tale narrates the sad discovery by caliph Harun al
Rashid and his vizier, Djaffar, of the corpse of a nameless woman, cut
in pieces, in a chest lying at the bottom of the Tigris river in Baghdad.
She was killed by a jealous husband who was tricked into believing that

she had cheated on him: he slew her and cut her in pieces, which he wrapped in a white veil, itself rolled up in a carpet, laid in a palm basket and placed in a wooden casket. The rest of the tale explains, via various detours, how the murder of the young woman came about. Through it all, the caliph threatens to kill his vizier if the latter does not produce a culprit. The husband's crime is eventually presented as understandable, and the blame is shifted to a lying, boastful slave. It is a story of amazingly detailed violence done to a woman, out of a belief that relies on a lie articulated by a passing stranger:

> "I plunged a knife into her throat. The throat of the one I believed to be unfaithful . . . Was it me, was it really me who, in the same blind rage, cut off her head and mutilated her body? Then, my heart growing ever colder, decided to wrap the body in pieces in a linen veil?"
> This is the confession.[22]

If the stabbing is revealed here as a hyperbolic reaction to the spouse's overwhelming feeling of love betrayed (not dishonor: the husband does not mention it in Atyka's retelling), his relentless, methodical mutilation of a body so passionately desired minutes beforehand still receives no explanation. Retrospectively, it even surprises the confessor of the crime.

While the vizier is trying to find the eunuch responsible for the "tragedy," "the body of the woman in pieces rests near the room where the caliph hears his counsel. Unburied. Unmourned."[23] Once the vizier has identified Rihan as the slave held ultimately responsible for the murder, he wishes to save Rihan's life from the caliph's wrath, and makes a deal with the latter: if Djaffar can tell him a story that surpasses the tale of three apples, then Rihan will be pardoned. The vizier thus becomes a daytime Shahrazad, "the sultana of the dawns."[24] Not a word, in the end, about the woman cut in exactly nineteen pieces. It is the justice of men with its competing narratives that has become central. But the only woman in the story has been forever silenced by death, and the extraordinarily ruthless desecration of her body is not itself investigated.

At this point in the story, Atyka is suddenly faced with agents of the FIS who burst into the classroom. "Atyka is at once there, in Baghdad – where the vizier and his strange master are struggling – and here, now, in the city."[25] One of the invaders, nicknamed "the madman" or "the hunchback" by Omar, a student, is accusatory: "You are Atyka F., a self-proclaimed teacher who, it appears, nonetheless tells these young children obscene stories."[26] He then shoots her, and does not stop there: "He sees the hunchback approaching Atyka's crumpled body and lifting up her head by her long hair – her long, red, flamboyant hair – with one hand. Then, with a long and sure gesture of his other hand, he slits Atyka's throat. He brandishes her head for an instant, then sets it upright on the desk. Watching, Omar thinks, 'The madman's laugh is straight out of a nightmare.'"[27] The same postmortem violence as that in the ancient tale appears in the contemporary text, and is immediately identified as nightmarish, insane, by the student. Constant as it may be, it is still unexplained.

The narrative continues after Atyka's death: "Atyka, her head severed, the new storyteller. Atyka speaks in a steady voice. A pool of blood spreads around her neck, across the wood of the table. Atyka continues the tale. Atyka, the woman in pieces."[28] The teacher resumes her reading, telling her pupils the happy ending of the *Thousand and One Nights*, with Shahrazad introducing her three children to the caliph. Eventually, Omar gets close to the desk to hear her very last words: "Each of our days is a night, a thousand and one days, here, at home, at ..."[29] Atyka becomes the vizier, the day sultana of contemporary Algeria. Omar remains in the classroom when the ambulance personnel arrive and watches what happens to her body: "Atyka's body and head, wrapped in white linen, rest within the chest inside the two coffins. The body of the woman cut into pieces."[30]

The listeners of the tale are identified in both cases: the caliph (the ancient image of male power) and the student in Algiers (today's next male generation), as they both mourn the loss of a woman who is destroyed and disfigured by male violence but whose story endures past her death. If both parables illustrate the reach and power of storytelling, they also posit the unfathomable cruelty of men toward women as age-old.

Rachida, in the footsteps of her sisters, keeps on telling her story (which is also the story of countless women before her): a narrative of male cruelty but also of female survival and, as clearly indicated in the title, of self-assertion. Just as Djebar had given her protagonist, Atyka, a name and agency, Bachir-Chouikh celebrates her heroine's name: Rachida. In that, both protagonists of the recent Algerian feminist rewritings differ sharply from the young anonymous woman of the ancient, oral tale. "'She remains nameless, alas,' Atyka says to herself. 'How can you name somebody who first shows up in pieces?'"[31]

Rachida: The Surviving Woman in Pieces

Apparently, Bachir-Chouikh can! For Rachida is introduced piece by piece in her film. The latter opens with a close-up on a lipstick that a hand then applies (cut to a second close-up) to a woman's lips. Here is our first "piece" of Rachida: very red lips. At this point in the narrative, several conflicting interpretations are possible: the lips on-screen are the first part of a disassembled body, a fetishized body part in keeping with a heterosexual male view of women "cut in pieces" by way of either Eros or Thanatos.

The next close-up is on the head and nape of the woman: again a second element of the female cutout, and still anonymous. A hand unties a ponytail and releases abundant black curls, shaking them free. This is filmed like the beginning of a classic seduction scene. Finally, Rachida's face appears in its entirety in a reflection framed by a small, rectangular mirror. Who is she? The insistence on body parts could signal a *papicha*, that is, one of these provocative young Algerian urban dwellers who, in the 1990s, left their home working-class area for another one, where, under the cover of anonymity they adopted "behaviors that flouted the order imposed by the Islamists. They shamelessly wore make-up and walked around wearing miniskirts and tight pants."[32] We finally hear her name, called by a woman's voice: Rachida.

The introduction of the female protagonist through anonymous body parts echoes the introductions of *The Woman in Pieces* and *The Three Apples*. But Rachida is soon given another role: neither a victim nor a *papicha*, she turns out to be a teacher getting ready for a class picture. She is then shown next to one of her colleagues, a veiled woman with no trace of makeup, who refuses to pose with her students for the photograph. "I don't want my kids to become orphans for a photo," she says. "I'm lucky my husband even lets me work." This first sign of potential violence against women appears right in the exposition scene. We now understand that, in her colleague's view, both Rachida's exposed body parts, red lips and unveiled hair, invite that violence.

The second sequence, in which we see Rachida tailed by two young men, is spliced with close-ups on anonymous hands finishing a home-made bomb complete with a timer. The juxtaposition of the medium shots of Rachida walking to school, riding public transportation, and the close-ups on the bomb is reminiscent of a parallel sequence in *Battle of Algiers*. In the latter, three women are walking out of the Kasbah to meet a bomb-maker. The same structure juxtaposes medium shots of each woman's walk through the city and close-ups on the homemade bombs.

But after his gang has caught up with Rachida, when Sofiane asks her to take the bomb to school, her refusal is adamant: "Not the school! Not the children!" – perhaps in counterpoint to Pontecorvo's film, in which one of the female bomb planters looks (in a lengthy shot) at a child who she knows is going to die. The processes of spectatorial identification with the women bomb planters in *Battle of Algiers* described by Stam are almost repeated in Bachir-Chouikh's film with Rachida[33] – not with Sofiane and his terrorist friends. The complex filmic intertext with *Battle of Algiers*, while reminding the present-day viewer that even *mujahidat* had second thoughts about collateral damage such as dead children, also starkly illuminates the different stakes of the 1990s "war." Rachida is presented as an unwilling potential bomb planter: she wants to save the lives of her students. She refuses to obey the order barked at her by Sofiane, a former student over whom she used to have authority: for a brief moment, there is a hint at a power game contested across gender lines. But violence will prevail, and she is shot in the stomach.

After Rachida is shot, an older woman, loosely wrapped in her white *haïk* (the Algerian traditional white veil) comes to kneel down by her side. She takes Rachida's hand and starts to whisper prayers. From a window above, another woman throws down what looks like a *haïk* or a shroud, to protect Rachida's body from view. The camera, having focused on the two women on the pavement, now takes an aerial view of Rachida, showing an eerie white and red tableau both distinct from, and evocative of, the one that opens *The Tale of Three Apples:* the white shroud or veil on one side of Rachida's inert body, and a growing pool of deep red blood on the other (see figure 7). However, the parallel stops there: Rachida is then transferred to hospital, the bomb is safely detonated by the police, the children will survive, as will Rachida – in contrast to Zekia Guessab, who did not (in her case, the bomb did explode).

The larger part of the film will be dedicated to Rachida's coming to terms with her survival in the midst of chaos and death. Emblematic of Algeria, Rachida's main concern is to survive. As Bachir-Chouikh declared: "One could talk about courage. But it is mostly a question of survival. The kids who keep on going to school everyday do not wonder about courage."[34] At some point, Rachida returns to Algiers for a checkup, and she is declared physically healed, but she complains about her nightmares and fears, which she diagnoses as symptoms of posttraumatic stress. "The whole country suffers from it," the doctor responds wearily. Rachida, now officially declared the embodiment of a brave, psychologically stressed country, gives the filmic narrative the dimension of a parable, itself sustained by the director's flexible use of multiple intertexts (film, news broadcast, literature).

SHOOTING THE VEIL: A CASE STUDY IN TRANSVERGENT COLLAGE

Bachir-Chouikh's project is not only to bear witness for future generations[35] to the state of siege to which women and children were subjected, but also to offer a corrective to competing narratives from the outside (e.g., the media, whether Algerian and state-driven, or European and/or French) and engage in self-reflection: "At some point, we had to take a good look at ourselves and hand out the image of ourselves that is not the image others give of us. . . . I wanted to look at myself and provide an image of us, of ourselves, because we are always told by others, narrated by others. And we end up being afraid of mirrors."[36] In "looking at herself" and at Algeria, she is peeling crude clichés off the surface of foreign representation and fashioning images as close to experience as possible in a fictitious yet realistic tale. It is as if she were filming a familiar world beneath – or on the other side of – the illusory mirror offered to the gaze of outsiders, with a view to correcting the tale of experience that has hitherto been told. One of her correctives is her treatment of the veil, an object with a deep resonance in the Algerian history of French colonization, the revolution, and independence.

As we have seen, Rachida is unveiled. Although she is not a practicing Muslim (unlike her mother), she is literate in the Qur'an. I do not intend to discuss the religious technical points raised by the Qur'an on veiling women (e.g., whether the Prophet wanted his wives to cover their *décolletés* or their hair), nor to engage in a feminist debate on who can or wants to veil whom (this has been done elsewhere in great detail). Neither do I wish to revisit the (ongoing) French and Tunisian debate about the role of the state in banning headscarves. However, it is important to briefly sketch the Algerian veil as a powerful and ambiguous polyseme. In his seminal piece, *Algeria Unveiled*,[37] Fanon (who was both a colonized insider and a male outsider) interpreted wearing a veil as a political act during colonization: (a) as a public show of cultural resistance against the French colonizer who wanted to unveil, "frenchify," "civilize" (violate women's privacy?) the female other; (b) during the war of liberation, as a militant way to resist the French invader by using the veil to conceal weapons or supplies for the FLN. Subsequently, the Fanonian reading of the veil has been either hailed as a positive stand against an oppressor and a way to assert one's cultural identity or decried as a "rationalization for Islamic patriarchal conservatism."[38] Since independence, myriad other interpretations of the veil still locate it at the intersection of Islam, culture, politics, and feminism. It would be foolish to try to ascribe a single value to it, but perhaps easier to ascribe one to its absence: bare-headed Rachida refuses to reduce herself to an agent of *fitna* (فتنة – i.e., the sin of temptation, seduction) upon the first glance of her abundant hair by men, by refusing to wear the veil. Bachir-Chouikh sees it as a separator, a curtain that divides men from women: "Everything is in the veils, in this film, I think: the veils that separate inside from outside, or men from women during the wedding ceremony. These materials are in turn symbols of happiness, prohibition or mourning. It is not necessarily discernible but it is part of my gaze, of my culture."[39] Hence filming a veil is filming a separation, the point of both contact and difference between inside and outside, the point of concealment and of revelation. In *Rachida* veils are used to produce different meanings, as the sequence of Zohra's return to the village abundantly illustrates.

Zohra's Veiling Sequence

The camera precedes her entrance in the village, and pans those who view it: the children and teachers behind the railings of the school (the first visual marker of a separation between the village and the young woman) where Rachida teaches. Her nephew's repeated call, "Auntie Zohra," is heard over the sweeping music, as he runs in a parallel line to her on the other side of the school enclosure. Cut to a medium, slightly low-angle, fixed shot of the teachers holding the bars of the railings, Rachida in the center, watching.

The camera now follows Zohra, still running, as she bangs on the various closed doors of her family's compound, crying, "Let me in." No door opens up. Exhausted, Zohra finally drops down on the street, out in the open public space of the village.

Two men immediately approach her: "Don't touch me!" she cries. "Don't be afraid!" one of them replies repeatedly. Cut to a medium shot then to a close-up on Zohra's face with the men's hands in midair, trying to allay her fears. The remainder of the sequence splices fixed camera frontal (slightly low-angle) shots of onlookers, their gaze steadily on Zohra, seated below. The camera now shifts to distinct, highly composed stills. The construction of these portraits and the poses of their subjects evoke, firstly, those of a journalistic report featuring a string of motionless (powerless?) witnesses of the event – three veiled women, one boy (What is he doing there? We know it is a school day . . .), and secondly, the enduring stills by Pontecorvo on the face of Ali la Pointe or the *mujahidat* (women freedom fighters) that punctuate *Battle of Algiers*.

An Older Woman Shoos the Men Away

Cut to a medium shot of three veiled women: one of them starts to remove her yellow veil.

Cut to a fourth, young, veiled woman: she is occupying the right side of the screen, leaving the other half empty, in a low-angle shot. She is taking off her red headscarf in a graceful arching gesture. Cut to the three women again: the one on the left, in counterpoint to the preceding shot, is in the last stage of removing her red veil (see figure 8).

All the women approach Zohra to cover her with their colorful, translucent veils: Zohra now has her legs and arms, her torn dress, her hair covered in yellow, red, and indigo. Finally, a fifth woman drops a pale blue scarf on her feet.

The women have thus stepped out of beautiful photographic portraits and out of their roles as mute witnesses in order to cover the victim with their own protection. Here, on-screen, we are given to see a powerful, silent story of female compassion. After the veiling, they stay, surrounding her. The final shot of them all together is a carefully staged tableau: Zohra is sitting on the ground at the center, her legs stretched out straight in front of her, framed by two crouching older women, while the younger ones have supplicant positions, as if paying homage. No one is placed in the foreground: Zohra remains the focal point of the shot (see figure 9).

This sequence illustrates several phenomena: the first is the estrangement of women by men, illustrated by her kidnapping and rape by the FIS thugs (off-screen) as well as Zohra's banishment from home by her own father, and the shockingly unwelcoming, closed doors of her father's house. Now the young woman, who used to live within the house, invisible to the outside, no longer has access to the customary "invisibility" and shelter provided by either the walls of a house or a veil. The protection from the desiring or envious "evil eye" of the other (unrelated men, the FIS, malevolent spirits) has vanished. It no longer envelops her. The communal bestowing of veils could be seen as a female attempt to restore Zohra's traditional defense against the evil eye, against the egregious brutality to which she was subjugated in the off-screen sequence of her kidnapping.

The second phenomenon is the ensuing female solidarity in the face of violence done to one of them. It is a gesture that might signal the return to the rules and protection of the home, which only women can now provide for Zohra. In removing their veils, the women tacitly agree to "disobey" the orders of the FIS men: they dare bare their heads in order to protect the one whom the FIS has savagely attacked. Bachir-Chouikh sees this sequence as women challenging the Islamists, by opposing their will to live to the terrorists' will to destroy and kill, by choosing Eros over Thanatos: "In this scene where women take off their veils to cover the raped young woman, there is a kind of challenge to the fundamentalists, the very people who forbid them to show their hair and who have kidnapped and raped the young woman. The veils with which they cover her have the colors of life; it is as if they were protecting her by transforming her in a little garden."[40] It is the victory of Eros over Thanatos, the embrace of a broken woman by her female companions: Zohra is no longer in pieces, as she was in the forest; she is one, and in this tableau, part of a community of women. Nothing is said, but everything is understood. There is no male narrative of (in)justice, and Zohra remains the focus of the picture. She is not ignored (as the Woman in Pieces was) and the women have taken over. Although the off-screen male violence done to Zohra is still perceptible on-screen (e.g., her wounds, her torn dress), women's solidarity has evicted all male protagonists from the public space of the village and relegated them to a peripheral position (none of them is seen frontally: there is no adult male face in this sequence) – hence the women-only final tableau of the sequence. The space traditionally occupied by women (the home) has spilled out into the street to succor Zohra.

Furthermore, the final, carefully composed tableau appears to the 2002 viewer as the counterpoint to a previous one that marked the media of the late 1990s: the famous photograph taken by AFP photographer Houcine Zaourar on September 23, 1997, after the massacre of Bentahla, which was published in the press across the world and called the "Madonna." The close-up shot shows a veiled woman, her face the expression of utter pain, supported by an older, veiled woman to her right. The face of the "Madonna" (a telling misnomer reflecting who "reads" a Muslim culture) became one of the most circulated clichés of the 1990s war. It showed two women: the younger one in pain (a victim in mourning) and the older one nurturing, solicitous (an *über*-mother); a victim, her face and scream frozen, next to a compassionate female companion (and to the Western outsider, an evocation of the pietà). The purpose of this image is hijacked in *Rachida*, however, for the final vibrant tableau of this sequence, instead of lingering on mourning, suggests a beginning, the possibility of a healing thanks to women.

Hence the possible reading of the film as a model of female resistance: women reconfigure the space of their agency as they regroup to heal. Since the patriarchal order has failed them and proven unable to protect them (against the male wave of egregious FIS violence that has brutally dismantled the gendered dichotomy between private and public sphere), women have started to (re)occupy the public space. Their traditional interior space having been "politically" invaded by outside male forces, women now begin to appropriate and share the outer political space within the city ("polis"), within society. Meanwhile, the FIS and its murky actions are relegated to the realm of the uncivilized, off-screen.

By the end of the film, women are prominently visible outside the home, reconstructing the village, and eventually, hopefully, Algerian society, as they start to teach the young again: in the last sequence of the film, Rachida is back in the classroom, writing on the blackboard, then turning her face to the camera, looking at us, defiantly. She will survive and so will her country. Bachir-Chouikh has thus signaled a crucial political renegotiation of spaces that clearly denounces the outdated, ineffective and, in the final analysis, dangerous old patriarchal boundaries. In that she has also inscribed her film as a counterpoint in the Algerian cinematic tradition of what Hadj-Moussa perceives as a construction of spatial territory:[41] while her predecessors behind the camera rallied to occupy and (re)define the national space of independent Algeria, she projects on a screen the occupation and redefinition of an Algerian women's space.

CONCLUSION

In her very first feature film, Bachir-Chouikh, by focusing on the story of a woman, has thus succeeded in breaking through the silence of the Algerian authorities, and in correcting the depiction of 1990s Algeria proposed by outsiders (in particular the media). Her subtle, transvergent negotiation of intertexts, which allows her to adhere to no prescribed regime of truths (neither that of the powers that be, nor that of the Islamists, nor that of the international media), allows her to tell a fictitious story with familiar Barthian *effets de réel*[42] (e.g., excerpts from the media, from other known films) to which her audience can relate. Her transvergent intertexts thus acquire an ironical realistic effect that supports the dynamics of the fiction. As a result, Bachir-Chouikh appears an embodiment of a cinematic Shahrazad, telling in her own artful terms yet one more episode of male violence perpetrated on women. But she also, ultimately, proposes a renaissance: the tale ends with the expectant faces of children in school and the determined gaze of Rachida – just as the *Nights* end with Shahrazad's determined face as she pushes her children to a finally welcoming, disarmed sultan.

4

Raja Amari's Screen of the Haptic: *Red Satin* (Tunisia, 2002)

PRELUDE

At the end of *The Nights*, Shahrazad marries the Sultan, and Dunyazad marries his brother. The description of the marriage feast is replete with details on the various attires both brides wear. Shahrazad's first dress is of a deep red:

> Presently they brought forward Shahrazad and displayed her, for the first dress, in a red suit; whereupon King Shahriyar rose to look upon her and the wits of all present, men and women, were bewitched for that she was even as saith of her one of her describers: –
>
> A sun on wand in knoll of sand she showed,
> Clad in her cramoisy-hued chemisette
> Of her lips' honey-dew she gave me drink
> And with her rosy cheeks quench fire she set.[1]

In Raja Amari's film, however, the bride does not wear red: her mother does. And the story is not about a fiancée's long journey to marital bliss; rather, it is the story of a beautiful widow who marries off her daughter at the end of the film, yet who dances seductively, all clad in a fiery red dress. One could see the film as a different take on Shahrazad's wedding to Shahriyar, or, better yet, as a new storytelling technique inspired by Shahrazad's but taken in an entirely new direction. Amari as postmodern Shahrazad tells us a secret story by going against the grain of the viewer's expectations.

At first sight, *Red Satin* seems to focus on the secret life of the widow
Lilia, who becomes a cabaret dancer at night. As we know, however, one
secret can hide another. Most incredibly, though, the secret it hides is
actually in plain view: in this film, Amari reverses the gazing strategy to
which we are accustomed and finally makes us rethink the very notion
of screen. The latter, no longer the smooth surface we have understood
it to be, becomes a space traversed by new forms of inquisitive gazing.
Here the veil and the screen also divide and unite, also stop from seeing
and allow to see.

AMARI'S DARING CHOICES

Raja Amari, born in 1971 in Tunis, epitomizes the daring spirit of the
younger generation of Maghrebi women directors unafraid of using cinema to test the limits of the permissible. Bicultural, Amari is the product
of two elite cultures: she studied French literature at the University of
Tunis, and then went to Paris to study cinema script writing at FEMIS
(École Nationale Supérieure des Métiers de l'Image et du Son),[2] from
which she graduated in 1998. She then divided her time between filmmaking, shooting a few shorts in Paris or Tunis, and cinema writing,
publishing a few critical pieces in *Cinécrits*,[3] in Tunis.

Her cinematic portfolio shows over a decade of diverse films in
various formats. Her first short, *Avril/April* (30 min, 1998), the exploration of a claustrophobic triangular relationship between two neurotic
older sisters and their new, very young, silent maid, reaped impressive
international awards.[4] Her second, *Un Soir de juillet/One Evening in
July* (2001), told the story of a bride who has cold feet and confides in
Saida, the old woman who has come to wax her body for her wedding
night. This 23-minute short was selected to be part of the *Mama Africa*
series.[5] *Red Satin* is her first feature film, which was followed in 2004
by *'Ala khoutta al nessyan/Sur les traces de l'oubli/Seekers of Oblivion*, a
52-minute-long documentary on writer and traveling free spirit Isabelle
Eberhardt (1877–1904), and the multiple images of herself that she left
behind after her untimely death in a flash flood in Algeria in 1904. Amari
teases out fragments of competing interpretations of a complex female
character but offers no resolution. Her chosen subject in this film raised

a few eyebrows on either side of the Mediterranean: today's Algerian writers of history view Eberhardt as a spy for France; the French viewed her as a woman of questionable morality; her cross-dressing has been interpreted as a sign of bisexuality by some and as a travel precaution by others. In short, Eberhardt's behavior outside the norms of nineteenth-century European and Algerian societies fed all sorts of gossip and legends that contribute to the aura of ambiguity that surrounds her.

Her second feature film, *Al Dowaha/Les Secrets/Secrets* (2009), shows a reclusive family of three women living secretly in an abandoned house in which the mother used to work as a servant. The film, whose Arabic title means lullaby, explores a triangular, female relationship reminiscent of *April*, and the repression of womanly desire as it appears in *Red Satin*. A lullaby haunts it throughout, and in one scene a song by Farid El Attrache (again a wink and a nod to Egyptian cinema similar to those in *Red Satin*) is heard playing on a turntable in the old villa, resonating as the song of the house, the latter both a mansion and a prison. In that film, Amari said, her "desire was to tell a modern, noir fairy-tale. [She] gathered all the elements of the fairy-tale: the castle, the ball, the evil stepmother, the sister, Cinderella's shoe, even Prince Charming. But [she] still wished to be realistic in her treatment."[6] In her nightmarish tale, Amari gradually unveils the dark secret of incest that ties the three women to a muted existence, and by exposing the crucial taboo that presides over their identities and relationships, she outs more than the incest; she outs female sexuality as "downgraded to the rank of an obscene reality (hence the secrets, the mysteries and prohibitions that border on the absurd and the silly)."[7] There ensues a bifurcated vision (exemplified visually through the filming of cold interiors and open, sun-drenched exteriors, for instance) that cuts from the social sphere to the personal, indeed the most intimate sphere of women's lives: sexuality. As Sonia Chamkhi rightfully highlights, "in both [feature] films by Raja Amari, the liberation and the rehabilitation of female desire is the sine qua non condition of women's sovereign existence."[8]

In all these films, Amari adopts a twofold approach to her characters: her camera focuses on one or more female individuals etched against the backdrop of what she calls "social hypocrisy."[9] This leads to a double vision: recognizable clues of a stifling social background in contrast to a female protagonist who gathers more and more complexities as the filmic narrative unfolds. Her choices of subject, character, casting, and approach in *Red Satin* further illustrate this idiosyncratic play on recognition and gradual uncovering.

When *Al sitar al ahmar/Satin Rouge/Red Satin* came out in Tunis in April 2002, it created quite a stir. The Tunisian audience, used to the images of respectable matriarchs in Arab cinema, for instance, could not readily relate to the mother-in-law, dressed in flamboyant red, who danced seductively in front of her daughter and her groom in the final scene. Critics avoided discussing one of the central themes (a widow acting on her sexual desires) and preferred, instead, to focus their comments on the casting choice of a Palestinian actress, Hiam Abbas, in the main role. In so doing, they could safely stay away from the delicate matter of sex in the city of Tunis. *Le Temps*, one of the main daily newspapers in French, titled its film review "Tunisia pays homage to the resistance of the Palestinian people."[10] Hiam Abbas attributed this take on the film to the date of its premiere – April 3, 2002 (coinciding with the day the Israeli troops entered the refugee camp of Jenin)[11] – and to the subsequent emotional response of Tunisians to both film and invasion in the presence of the Palestinian star.

Yet, even with the luminous screen presence of Hiam Abbas (an international star in the Arab world as well as in the West) emptied of its possible Middle Eastern political weight, one still wonders why Amari cast a Palestinian actress instead of a Tunisian one. Although Roy Armes explains that selecting a foreigner for a Tunisian leading role is far from new, citing the previous examples of Abdellatif Ben Ammar and Taïeb Louhichi,[12] I would suggest that this is the exception rather than the norm. In order to sound authentic in her role, Hiam Abbas had to be coached in Tunisian Arabic (as well as trained in "oriental dancing"). Meanwhile, the presence of Abbas on-screen gives the film an added international flavor that reflects various elements of her star image in her previous roles in a variety of Arab and European films. In the end, Abbas embodies a character who is Tunisian but who could also be emblematic of Arab dancers from the Mashreq to the Maghreb.

When asked where the subject of her film originated, Raja Amari always answers that she wished to pay homage to the classic Egyptian musical comedies of the 1940s and 1950s, and its star couple. "I was a fan of dancer Samia Gamal and singer Farid El Attrache," she confesses in an interview,[13] and further expresses her nostalgia for the freedom of expression and sensuality that Egyptian films exuded at the time.[14] She herself studied oriental dance in Tunis. Her conscious choice of inscribing her film in that particular cinematic tradition (even if, as Roy Armes underscores, she also cites Italian and French filmmakers' influences) goes against the grain of today's Tunisian filmmaking. It can be seen as both a nostalgic return to her own dancing and childhood television-viewing years, and a challenge: how to win an audience for whom cinematic codes and expectations have drastically changed since the golden age of Egyptian musical comedies. Hence the "oriental dancer" of *Red Satin* is a carefully constructed polysemic figure from the very first image of the film.

THE NARRATIVE INVERSION OF MARGINS AND CENTER

Film Synopsis

Lilia, an attractive forty-something, leads a rather dull existence as a housewife in Tunis with her only daughter, Selma (Hend El Fahem in her first role on-screen). She spends her days cleaning her apartment, food shopping, cooking, sewing dresses for neighbors, and knitting sweaters for Selma, who does not like them. Her only occasional solitary pleasure, we are led to believe, is the amateur oriental dancing she sometimes performs for herself in the privacy of her bedroom.

Meanwhile, Selma, a senior in high school, is in love with Chokri (cinema and TV actor and director Maher Kamoun), a drummer – a *darbouka* player – whom she has met at the school where she takes oriental dance lessons. Lilia guesses that her daughter sees Chokri in secret. The latter has a second job, playing for women dancers in a cabaret where Lilia, worried about her daughter, follows him one day. At first overwhelmed, then fascinated, by the cabaret dance show, Lilia soon strikes up a friendship with Folla, the dancing star of the place. In short order, she finds herself on stage as well and starts to lead a double life: that of a dutiful housewife spied upon by her neighbors during the day and a secret performer on the cabaret stage at night.

This initial dual situation becomes further complicated by the fiery relationship that develops on stage between the drummer (Chokri) and the dancer (Lilia). The *darbouka* beat feeds into the frenzy of the dance, and the dance spurs on the drumming in a mutual and shared exhilaration. The sensual paroxysm of dance and music on stage is translated into an intense sexual encounter. However, Chokri puts an abrupt end to the affair with the radiant Lilia after hearing that Selma finally wants to introduce him to her mother (who, still unbeknownst to him, is Lilia).

Chokri finally meets Lilia as Selma's mother. Lilia behaves as a powerful woman in perfect control of the situation. The wedding of Selma and Chokri takes place in a final scene in which groom and bride are sitting side by side, motionless in their seats, while Lilia, dressed in red, dances boldly in the foreground.

This final tableau, while reminiscent of the Egyptian musicals of yore in its trappings of a classical dancing feast and wedding, actually offers no explicit resolution of the Lilia-Chokri story. It also marks a radical shift in perspective. While the rest of the film seems to be shot from Lilia's perspective, the final scene is shot at mid-distance from her, and points her out as the highly unconventional focal point of her daughter's wedding ceremony.

Choosing the Female Gaze

The overture of *Red Satin* immediately signals that something is up with the spectatorial gaze: instead of identifying with what feminist cinema critics have called a male voyeuristic gaze, the viewer is led to follow the gaze of a woman contemplating herself in a mirror. Her body is not fetishized, her allure is not one of seductiveness, she is not applying makeup. No, she is a housewife in a loose, drab-looking dress, busy dusting her bedroom. In this first scene, Lilia performs the gestures of her daily life to the sound of a popular song from Egypt playing on the radio. Yet, as she catches a glimpse of herself in the mirror, she shakes her hair loose, unties her belt, and starts to dance. This sudden transformation of the housewife into a playful private dancer is shot from behind: the extra-diegetic viewer is thus looking over Lilia's shoulder at her image in the mirror (see figure 10). The position of the camera behind or over the shoulder of Lilia recurs throughout the film, and each step of her conscious development from a reclusive housewife into a cabaret dancer on stage is clearly highlighted in scenes shot close-up in which Lilia watches her reflection in the looking glass. In the inaugural scene, she moves from the mirror to a framed picture of her dead husband, thus aligning the pleasure of dancing with the nostalgia of past, shared sensual pleasures. Later in the film, she tries on Folla's stage costume in Folla's changing room in the cabaret and transforms herself into a public dancer right then and there (see figure 11). Later again, we see her staring at her face next to Chokri's in the mirror of Folla's changing room and realize, with her, that she will succumb to his charms.

The notion of a mother sharing a lover with her daughter establishes a new form of female power as it inverts the traditional masculine triangulation trope that haunts, say, classic French film: the older man who "steals" a younger female lover from his (proto)son is replaced by an older woman stealing her daughter's lover.[15] This transgression not only empowers women but also locates desire and the erotic charge in the mother, thus highlighting (older) female desire rather than male desire. Finally, at the last point of her transformation in the film, we see her staring at her carefully composed face as she tries on her new role as mother-in-law to be: she has readied herself for Selma's official introduction of her fiancé, Chokri. This recurrent use of mirrors in the film signals self-reflexive moments on the part of the protagonist; meanwhile the position of the camera (and therefore the viewer) that relays Lilia's (obviously feminine) gaze leads to fascinating reversals in both the narrative itself and the projection of woman's image onto the screen.

For instance, Lilia's first encounter with the nocturnal world of the cabaret is translated into shots of the male audience staring at the female dancers and at her, a woman out alone in this place of (male) pleasure. The medium to close-up shots of the faces of men who are drinking, laughing, cheering the dancers are united in a dizzying, whirling pan over an audience intently staring at Lilia. Here the camera is recording the male watcher contemplating the female object of his desiring look, as opposed to recording the object of the male gaze. In this montage, Amari seems to launch the first stage of reversal of the classic gendered order of the shot/reverse shot, as seen by Kaja Silverman: "The most paradigmatic of all shot/reverse shot formations is that which aligns the female body with the male gaze. This two-shot not only covers over the absent site of production, but places the male subject on the side of vision, and the female subject on the side of spectacle."[16] In the cabaret scene, Lilia actively gazes at the gazers, who then become the passive objects "on the side of spectacle" of her own vision. The reversal does not go smoothly at first: the female protagonist, as she faces what looks like a multiplied male gaze of desire, cannot bear it initially. Lilia promptly faints, and is transported to the safety of a female space: Folla's changing room. Lilia, who has ventured inside the cabaret to see if her daughter is there with Chokri, is clearly a brand new gazer, a brand new member of the audience in the cabaret, and she is unprepared for the onslaught of male gazes that have thus propelled her onto their stage. This first encounter of the male gaze is an aggression (as illustrated by the infectious rhythm of the intra-diegetic music, and the overwhelmingly rapid succession of images of the audience) and already contains a shift in gendered role distribution in the gazing game.

(Of course, this gender reversal in Maghrebi women's gazing agency is not unique to *Red Satin*. In Djebar's *Nuba of the Women of Mount Chenoua*, Leila's husband is often the object of a spying gaze: that of a young woman who fleetingly appears, framed by an open window or door, observing him. Similarly, in Moufida Tlatli's *Season of Men* (2000), the camera's perspective is that of women stealing looks at their husbands watching an oriental dance show, from behind a wall. Yet, nowhere in women's Maghrebi cinema is it as clearly demonstrated as in Amari's *Red Satin*.)

Later in the film, when Folla leads Lilia on stage to perform, Lilia's dance scene is edited in a telling montage of shots of her audience reminiscent of Lilia's first entrance into the cabaret, spliced with close-ups of Lilia's ecstatic face as she lets her body perform what looks like a solo expression of sensual longing and pleasure (a fact not lost on the cabaret manager, who tells her she needs to learn to dance for an audience, not have a good time on her own!). The montage, however, seems to be structured along a call-and-response pattern, illustrative of the possible illusion of a superficial, coded exchange: the gaze of the looked-at woman as she twirls around the room and loses herself in a trancelike state of dancing pleasure supposedly "responding to" the avid stares of the men. That structure underlines for the extra-diegetic audience the misunderstanding between the intra-diegetic cabaret audience and Lilia: the watchers (except for the manager) believe that they are part of the dancing moment, part of the exchange that occurs in a live show. The intra-diegetic audience still functions along the old dynamics of the gaze: the male as the subject of vision and the female as the object on the side of spectacle. But the extra-diegetic audience knows, having seen Lilia dance for herself before, that such is not the case: her dance is strictly her own, performed for herself, for her own fulfillment. It will take another phase of her development for Lilia to actually break out of her self-reflexive, isolated dancing mode. For the time being, she is, simply, not participating in the dynamics of the show, in the (gendered) gazing game. In fact, once she dances, she seems impervious to the male gaze.

Put differently, Amari suggests a renegotiation of what Laura Mulvey called "viewing pleasure": instead of appearing as the fantasized result of (heterosexual, male) scopophilia that usually fills the screen with the titillating image of an attractive female object of male desire, male scopophilia here is represented directly on-screen in the guise of aggressive, unpleasant images in the eyes of the female protagonist. Lilia takes on the role of an active watcher, while the patriarchal gaze of men is rendered passive by the spectacle of their scopophilia. In the end, although the filmic narrative derives some of its elements from a melodrama with Western and Egyptian overtones, it is not projected onto the screen in the latter's usual forms of excess. Moreover, the gaze logistics seem to be superseded, perhaps even displaced, by another sense at work in the film: the sense of touch.

RED SATIN: A STUDY IN HAPTIC (UN)VEILING

As is often the case in Maghrebi cinema, the Arabic title ascribed to the film differs from its simultaneously given French one (the latter subsequently translated into English). Here, *al sitar al ahmar,* "the red curtain," distances the viewer from the "red satin" of the other title. The first one introduces the notion of a spatial separation and reminds the audience of the intra-diegetic cabaret stage and Lilia's double life, while the second one focuses on the guiding sense that leads Lilia through her transformation from housewife to dancer. Yet, I would contend, both titles taken together also further illustrate a productive reading of the film as both haptic and double.

At the core of it all lies the illusion of cinema that projects flat images onto a screen. Yet these images elicit, through various manipulations, feelings of closeness that appeal to our senses: sight, hearing, and also smell and touch. Images of the latter abound in *Red Satin* and have both narrative and aesthetic functions that correspond to Deleuze and Guattari's concept of the haptic: "A haptic space can be visual, aural, as well as tactile. . . . 'Haptic' is a better word than 'tactile,' since it does not establish an opposition between two sense organs, but rather invites the assumption that the eye itself may fulfill this nonoptical function."[17] In other words, the eye can touch as well as see. Yet, sight does not merely assume a synesthetic function (with sight leading to a multisensory perception of the world) for the extra-diegetic viewer. Rather, it provides an entirely different mode of "sensing" the film on-screen. It is the conversion from a projected tactile scene on-screen into the audience's haptic viewing of it that gives *Red Satin* its power to offer new ways to produce meaning, or, rather, new ways to apprehend the film. As a viewer, I am led to see and then reconceive the object of my gaze as touched, felt, sensed, and not merely seen. According to Laura Marks, the haptic actually gives the viewer a novel way of "interacting" with the film, as it proposes a to and fro between intimate closeness (the sensation of an object) and distance (the screen is still the screen, thus separate, indeed away, from us):

> In the sliding relationship between haptic and optical, distant vision gives way to touch, and touch reconceives the object to be seen from a distance. Optical visuality requires distance and a center, the viewer acting like a pinhole camera. In a haptic relationship our self rushes up to the surface to interact with another surface. When this happens there is a concomitant loss of depth – we become amoebalike, lacking a center, changing as the surface to which we cling changes. We cannot help but change in the process of interacting.[18]

I wish to first explore the optical representation of touch in the film, and then carefully observe how it leads to the viewer's haptic experience. As we have seen earlier, the emblematic overture of the film shows Lilia dusting her bedroom. Yet her ordinary gestures (the hand gliding on the mirror surface to clean it, or displacing objects to wipe away the dust under them) shot left to right in a circular pan, also show a woman caressing the familiar objects that delineate the limits of her private space: her bedroom. The viewer is invited to apprehend Lilia's world immediately in an intimate fashion, mimicking hers, as she follows Lilia's hands, and comes to see Lilia's reflection in the full-length mirror that adorns the bedroom armoire. While, in the emblematic scene, extra-diegetic viewers are ushered into Lilia's space, sounds, and routine, they also "feel" invited to partake in her routine touch of things, to be initiated into her own tactile relationship with her world.

Three other significant "haptic moments" in the narrative illustrate the "sliding" from the optical to the "haptic" even further: the pivotal scene in which Lilia changes into Folla's dancing costume and tries on this new persona; her first dance with Chokri playing the *darbouka;* and her furtive moment of sensual pleasure as she fingers the red satin of a feminine slip in a lingerie store.

[30:25] In Folla's room, Lilia's face and bust appear between a row of shiny costumes in the foreground and hanging ones of various colors and textures behind her. She has been invited in as Folla's seamstress, to sew dancing outfits or mend those that break after particularly energetic numbers on stage. She smiles, alone in the room, stroking the various materials, and clearly feeling tactile pleasure. She holds up a dancing top (an adorned, golden, shiny brassiere) to her bosom in front of the mirror. The camera modestly turns away. And here starts a slow, right to left pan of the room that details the objects of the night world of the cabaret: rich costume fabrics, some smooth and silky or satiny, others striated or rough with sequins, their colors bright, bold, varied; the camera slowly glides over a few bottles of Celtia Tunisian beer, a half bottle of whiskey, a full ashtray, before it finally rests on Lilia from the back, now fully clad in a glittery, gold dancing outfit, looking at herself in the mirror and putting on red lipstick. Lilia engages in a femme fatale–like "masquerade," as Bruzzi would say, for her own pleasure (and not with a male audience in mind).[19]

This scene, although in sharp contrast with the opening one (e.g., the muted tones of the bedroom in contrast to the brilliant, even garish, colors of Folla's garments; the direction of the panning; the sounds of the cabaret filtering through as opposed to the radio), can also be seen as its prolongation. Here, the viewer first recognizes the fleeting pleasure of touch as experienced by Lilia in the first few seconds of the scene, and then is left to see the room with no guiding hand to finger its objects. As the camera slowly, almost languidly, brushes by each costume, each object constitutive of the cabaret room, the viewer is touching them too. In other words, once Lilia has shown the way to touch, in the inaugural scene, the viewer knows to follow the tactile injunction given by the camera. This entire, circular panorama of Folla's den can be seen as an illustration of Laura Mark's concept of a haptic image: "The term haptic *visuality* emphasizes the viewer's inclination to perceive haptically, but a work itself may offer haptic *images*. Haptic images do not invite identification with a figure so much as they encourage a bodily relationship between the viewer and the image. Thus it is less appropriate to speak of the object of a haptic look than to speak of a dynamic subjectivity between looker and image."[20] Once the dynamics of this subjective encounter have been established, other haptic phenomena can occur and further a multisensory approach to the film that is so intense, and almost independent of the characters at this point, that the extra-diegetic viewer loses ground as "extra-diegetic" and becomes part of what is on-screen. In such moments when she loses her safe remote position, the viewer experiences a vertiginous sense of indistinctness of ontological proportions: she is no longer who she sat down to be in front of the screen.

Immediately after this pivotal scene in Folla's room from which Lilia emerges as a dancer, she is led onto the stage and starts to perform to the sound of an increasingly ebullient *darbouka* played by Chokri. The scene is structured as a shot/countershot dialogue between Lilia and her audience, and further complicated by a few close-ups of the *darbouka* filmed from the inside. We see the opaque membrane of Chokri's drum from beneath, its bluish round surface trembling under the musician's fingers. The extra-diegetic viewer is thus positioned as closely as possible to Chokri's drum beating, and feels its infectious rhythm in synch with the quick glimpses of Lilia's movements on stage. At this point in the film, we are not only on-stage, on the other side of the red curtain (of the Arabic title), but also on the underside of the playing instrument.

Not only do we "lose" our optical distance to the screen, but we also almost lose our aural distance to it: we are thrown beneath the fingers of a drummer (see figure 12). We need no further visual clue, no further explanation: by metonymy, we "know" – intimately so because we are positioned right there, beneath the hands that beat the *darbouka* – the rhythm shared by Chokri and Lilia, and we have even become able to "sense" through these instants of tactile viewing that the dancer and musician are sharing an ecstatic, sensual performance.

The viewer is therefore not surprised when Chokri is filmed against Folla's costumes in an eerie parallel to the earlier scene, as Lilia watches him in the mirror. He comes to stroke her shoulder with two light fingers and confesses: "Since I have been seeing you dance, I can only think of you." The tactile means of the protagonist's apprehension of the world is then recognized in Chokri's touch. The clue once again functions metonymically thanks to both spatial and haptic recognition (Folla's place = a place of touching pleasure for Lilia) and the codifying of characters along the axis of touch (Chokri's fingers literally make Lilia dance). Chokri's light touch provides a direct resolution of what we have suspected all along, for while, in performance, both protagonists were at a distance, not "touching" with their fingers (though sharing the elation of music and dance), we, extra-diegetic viewers were in touch with both distinct bodies. We become the link between them. To quote Marks once again, "it makes sense to talk of touch participating in what we think of as primarily a visual experience, if we understand this experience to be one of the lived body."[21]

It is this lived body, then, that feels the red satin of the French title in the scene when Lilia ventures out of her neighborhood to enter a lingerie store and, mesmerized by the red satin slip displayed on a mannequin, starts to finger it slowly. There is no need here for a close-up on Lilia's fingers: at this point of experience in the film, the extra-diegetic viewer can apprehend the film haptically at the slightest hint.

In *Red Satin*, then, the viewer is projected into the filmic narrative itself; her interaction with the filmic world is tactile, visual, aural. The experience is not one of sensory overload, in which meaning would be achieved only through a state of saturation of the various senses. Instead, the experience is one of a new kind of transvergence that gives the viewer the sensation of having traversed the screen, of being on the other side of the mirror. That very journey through perception is one that is entirely suggested via the body, not the intellect. As Marks states:

> Haptic cinema appeals to a viewer who perceives with all the senses. It involves thinking with your skin, or giving as much significance to the physical presence of an other as to the mental operations of symbolization. This is not a call to willful regression but to recognizing the intelligence of the perceiving body. Haptic cinema, by appearing to us as an object with which we interact rather than an illusion into which we enter, calls on this sort of embodied intelligence. In the dynamic movement between optical and haptic ways of seeing, it is possible to compare different ways of knowing and interacting with an other.[22]

I would argue that more is at stake than Marks acknowledges here: the haptic viewer temporarily loses her own willful imagining of the other (from a projected image) to slip into her own interaction with the other, no longer seen as a simulacrum but experienced as the vivid presence of another body. Hence the relationship that ensues is one of closeness that in some ways defeats the necessary remoteness of the gaze. (Marks even talks of that relationship as "erotic," in that it meets the other in her/his own closeness and abolishes all distance.) In that state of viewing/being a viewer, the two titles of the film finally merge: the curtain that separates becomes the touched satin, and the satin that I touch becomes the curtain of the screen. The images on the cinematic screen have thus become both within my eyes' reach and at my vividly imagined fingertips. The collusion of both senses here is simultaneously consonant with the Tunisian culture off-screen (which is tactile in its approach to objects – say, to fruit or bread at the market) and dissonant with it (interpersonal touch across genders is not allowed in public). Amari's haptic cinema suggests both the intimacy of touch that usually remains private, hidden, and a daring gaze that stares at and around the veil of the projected character.

SCREENS AND VEILS

حِجَاب /hijab

Not a single woman wears the veil in this film: neither the protagonist, nor her nosy neighbor, nor the women shopping for food at the market. This clear choice on the part of Amari, can receive this rather unexceptional explanation: the director is making a feminist political statement (in agreement with her government at the time),[23] and, by erasing it from her film, is stating that the veil is not an issue. Such a position would then tend to ignore the recent phenomenon of "new veiling" (as McLeod calls it[24]) in the Maghreb, that is, women donning the hijab, the dark veil from the Mashreq, as a political statement, instead of the traditional white *safsari* of their grandmothers. Hence, my invocation of the hijab in the discussion of this film is located on a symbolic level: that of the dynamics of the cinematic gaze.

Hijab comes from the root *hajaba* [حجب]: to hide, to subtract from the gaze. Thus, it takes on the meanings of the veil (that protects from the gaze) but also the meaning of "curtain" or "screen," a surface that separates, hides away (as in the curtain through which a male doctor can examine a female Muslim patient in some regions of the world). It is a screen that bars from seeing. It is the veiling surface that prevents from touching, seeing, reaching the other behind the hijab in an act of seduction and/or transgression.

In other words, it is diametrically opposed to Amari's use of the cinematic screen, as she invites the viewer to see, indeed to feel, cinematic bodies.

The Cinema Screen

The history of cinema in the Maghreb, as indicated in the "Overture," has its recognized roots in the itinerant theater of the shadows. In that tradition, the screen presented to the audience showed the projected images of puppets held behind it, against the light. Hence the viewers were facing the two-dimensional surface images of a spectacle performed behind and beyond the screen. That screen both separated the viewers from the origin of the show, from its making, and conjoined the spectatorial gaze with the show.

Similarly, the veil, taken as a symbolic cultural marker, isolates and attracts, separates and points out the (female) element that is separated, subtracted from the gaze. The illusory nature of the theater of the shadows, with its play on silhouettes that signal representations but do not present any "real" body, still fulfils the function of the hijab: it sets up a screen that prevents the audience from touching, seeing fully, reaching. The shadow narrative, so disembodied and symbolic, keeps the viewer remote.

In such a segregated environment, how does a woman "show" another woman? How does a woman director film and project a woman's image onto a screen, given the fact that women are culturally and socially located behind a screen that forbids closeness? In *Red Satin*, the viewer is offered a look from the other side of the shadow screen, invited to touch, see, reach fully through a haptic apprehension of Lilia's world. In this type of cinema, the cinematic screen becomes a meeting surface but also the plane on which what usually goes on beyond the veil of women is projected from the other side or from – dare I say? – its underside (like the side never shown of a *darbouka*). It is as if the director were turning the hijab inside out (like a pocket). As a result, the viewer is given license to see the inverse projection of the usual imagery of woman in Maghrebi cinema (or even Arab film in general), since the forbidden, cloistered space of woman's body appears within reach. This, in turn, reshuffles the rules of scopophilia, now no longer the exclusive province of male gazers. Instead, it becomes the delicious impulse, shared across genders, to open oneself to the womanly side of the spectacle and vision. Paradoxically, the cinematic screen, in a haptic perspective, then becomes a type of skin: both the end of the gaze and the porous membrane that allows the eye to pierce through it and into another world, thus leading the viewer into the deeply felt illusion that she has traversed it, and attained the interior world of the filmic narrative. This conception of the screen can hold only through a transvergent move between sight and the haptic gaze.

The Transvergent Veil and Screen

So far we have seen how a haptic visuality can result in a new sensory and ontological perception of an other and her world on the cinematic screen. Yet what is left unclear is what happens to the gazer's subjectivity when she switches from the visual gaze to the haptic one. This is where Novak's notion of transvergence can productively illuminate the process, since it focuses on the flexible aspect of a subjectivity constantly in becoming, instead of being fixed in one position, and always/already other from one moment of being to the next.

Invoking the notion of transvergence to rethink the cinematic screen, the latter can become an interface: a plane with portals that give access to other virtual or cinematic worlds, and that allows the viewer to come to experiment with that other projected world from beneath the screen that we have just described. Hence two phenomena occur on the transvergent screen, as it provides a viewing surface to the gaze, and opens up, beyond it, the possibility of engagement with the cinematic world it images. The interface allows the coexistence and negotiation of two worlds. The extra-diegetic viewer can then opt either to explore the world proposed cinematically and/or to retreat into her own. In the former case, her exploration of the "shadows" behind the screen will last the entire 100 minutes of the cinematic illusion. What feels, however, genuine is her moment of engagement with the filmic world. That the latter is artificial does not matter: it is the shared received projection of it that is crucial. To illustrate that point, let's take a look at what Novak describes as his Virtual Dervish project:

> It began with the observation that virtual reality allows us to share visions. Consider the image of a 'whirling dervish': a Sufi mystic blind to the world but spinning in a secret vision. We can see the person, we can see the spinning, but we cannot enter the mental universe within which she dances. Now, compare the image of the dervish to that of a person donning the late-twentieth century's version of the mystic's robe: the head-mounted display, the dataglove, and a tangle of wires. Confined to the narrow radius of sensor-reach, joined to the ceiling by an umbilical connecting brain to computer, eyes blind to the world, this spinning person is also lost in a vision. The parallel is strong, but there is a key difference: this vision is constructed, and can thus be shared.[25]

Here, the constructed film is the shared vision. A cinematic audience can access the latter through the interface of the screen and actually participate in the vision, not only in its sight dimension (the "view," "visual show") but also in its visionary one. In that vision which I actively share, I virtually enter the underside of the constructed cinematic world, virtually become part of it, as I, too, spin within the dervish's whirl, dance within Lilia's movements, feel the rhythm of music from the underbelly of Chokri's *darbouka*. I experience becoming an "other," or what Novak terms an *allo*. I experience moving and sensing from within that *allo*, that avatar that I have grown out of my own subjectivity. When I switch from optical to haptic viewing, I extend my epistemological perception not only from sight to other senses, but from the "dark room" of my physical world to a virtual *allo* world, and experience myself there. In that fleeting contact with the *allo*, I become joined with that part of myself that is *allo* and can navigate that other world. In short, the transvergent screen activates my power to produce otherness, the *allogenesis* that Novak claims is at the basis of "transmodernity" (i.e., our current condition, which is no longer "post-" but "trans"-modern, which is born from the multiple connections and plural consciousness that the main narrative of globalization has engendered, and in which we can no longer think of the Otherness as static, but as simulated, in becoming, multiple[26]).

CONCLUSION

Once haptic cinema has clearly set up the screen as transvergent, then the screen is no longer a static, rigid surface passively receiving the images of a film projected from behind the spectator but, rather, the interface that allows the spectator to peek in and interact with an *allo* world: the world of a Maghrebi female character, who is woman, mother, widow, dancer, lover, and more. All of the dimensions of her world become available to be sensed rather than seen, shared rather than shown, thus erasing in the process the old gendered spectatorial lines of agency and desire. Amari is not the only director to use the screen "transvergently," and thus complicate the position of her extra-diegetic viewers, but *Red Satin* is a masterful example of such a use of the cinematic hijab. Nadia El Fani, a fellow Tunisian, proposes an alternative transvergent use of the screen, away from the intimate, on the global scene.

5

Nadia El Fani's Multiple Screens: *Bedwin Hacker* (Tunisia, 2002)

PRELUDE

How would a contemporary Shahrazad convey her multiple, embedded stories? Her *mise en abyme* of several stories could, of course, take the form of the hypertext linkages of today: at the click of the teller's finger, a new story would unfold, like a Japanese paper flower. Another possible way to open up story after story is through embedded screens. Such is Nadia El Fani's storytelling technique.

In Nadia El Fani's film, the cinematic screen acts as a revealer of a multitude of screens, each of them referring to a distinct world. Hence, not only does one secret hide another, but also one screen hides another, and another, and another. The film flashes a series of embedded screens that frame multiple narrative fragments, destabilizing the hijab screen we have just explored in *Red Satin* in the process. In the end, of course, all the fragments, like pieces of an intricate jigsaw puzzle, fit together to propose a unifying, variegated meta-narrative. Each screen is a portal that leads to a particular plane of a globally shared cyber-vision rather than to a haptic apprehension of the world under the hijab. Here, El Fani proposes another interpretation of the filmic veil and screen distinct from Amari's in *Red Satin*.

BICULTURAL NADIA EL FANI

Born in 1958 to a French mother and a Tunisian father, Nadia El Fani grew up in Tunis and later traveled back and forth between Tunisia and France. She came to cinema in her early twenties as assistant to Jerry Scharzberg, and then to a host of international film directors (e.g., Romain Goupil, Roman Polanski, Franco Zeffirelli) who shot their films in the Tunisian studios, as well as to Tunisian directors such as Nouri Bouzid.

Her first short, *Pour le plaisir/For Pleasure* (1990, 7 min) about two girl friends sculpting the naked body of a man and wondering whether or not to endow him with a penis, was noticed at various festivals in Europe and in the United States, and was even broadcast on French Canal + and FR3. She then went on to create her own production company in Tunis, Z'Yeux Noirs, and produced a variety of films including ads, institutional projects, a few clips for singers such as Francis Cabrel of Cheb Mami, and a documentary coproduced with Quebecois director Louise Carré, *Mon Cœur est témoin/Cross My Heart* (1996) – an homage to Muslim women worldwide.

Her second short, *Fifty-Fifty, mon amour/Fifty-Fifty, My Love* (1992, 20 min) follows a young woman between Tunis and Paris, between two men, between two identities. The issue of identity comes back full force in *Tanitez-moi/Give Me a Tanit* (1993), a whimsical, 26-minute-long documentary on today's Tunisian women, tracing the significance of their ritualistic gestures all the way to Tanit, the Carthaginian deity of Punic times. Its punning title also offers an ironic commentary on the plight and hopes of women directors, as it refers to the meaning of *tanit* in the contemporary world of cinema – the name of the prize awarded by the Journées Cinématographiques de Carthage (the International Film Festival of Carthage, held every other year in Tunis). Loosely based on Emna Ben Miled's initial version of what would later become her book *Les Tunisiennes ont-elles une mémoire?* (Do Tunisian Women Have a History? 1998), the film subverted the genre of the documentary in its personal exploration of the Tunisian past.[1] Similarly, her latest work, *Ouled Lenine* (2008), is a documentary on El Fani's father and his fellow communist militants, and includes elements of autobiography in its approach (e.g., the director appears on-screen, talking and walking by her father's side in Sousse, or Sidi Bou Saïd) and a larger political agenda in conveying the hitherto untold history of communists in Tunisia. All in all, her cinema is one that interrogates identity and the past stories that have contributed to the hybridity of today's Tunisians.

Her initial double culture, double nationality, and subsequent choices (she now resides in Paris) gave her both material for her films and a type of fluid identity that culminated in the making of her first feature film, *Bedwin Hacker* (2002). Tahar Chikhaoui sees her as one of the cinematic representatives and proponents of "identity glides" (*glissements identitaires*): "These identity glides are linked to historical and geographical factors, but are also linked to the very status of cinema, which has become an element within a cyber-cultural whole. The wandering of characters, the unrelenting presence of the outside world's materiality, the crossing of borders are all expressions of this movement."[2] These gliding moments haunt her first feature film, as if to offer a resolution to her previous short film, *Fifty-Fifty, My Love,* in which each departure, each crossing of the Mediterranean, felt like a painful cut, a duality to be overcome. *Bedwin Hacker* negotiates various spaces that bridge and/or divide cultures and languages, as we follow Kalt, a Tunisian hacker, who travels between Paris (France) and Midès (Tunisia), and proposes a cultural detour to a third – and global – site: the at-once familiar and unfamiliar virtual world of computer hackers. It can be read as a reflexive piece on the state of Tunisian cinema – perhaps even culture – as Chikhaoui states, since it travels back and forth between France and Tunisia, the national and the transnational, the tangible and the virtual. As such, the filmic narrative works along a very old-fashioned structure: that of time-tested *mise en abyme,* already practiced in mythical times by taleteller Shahrazad.

A Screen May Veil Another: Film Synopsis

The narrative starts simply and is, at least superficially, inscribed in space, as we follow Kalt (played by Sonia Hamza, not a professional actress), a young bisexual Tunisian woman also called "Pirate Mirage" (Mirage Hacker) as she travels between France, Tunisia, and the virtual space of television, the World Wide Web and the murky, high-tech world of computer hackers.

The cartoon of a funny little camel starts appearing on French television (as well as the other European channels). The camel merely states "we exist" and promotes messages of peace in Tunisian Arabic. But its presence on-screen has the French secret services, or DST (Défense Secrète du Territoire), and the Tunisian government up in arms in the face of this feat of hacking. Although there is no discernible "terrorist" threat, the camel indicates that someone has managed to infiltrate the television airwaves. All the DST's attempts to locate the hacker's transmitter keep failing. The Parisian agents can only muse about the mysterious signature: *Pirate Mirage* (Mirage Hacker).

One of these agents is Julia (code name: "agent Marianne," played by actress Muriel Solvay), who works for the French secret services unbeknownst to her boyfriend Chams (played by cinema and TV actor Tomer Sisley), a Tunisian reporter who has been raised in France and is awaiting his French naturalization documents. He is writing a story on undocumented immigrants in Paris and is hosting an Algerian musician friend, Frida (Nadia Saiji, who also starred in Moufida Tlatli's *Nadia and Sarra,* 2004), who has brought along her mysterious and beguiling Tunisian friend, Kalt. Chams spends the night with Kalt and soon finds himself in the midst of several intersecting narratives.

He flies to Tunis, a few days after Frida and Kalt leave, most obviously to follow Kalt, but under several official pretexts: for his employer, to continue his investigation of illegal immigration; for the Tunisian authorities, to interview an old poet, Salah, who is none other than Kalt's uncle (played by Bechir El Fani, Nadia El Fani's father); finally, for Julia, to help her locate Mirage Hacker.

Julia starts to suspect that Kalt, who used to be her lover when they both attended École Polytechnique in Paris, is Mirage Hacker, and she uses Chams to try to corner her.

Meanwhile, Kalt and her "tribe" (a family of friends and their children) operate from a house that hosts a homemade assemblage of wired technology in the southwest of Tunisia, near Midès, the "gates of the Tunisian desert" near the Algerian border. In the end, Julia does catch Kalt, and the camel disappears from the airwaves. Yet the last image of the film shows Kalt looking defiantly across the screen in a clear sign that her own brand of wandering freedom has not been endangered. Hence, then, although the camel cartoon is now off the air, its creator powerfully reaffirms her freedom to create other cartoons, further disrupt the status quo, and move from one space to another.

The film tells more than one story on several levels, as it pushes the limits of what can be said on the airwaves, via satellite, as well as on the cinematographic screen. It is, again, an exercise in fluid cinematic narrative: Shahrazad telling a story within a story within a story. Yet, El Fani also plays with spaces, provocatively negates borders, and seamlessly glides from the dimension and space of one narrative to the next, thus constantly refocusing the central question of the film. "Nadia El Fani's *Bedwin Hacker*, in 2003, expresses explicitly and frontally the questions of belonging to a double culture, of moving in space, and, in its provocative approach, the necessity to rethink the identity of woman and the nation in light of cyber-cultural transformations."[3] Because, in the end, her cinematic narrative takes us into cyberspace, the narrative *mise en abyme* quickly morphs into a *mise en abyme* of screens: the cinematic first screen opens up onto another one, which opens up onto another one, and so on.

Bedwin Hacker's *Series of Screens*

The emblematic, opening sequence of the film shows the various spaces of the narrative imaged on a series of embedded screens: the Tunisian desert, Paris, and the Web are projected on television and computer screens. In that, the scene foreshadows one of the central dynamics of the visual narrative: a screen literally always lies over another, but also relays information from one world to another. Hence, the *mise en abyme* of screens is the main vehicle for narrative progression, and offers a cinematic version of the seemingly haphazard (yet logical) way knowledge is gathered via hyperlinks on the World Wide Web.

The overture is structured in three moments:

1. The very first shots show a juxtaposition of images reflecting a montage of various narratives along a hip-hop mix of aesthetics and politics, as the hacker imprints the colorful image of her little camel over the

black-and-white film of the known historical speech delivered by U.S. president Harry Truman in 1945 when he inaugurated the Tennessee Valley Authority dam in Gilbertsville, Kentucky. The television screen already shows two stories: the archival footage of the speech, spliced with shots of an atomic mushroom cloud. The whole program looks like a television documentary on the atomic age, with the French subtitles of Truman's speech aiming to reassure ("we now have this tremendous responsibility instead of our enemies . . .") belied by the ominous visual mushroom cloud. This first muted look at a black-and-white screen might hint at a televised continuum that stretches from the old dichotomous discourse of the Cold War (which opposed the United States and Western Europe to the USSR) to today's discourse on immigrants (which opposes those from the wealthy North to the "others" from the South). Television would then formulate the same type of duality in a repetitive, endless loop.

In this emblematic sequence, the soundtrack features, over a silent television (hence we literally have to "read" President Truman's speech; we can never hear it), extra-diegetic music (a sampling of synthesized music evocative of a modern-day Maghreb), the intra-diegetic clicking sounds of someone typing on a computer keyboard, and a French-speaking female voice off-screen announcing "enemy on the right" as another camel leapfrogs onto the television screen. The subtitles now read: "We have just now discovered the source of the power of the sun . . ." as the female voice says "enemy on the left" in synch with the sudden appearance of the same camel on the left. "Nuclear power. This incredible source of energy ushers us into the greatest era of all times," the subtitles now predict, as the French-speaking voice warns: "Careful: there is one in the back." Now, both previous camels are gone, but one emerges in the center of the screen, seemingly from the back, zooming all the way to the foreground, invading the screen. It is wearing blue jeans and a green shirt, and has bare, human-looking feet. The historical documentary, already reduced to a mere background framing the invasive, enormous camel, now fades to black: the camel is the only visible figure left on-screen. Here, the new colorful cartoon literally shakes up the old black-and-white vision of the world of the Cold War era and suggests a radical change (see figure 13).

Hence an unknown animation figure emblematic of nomads, of the South, has invaded European television sets. Interestingly enough, its appearance: (a) coincides with a program on the nuclear hegemony of the North; (b) mutes the discourse of the latter and replaces it with a friendly, nonthreatening alien presence in stark contrast with the nuclear mushroom cloud, thus suggesting that aliens (whether legal immigrants or not) might be much less hazardous to the world's health than the Northern/Western leaders' foreign policies. Moreover, while this visual transformation is taking place, the masculine speech is silenced, rendered only through translated subtitles, while the feminine voice of the hacker is heard forecasting the arrival of the camels on-screen. In that audiovisual montage, the clearly outdated patriarchal power is stifled, superseded by the cool and composed voice-over of a yet to be revealed female form of power.

2. Cut to a canyon in the desert near Midès, with a smooth aural transition: the same extra-diegetic music accompanies the second sequence, this time with cries of children superimposed on it (as opposed to the computer clicks and female, disembodied voice). The camera is still fixed, this time filming a canyon in the desert.

Credits appear on the left side of the screen, in the same fashion the cartoon appeared on the television screen beforehand. The information (in Arabic lettering above the Roman alphabet) seems to be springing from the depth of the canyon. The viewer finally distinguishes a group of happy children coming up a trail to the right.

Cut to the head of the band of children: a close-up shows that a little girl, Qmar, is at the head of the group, and leads a donkey. The camera tilts toward an intensely blue sky before reaching Qmar's house ahead of her.

Cut to a medium shot of Qmar's father, Mehdi, bent over what looks like an old wooden barrel, outside the house. The camera follows him as he calls: "Kalt, it is already plugged in." Kalt is seen through the window. She comes to the threshold of the house and puts on her military-style cap before she joins Mehdi at the barrel. "Go ahead! After you!" he tells her, as he hands her a remote control.

Qmar, still in her pink schoolgirl smock, reaches Kalt and her father and exclaims: "I knew you'd do it. You're the best, Auntie," to which Kalt retorts: "Please don't call me that! . . . You'll keep your promise, right? School comes before everything else."

Cut to an antenna coming out of the barrel, with the last inscription of the Arabic credits over the French ones, a dedication to Nadia El Fani's grandmother: "To my grand-mother, 'Bibi', who still inspires in me the courage to resist." In keeping with the bilingualism of the credits, the first dialogue, between Mehdi and Kalt, is in French, and the second one, between Kalt and Qmar, in Arabic.

The ending frame is a close-up on the antenna, now fully extended out of the barrel, reaching up to the sky.

Here we see where the cartoon camel comes from: a tiny house in a remote hamlet in the Tunisian South. We also realize that this hacking coup is, literally, *un jeu d'enfants* (i.e., as easy as "a kid's game," a piece of cake) for Kalt and her "tribe" of hackers that even includes a child (Qmar), performed in a low-tech environment, symbolized by the old barrel concealing the hacker's antenna (like one of Ali Baba's jars concealing a thief).

3. Cut to an indoor space hosting a meeting of undocumented immigrants in Paris. A cross on the wall suggests that they are probably in a church. This sign alone echoes the factual narrative of three hundred undocumented immigrants from Africa who occupied St. Ambroise Church in Paris on March 18, 1996, and were forced out of their sanctuary by the police four days later. (They then moved to St. Bernard Church on June 28, to be, yet again, evicted by the police.)[4]

The media are here: Chams is one of the reporters interviewing the immigrants. He is shot at eye level with them (a visual clue to his egalitarian views as well as to his own status as an immigrant).

Cut to a panning shot of the demonstrators' faces, with a few close-ups that individualize them, and of signs that read "Documents for all" and "No to exclusion." Close-up on Frida clasping her *'ud* (Arabic lute): she is sitting next to a woman who looks French, wears a Palestinian *kafiya,* and is clapping to the rhythm of the drums that others are playing. Whistles are heard. The police come in and invade the place. Mayhem ensues.

Here the off-screen narrative is complex: it refers to historical events (in 1996, for instance) and to the various peaceful marches of the undocumented immigrants in Paris that turned into musical performances in the streets. It also foreshadows the role of Kalt, on- and off-screen, and the role of Chams, the reporter who tries to know the truth and ends up being manipulated throughout the narrative; finally, and perhaps most importantly, it foreshadows the semantic polyvalence of "screens" that unfolds in *Bedwin Hacker*. This opening scene reveals the film as a succession of apertures: one screen is both the surface on which images are projected and the mask for yet another screen that it may or may not reveal in one slide of its shutter.

In this way, Nadia El Fani also plays on the "framing" aspects of her screen: not only can we see each frame liable to – precisely – frame another one, but she also makes clear that our understanding is "framed" by the limits of what we see. And it is these limits she wishes to push on the airwaves, via satellite and on-screen, by gliding from one to another: the initial television screen supports a second one – that of the camel/ Kalt's hacking. One computer screen in Midès can show the command to a local relay that will affect screens far away (in Europe). Conversely, the television screen in Midès reveals to Qmar that her mother, Frida, is in trouble in Paris, as the police take her away "live" on television. From the very first sequence, then, we are shown that space is movable, dynamic: the film opens with a screen onto the virtual, before it even starts to move from Tunisia to France. *Bedwin Hacker,* squarely located in the global dimension of the virtual world as it is, destabilizes notions of distinct nations (whose borders can be crossed virtually) and *grand récit* (master narrative), since the later can be subverted, derailed, played with by as innocuous a figure as a cartoon! It even destabilizes the very notion of space as finite: the space we see is embedded in another one; one screen contains another screen; one locus points to another, repeatedly, along a line of flight. A hacker needs a transmission point (which we are given to see immediately), but it is a portable one (as we shall understand later in the narrative). Here, what is left silent and invisible is also what is most significant, for it presupposes that the viewer is going to fill in the blanks of the narrative: how do all these screens fit in with one another?

Double-Screening: *The* Allo *and the Self*

The extra-diegetic viewer will feel some degree of confusion when faced with this plethora of screens revealed in front of her, unless her mode of gazing changes or adopts a new type of consciousness. For this first *mise en abyme* of screens launches a mode of viewing that zigzags between recognition and puzzlement, along vertiginous dynamics that mirror Novak's transvergence. The latter oscillates between two poles: the creator's inward motion toward the self-referential – the self – and the outward creation of the alien self – the *allo*: "This *alloself*, the *self* of the *alien*, is other to us, and yet of our own production: as we produce the *alien*, so do we produce the *alien self*, as we produce the *alien self*, so do we begin to modify, reflexively, our present self."[5] This inaugural phase – at this point still steeped in postmodernity – mirrors, in a cinematic situation, the reception of film. If we now imagine that, once confronted with an *alloself* projected onto the screen (the director's creation), we incorporate shades of that *alloself* in our consciousness (much the same way we import characters as we read fiction into our own personal world, for instance), then we become "other," while still retaining some of our original "us."

That is not news: Freud's *Unheimlichkeit*, Rimbaud's *Je est un autre*, Nietzsche's "internal enemy" have already offered representations of the *alloself*.[6] What is novel here is that the *projection* of an *alloself* (created by another altogether) still reveals the presence of the *alloself* within the viewer's self. A most striking example of such an incorporation of meaning, and resulting modification of the viewer's *self*-consciousness, occurs in *Caché* by Michael Haneke (2005): the French viewer does not "become" Georges (the protagonist played by Daniel Auteuil), yet, when all is said and done, that viewer suffers from the same nationally repressed trauma (the French refusal to acknowledge the massacre of Algerian workers on October 17, 1961). Hence both the viewer and Georges experience the same lack of closure at the end of the film, a lack of closure that is both represented on-screen and suddenly awakened outside the cinema theater. Here, the spectator has first to face on-screen the image of the alien dormant in him or her, and then, immediately past the shock of recognition, to appropriate and thus (re)produce that alien momentarily dislodged from the self.

Looking at the *alloself* and the self not as two distinct, static concepts but as two poles between which shifting relationships are forever active, in motion, leads to Novak's concept of "endless allogenetic transvergence."[7] This dynamic notion clearly departs from Deleuze and Guattari's notion of "assemblage," or "*agencement*" in the original French text,[8] which hints at the putting together of eclectic elements, rather than describing the élan of their shifting relationships in motion, and that of their individual and collective becoming.

Cinematic images may help us visualize this élan in the seemingly disrupted form of the incessant shot/countershot series between the alien and the welcoming self. The viewer is thus able to continue to produce meaning(s) as she glimpses, through a flighty, seductive succession of recognizable images, the sudden flashes of the alien suddenly appearing on and disappearing from the surface of the familiar.

In *Bedwin Hacker,* this "allogenetic transvergence" takes on several forms, its most immediately visible one being its double nomadic project. Hence, film viewers in France recognize Parisian locations before being taken to Tunis, then to Midès, and being led to Paris again through the intervention of Julia, along the following pattern: self – *allo* – self. Meanwhile, viewers in Tunisia recognize some of France but, above all, Tunisia. To them, the pattern is: *allo* – self – *allo/self.* Both sets of viewers are now mixed and matched. From beginning to end, the film always addresses two distinct audiences: one Tunisian, one French (or living in France). Both know about the other, indeed have adopted qualities of the other, but still maintain that the other contains alien elements (e.g., different culture, sexual mores, aesthetics). Both sets of viewers are led to the other and experience moments of *allo*-selves.

This logic leads to a first paradox: if the alien keeps coming to my familiar world, how much longer can it remain alien? In other words: what quality of otherness is it able to keep, or recycle, or add to itself? And, conversely, how familiar is the familiar going to remain if it is always welcoming new shades of the alien to its midst? This conceptual quicksand fragility does not escape Novak, who is minded of Kurt Gödel's 1931 incompleteness theorem (stating that all logical systems of any complexity are, by definition, incomplete: each of them contains, at any given time, more true statements than it can possibly prove according to its own defining set of rules). Hence, the alien needs the self (outside the alien) to define him, just as the self needs the alien to return the ontological favor. Similarly, the viewer can only remain a viewer if confronted with the other on the screen whilst reassured that he is the viewer at a distance from the screen. In doing so, the viewer protects his own identity as viewer while fleetingly identifying with the other on the screen.

Once the viewer has identified the two poles of transvergence, the question becomes: How does the movement of transvergence proceed? Which paths does it choose to take? Novak describes it as a seemingly erratic journey along a geography of ethics: "While convergence and divergence contain the hidden assumption that the true, in either a cultural or an objective sense, is a continuous landmass, transvergence recognizes true statements to be islands in an alien archipelago, sometimes only accessible by leaps, flights and voyages on vessels of artifice."[9] Transvergence allows for explorations and *flâneries* (aimless strolls) outside cultural hegemonies and their modes of representation, while still referring to them; it also opens passages and designs *lignes de fuite* (lines of flight) away from totalitarian regimes – whether the latter be cultural, political, or religious. In that, it provides a useful tool to negotiate art among plural cultures. Yet if we were to look at the multicultural in motion, in becoming, we might be able to map out various passages from one culture to the next, observe their clashes in movement, "live" as it were, and see how they diverge while joined at the hip.

Cinematic transvergence, then, has an important political role to play, in that it can give both the filmmaker and the viewer ways to resist a totalitarian regime of truths by allowing them to meet outside its anchored discourse. They would first follow one particular regime's prescribed tracks, but then veer away from them, and project ahead various new possibilities of meaning. Its translation in *Bedwin Hacker* takes on the form of a *mise en abyme* of screens: the film thus seems to be shifting endlessly from one regime to the other, postponing the last word, the last image, in a form of restless freedom. The extra-diegetic viewer derives meaning from each screen separately as well as from the relationships of complementarity and/or contrast that link them.

What better image to symbolize this journey than the silhouette of a virtual camel on European screens? The icon is neither an invader (it has no colonizing goal) nor a "terrorist" (it is not out to destroy, or annihilate), but simply occasionally occupies space as it nonchalantly walks in; it simply alludes to the sharing qualities inherent to the old ways of nomadic life: the desert – and the airwaves – can be anyone's space to be traversed, for they belong to no one in particular. The incongruity of its sudden presence on the screen is toned down by its cartoon quality: the latter makes it at once familiar, an echo of shared childhood television narratives for the audience. It evokes both *A Thousand and One Nights* and the Saharan caravans on the southern shore of the Mediterranean, and Disney, Asterix, or even Cinderella, on its northern shore. It is a dromedary, not Joe the Camel of the cigarette brand: it is metonymous with it, but clearly not as hazardous to the viewer's health.

Nomadism On-Screen

Bedwin Hacker can be considered the first Tunisian spy film. Yet, apart from a smattering of high-tech details pertaining to virtual communications, it features none of the James Bond spying gadgets. This film never forgets that Tunisia is a developing country with few means (but great imagination and brains!). Nadia El Fani claims she wanted to make a film to open a dialogue between the South and the North but not through the usual channels: "I thought of a female hacker to illustrate access to speech. I wanted to show that there are free spirits, south of the Mediterranean. Our images are not broadcast in the North, thus leading to a misunderstanding: people here believe that we are backward people not living in 2002."[10]

Kalt uses an innocuous little cartoon of a camel to impose a cute but alien image from the South on the screens of the North. The cartoon figure never stays long. It appears (against the backdrop of a much-watched soccer game, for instance) together with a message in Arabic scrolling across the screen from right to left, soon followed by its French translation moving in the opposite direction. The message is signed "Bedwin Hacker." The cartoon figure does not move, but its presence gathers more meaning at each of its appearances (see figure 14).

Its first message is: "The third millennium features other ages, other places, other lives. We are not mirages." Although its words are not threatening, the message, by virtue of its interruptive quality, hence by its mere presence, is seen by the people in power (emblematized here by Julia's boss) as a potential terrorist message that is to be deciphered, and whose authors, of course, need to be caught at once.

The second message responds to the DST's disinformation campaign that has announced in the press that the cartoon and its message were "technical errors": "I am not a technical error . . . I keep on walking, down my path, step by step . . . If you don't like the sound of boots, wear *babouches* . . ." (ellipses in original). Predictably enough, TV viewers in Paris start wearing *babouches,* or North African leather slippers, the following day.

The third and aural message also invites viewers to act: the camel pops up on the screen, his "arms" and "fingers" displaying the ambiguous "V" of the peace or victory sign, while an Arabic-speaking, genderless, computer-generated voice utters: "Zap reality, at one minute to midnight. Call 01 50 40 30 20, then dial 666. Bedwin is not a technical error!" This message scares the French DST into cutting all phone lines to the financial and commercial district of La Défense before any influx of calls has a chance to crash the system (thus, ironically enough, transforming the DST into the hacker's accomplice!)

In its last appearance, the camel is multiplied, as if cloned into numerous others who are now demonstrating on the screen (much like the *sans papiers* at the beginning of the film), holding large signs in dialectal Tunisian Arabic and in French saying: "We are not mirages! . . . What about you?"

The cartoon figure that simply occupies the virtual space of television, much like a camel in the desert, asks for no visa or pass. Its alien presence superimposed on the broadcast program makes it both intriguing and funny. Yet its disruptiveness also elicits feelings of potential threat. As the alien signifier on a familiar landscape, it receives various meanings from intra-diegetic French observers.

At the site of power and law enforcement, Julia's boss offers a surprising explanation for its signature. He seems both threatened in his masculinity and attacked in his Frenchness (not to mention his linguistic skills) as he exclaims: "Un rosbif qui se prend pour le champion du plumard. Bed, c'est lit; win, c'est gagner. Le gagnant au lit." (A Brit who thinks of himself as a champion in bed: "bed" and "win." The winner in bed.) Curiously, though, agent Marianne (a short-haired, computer-savvy, female personification of the French Republic eager to integrate its Maghrebi population, as exemplified by her own relationship with a

Maghrebi boyfriend) tells him that *bedwin* is the feminine form of *bédouin*, which can be explained by the fact that "computer languages ignore spelling." This bizarre exchange around crude linguistics reveals not only the monolingual character of the French (further illustrated in the film by a French cop accusing Kalt and Frida of babbling [*baragouiner*], when they speak Arabic), but also the perception that English, as a global computer language, is really French misspelled! Agent Marianne, who guesses (rightly) the gender of the hacker, does it through an apparent erroneous reading of "bedwin," a gender-neutral term in English.

Language, spiraling out of computer encryptions that the French secret services fail to decode, plays an important part in this film. The same failure to decipher language or meaning applies to a variety of characters in this film: the French, who cannot understand dialectal Arabic; the older generation, who do not understand second-generation *verlan* (the slang of the French suburbs that consists in inverting syllables – hence its name *verlan*, i.e., *à l'envers*/in reverse). Chams's sister says upon seeing the dromedary's message, "c'est en rebeu" (it's in Arabic); the DST boss cannot quite grasp agent Zbor's statement: "je kife mon métier"(I love my job). The most adept at playing with languages (whether the latter be music, computer, French, Arabic, poetry) are Maghrebi: Kalt's uncle writes Arabic poetry and speaks elegant French; Kalt's "tribe" speaks dialectal Tunisian Arabic peppered with French words and phrases. Chams, who has stayed too long in France (his "Arabic is French" according to his Tunisian friends), can navigate both linguistic mazes, but is illiterate in the mores of Tunisia; and his linguistic skills are of no use when he tries to understand Kalt or Julia.

In her representation of language – or rather languages – in action here, the director shows how French has permeated dialectal Arabic, and how Arabic has traversed and refashioned French. Even though the languages are still two distinct entities, they each contain traces of the other's passage or contiguity, and continue to evolve with transvergent dynamics at work. The same goes for a form of transvergent "biculture" expressed through one or the other language indiscriminately. For instance, Salah, the wise poet who writes verse in Arabic, quotes Bernanos in French: "Il faut beaucoup de fous pour faire un peuple libre" (It takes many insane people to make a free nation). This line echoes Tunisian poet Chabbi's text, which inspired the nationalists to resist the then French oppressor, and which is now part of the Tunisian national anthem. The thematic continuum points to tropes and concerns that have crossed borders, as if language and language artists and performers had always met in some space that transcended the alien/self dialectics, much like the dromedary in cyberspace.

In some ways, the film is about the complicated relationship between the French and the Tunisian, and their shared history (symbolized by the former relationship between Julia and Kalt and the way it has shifted into its present stage), but it also gravitates around the notion of freedom: "Kalt represents freedom: she could have chosen to 'become somebody' in French society but she preferred a society in which she is not free, and that is the epitome of freedom. Julia is the one who tries to contain the freedom of others and Chams is the one who, like most people, believes that he is free but is always wrong."[11] Again, such a fluid concept is hard to film: by definition, freedom "escapes" the limits set by a frame. Hence the particular mix of media used in the film and the dialogic relationship established between characters on-screen and the viewer (as illustrated by the very last frontal shot of Kalt staring at the extra-diegetic viewer – see figure 15).

El Fani shot her film about the digital manipulation of images with a digital camera. Gradually, one screen peels off to reveal the hitherto masked screen beneath. Each image then hints at not what is outside the frame necessarily but what is concealed under its photographic surface. El Fani plays with the meaning of photographic "revelation" as the thriller goes on. Hence, the juxtaposition of the camel cartoon figure on a TV screen that is broadcasting something completely unrelated emblematizes a series of insertions of various extraneous pieces into the main visual narrative: the cartoon is superimposed onto excerpts of televised news, soccer games, porn, games, talking heads, films, black-and-white archival material. The scenes of the investigation on the one hand, and of Kalt's hacking on the other, both contain shots of computer screens coming alive with computer animation. But the latter also reveal scrolling pages of encrypted data – the same encryptions that make the surface screens with their animations possible. All these shots are both *allo-* and referential to the familiar. At this point in visual culture, they do not surprise us, even if we do not understand the computer languages the scrolling screens show us.

These photographic revelations serve as the visual metaphor for other revelations. The viewer is then faced with intriguing screens. Immediately after Kalt realizes that Julia is on to her scheme, Kalt changes hard disks in order to escape Julia's surveillance. There is an abrupt cut to a close-up of the insides of a computer. The camera slowly pans in a circular fashion from right to left, showing a motherboard, various computer tools, bits and pieces of a dismantled computer. This shot is intriguing in more ways than one: (a) although the computer is a known object to the viewer, its motherboard and wires trigger no recognition for the non-expert: the alien buried deep within the familiar, is suddenly exhumed; (b) the viewer is tricked into thinking that Kalt might be rebuilding her computer in her garage in Tunis but, as the direction of the panning implies, this is a flashback; (c) the viewer discovers Kalt and Julia as students collaborating on this computer project and finally understands they used to be lovers. It is as if the film embodied Balzac's famous fear of photography that would rob a subject, envisaged as structured like an onion, of all his protective skins: each image is a layer of reality superimposed upon another one. El Fani films until most layers are laid bare, yet still keeps us guessing as to the next one. With this transvergent way of filming, we, as viewers, are both on the "in" and on the "out": we recognize and adhere to the familiar and learn to recognize the alien within it, an alien to which we still have limited access but of which we have been made, at least, fleetingly conscious.

El Fani's film is transvergent in some of its soundtrack as well, as she is careful to mix other traditions in the music of the film: for instance, she uses electronically composed music mixed with Arabic vocal melismas (around the peaceful message *assalaam aleykum*). She explains that French musicians are "sampling" musical pieces from Algeria and Tunisia these days. The resulting compositions, far from being watered-down Arabic pieces inflected to suit Western tastes, reflect a transvergent form of music harmonizing to North African inflections and European ones, and beating to their cross-rhythms.

Finally, *Bedwin Hacker* also veers away from cinematic genres, notably the spy thriller genre (à la James Bond). Some elements persist:

police-escorted car rides, high-tech gadgets, a hacker operating from a hideaway in the desert. But these signs are turned on their heads and signify something else altogether: the hacking superwoman is helped by a little girl (Frida's daughter); what looks like a protective "escort" is actually a way for the omnipresent Tunisian police to control Kalt and her friends as they are driving south; the high-tech equipment has amazing capabilities but was reworked and engineered mostly by Kalt (and not by the secret services, although they manage to infiltrate some of it). The film, under the guise of a light parody of the spy thriller, seems to have a political dimension. It shows how to beat the information system both in France (and Europe) and in Tunisia, where the regime tightly controls information and arrests "cyber-dissidents" (as well as routinely takes down sites on the Web to further monitor the flow of information coming from the outside into the country). It shows how to fight against the various campaigns of disinformation started by both governments and to rebel peacefully against them.

Who, then, are the viewers/listeners? The viewers reside on both sides of the Mediterranean (although the film was not widely distributed in Tunisia despite having been shown at festivals there, probably – although never officially – because of its treatment of women's bisexuality and lesbianism, a taboo topic in Tunisia). Therefore, they relate to different cultural landscapes and customs. However, if some of the familiar in one site might create the *allo* in the other, the film presents both that first as well as a second level of the allogenetic as it manipulates images and music. That supra-level contains the always/already recognizable, but in flashes, mixed in with the alien (as we have just seen). The viewer is hence constantly on the watch, so to speak, awaiting the next bending of the familiar into an alien form, the next transgression of the familiar rules, the revelation of the next screen beneath the one in full view.

On Cinematic Transvergence as a Form of Dissidence

I would, then, use the term "dissidence" to designate that quality of transvergence that is at work in films made by Maghrebi women, as exemplified by *Bedwin Hacker*. Or rather, these authors film in a transvergent fashion in order to signal traces of disobedience or dissidence within one system and the other. El Fani films neither along the norms of a Tunisian, native cultural system, nor according to the French model; rather, she negotiates her way(s) from one to the other, endlessly. Hence, the form and the contents of her film are constantly on the move in between both spaces and hegemonies, at once fragmented and linked on a series of screens. In that, *Bedwin Hacker* evokes other films by diasporic women directors, such as Yamina Benguigui's *Inch'allah dimanche* (2002). The latter shows a female protagonist, Zouina, a recent immigrant in France from Algeria, finding ways to negotiate her way between the rule of her husband and mother-in-law and French rule. This is a story of individual dissidence against both the Algerian and the French social orders.

Transvergent cinema also proposes, as we have seen earlier, a form of resistance to various hegemonic discourses: that form is political at both the macro and the micro level. It might even blur, as *Bedwin Hacker* does, the line between both, as it keeps on shifting the locus of disobedience: first France (where the *sans papiers* demonstrate and Kalt hacks into the police system); then Tunisia (where Muslim women drink at night, and men talk about a free press); finally the virtual site of information technology (where a cartoon figure invites people to distance themselves from the army and the police by refusing to wear boots).

Transvergence is a form of (possibly acceptable) disobedience since it borrows from the familiar and the allowed and signals the life of the other, the different, the *allo* beyond the established boundaries: the forbidden that is always "differed" in a Derridian way (both deferred and different always), out of reach, in a totalitarian system.

Tunisian cinema reflects the boundaries of Tunisian life, prescribed by Ben Ali's dictatorship (and before that by Bourguiba's) and by Europe's stern immigration policies (and law-enforcement agencies). The space of free circulation of people is shrinking. As a result, the cinema screen sometimes opens up a fantasy space, forever "differed" and never reached. At least, this is what Sonia Chamkhi suggests as she analyzes the various spaces of "New Tunisian cinema" (between 1980 and 1995) in her in-depth study of "enclosure" in a representative sample of films. She convincingly argues that containment, visualized through enclosed spaces (e.g., the bedroom/cell, the family house, the walled-in medina), represents "the unifying and 'enclosing' goal of a collective, i.e. socio-cultural identity, and its radical opposition to all forms of subjectivity or individual singularity."[12] Film narratives of that period depict characters caught between their being imprisoned in their family spaces, complete with knots of obligations from which there is no escape, and their desire for an open space away from the stifling patriarchal rigidity in which they feel cornered, spied upon, and miserable. The characters yearn for a dream *locus*, far from their present jail-like location (e.g., Alia in *Silences of the Palace* dreaming about the other side of the gate of the palace). Chamkhi defines the experienced space of oppression as *l'espace des profondeurs* that always represses the desiring subject, and the desired space of freedom of movement and expression as *la surface.* The latter, magically detached from filial duty to the Father, is clear, limitless. Yet the protagonist cannot "surface," and remains glued to his or her "locus of depths."

A decade later, our whimsical camel does surface, but unsteadily and unpredictably so: he comes, goes, returns onto the literal and symbolic screen surface. The character is successful at derailing the patriarchal system (the DST, the French police) and nonchalantly ambling onto the French screen for a while, just as his creator (a woman, finally!) is successful at hijacking the French police's computerized ID control of her friend Frida, at passing through the ubiquitous police roadblocks of Tunisia with illegal material for her hacking purposes, at taking refuge in Midès, at showing that there is a solution beyond the ruthless alternatives: confined helplessness in Tunisia and hidden helplessness in France.

Transvergence thus proposes a way to reconfigure the appropriation of space, for it allows for nomadic incursions into alien zones, located outside the contained, policed space of the territory reserved to its citizens only. These incursions are too brief to be forbidden. You do not need a visa to get a glimpse of France on-screen, nor a pass to see the secret recesses of the Sahara, near the Algerian border. All you need is a digital camera . . . or a hacker!

This form of dissidence, which operates from within and reaches outward, is not alien to Tunisian women's culture at all. It echoes two different histories: the history of Tunisia, invaded, conquered by the

Phoenicians, the Romans, the Arabs, the Andalou, and the French, and the women's history of *nushuz* in the Maghreb, a particular form of disobedience that women would exert in private. From that tradition of female disobedience, women have learned to stand up to men in the privacy of the home, thus, claims Moroccan feminist Mernissi, are already equipped with a "woman" consciousness. In *Bedwin Hacker,* the female hacker expresses her dissent away from the bedroom, the home, the country: on very public, indeed international, screens of power (and not, we are told, African or Asian ones). She breaks the rules of two patriarchal systems at once: Tunisian and French. A clear example of such trespassing is the fact that Kalt, the protagonist, is gay – the first female gay character in a Tunisian – indeed in a Maghrebi – feature film, as far as I know.

Furthermore, her camel does not address an intellectual elite but a large audience, as if responding to Mernissi's call for a wide array of expressions of resistance: "One of the steps necessary for intellectual women to share their privileged access to knowledge and higher consciousness is to try to decipher women's refutation of patriarchy when voiced in languages other than their own. One such endeavor is to grasp and decode illiterate women's rebellion, whether voices in oral culture or in specifically dissenting practices considered marginal, criminal, or erratic."[13] The visual language of the camel and his intrusion into the world of others is "considered marginal, criminal, or erratic": the ways of transvergence might also suggest that some rules do not apply, that some borders need erasure in order for the power of imagination to flourish.

With transvergence, cinema moves away from a static mélange, or "synthesis" as Ferid Boughedir calls it: "What you call hybridity I prefer to call synthesis. Synthesis consists in saying that, after all, we have an incredibly rich popular culture. . . . Thanks to it, as a cinephile, I can manage to steal modernity from the West in cinema and give the Tunisian citizen a likeable mirror of himself and of his own culture: a likeable Tunisia, but not a simplistic, caricature-like, credulous or folkloric Tunisia."[14] For El Fani (see figure 16), there is nothing to "steal" from the West. She simply proclaims the right to traverse its screens, just as her peers in the Maghreb proclaim the right to make films steeped in images from the South and the North, without subscribing to the patriarchal rules of either, and/or to the codes of either. In the end, the Western screen is only a cultural detour for the camel, rather than a fixed sign. It is just a camping site, a momentary space where nomadic images alight.

CONCLUSION

Through her brand of cinematic transvergence, then, El Fani multiplies screens to better unveil what lurks beneath the surface of each confining space for women and men alike. Her use of the screen/hijab is that of revelation: on the surface of her screen she embeds the powerful image of the potential freedom that all societies north and south of the Mediterranean systematically cover and stifle with layer after layer of economic, political, social, and cultural oppression. Yasmine Kassari picks up a similar theme in *The Sleeping Child,* as we shall see in the next chapter, but with a much less optimistic view of women's agency in the private – and therefore political – world they inhabit. There, in the stifling interiors of motionless women left at home, the screens of the North and the screens of the South seem to further isolate women and offer them no exit except through transgression.

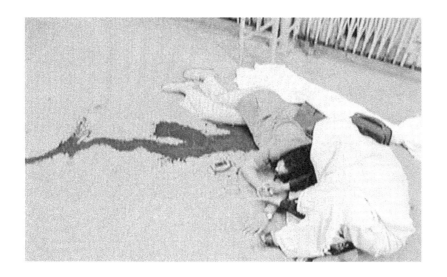

7. Rachida: the woman in pieces. (*Rachida*.
Dir. Yamina Bachir-Chouikh. Algeria, 2002).

8. The communal bestowing of veils. (*Rachida*.
Dir. Yamina Bachir-Chouikh. Algeria, 2002).

9. The silent story of women's compassion. (*Rachida*.
Dir. Yamina Bachir-Chouikh. Algeria, 2002).

10. Lilia dancing in her bedroom. (*Al sitar al ahmar/
Satin Rouge/Red Satin*. Dir. Raja Amari. Tunisia, 2002).

11. Lilia dancing in Folla's changing room. (*Al sitar al ahmar/
Satin Rouge/Red Satin*. Dir. Raja Amari. Tunisia, 2002).

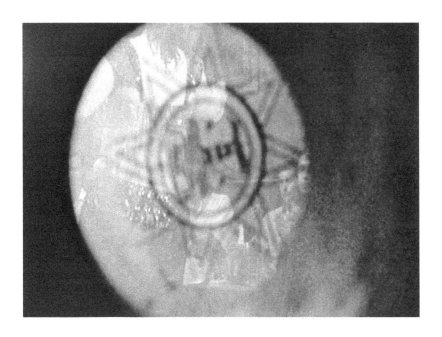

12. Lilia's dance through Chokri's *darbouka*. (*Al sitar al ahmar/
Satin Rouge/Red Satin*. Dir. Raja Amari. Tunisia, 2002).

13. The colorful camel shakes up the old black-and-white view of the world. (*Bedwin Hacker.* Dir. Nadia El Fani. Tunisia, 2002).

14. The camel endures on TV screens. (*Bedwin Hacker.* Dir. Nadia El Fani. Tunisia, 2002).

15. Kalt boldly staring at the extra-diegetic viewer. (*Bedwin Hacker*. Dir. Nadia El Fani. Tunisia, 2002).

16. Nadia El Fani, Paris, April 2010.

Act III

From Dunyazad to Transvergent Audiences

6

Yasmine Kassari's "Burning" Screens: *The Sleeping Child* (Morocco, 2004)

In the twenty-first century, how would Dunyazad be able to hear and respond to a transnational incarnation of Shahrazad? To a sister who has migrated far away into a different culture and still whispers tales meant for her sibling left at home? For, although Dunyazad can recognize her sister's world, lexicon, stories, although both have been sharing secrets, narrative twists and turns since childhood, Shahrazad's narrative comes from afar, across various borders.

Directors from the Maghrebi diaspora such as Yasmine Kassari can address both a sister in the know, locally, and a more distant, global audience. These latter-day, diasporic Shahrazads then cross borders, switch languages, and alternate modes of communication in order to construct a narrative with at least a double audience in mind. Yet, such double-edged narratives also cause them to cross unimaginable cultural boundaries and lines of permissible conduct.

In her first fiction feature film, *L'Enfant endormi/The Sleeping Child* (2005), Moroccan director Yasmine Kassari shows how "burning" (i.e., crossing borders illegally to become an immigrant worker in Europe) is experienced and seen by the wives and mothers of the migrants.[1] In the process, she shows how the initial male crossing of borders upsets traditional behaviors at home and leads to a series of transgressive acts by the women left behind.

This film, from the Moroccan diaspora, stages a return to Morocco and the gaze of Moroccan women. This is the standpoint from which Yasmine Kassari films: she is not showing the illegal crossing of borders by the migrating husbands but the hushed, lackluster narrative of the women waiting at home for the men's anticipated yet highly hypothetical return and remittances. The theme of emigration from the Maghreb to Europe appears in other films by women directors from the Maghreb or from the Maghrebi diaspora. Some of them are fiction films: for example, *Salam* (El Bouhati, 1999), *Bedwin Hacker* (El Fani, 2002, see chapter 5), *Française/French Girl* (El Bouhati, 2008) or *Trois Visas pour un charter/ Three Visas, One Charter Plane* (Krim, in production at the time of writing); others are documentaries: for example, *Quand les hommes pleurent . . . /When Men Cry . . .* (Kassari, 2000, see below) and *Tanger, le Rêve des brûleurs/Tangiers, the Dream of Illegal Migrants* (Kilani, 2002). (One should also mention Bouchra Khalili's experimental videos in this context, for, although she is not a filmmaker, this conceptual artist mixes media in her installations and creates experimental videos that redesign a cartography of clandestine Mediterranean migration.)[2] However, if they expose the ordeals of the journeys and of the immigrants in Europe, they do not present the view of the women left behind.

"Burning" reverberates on several levels in the filmic narrative and illustrates the immense changes in the rural culture of Morocco created by illegal emigration. Furthermore, the director herself returns from Europe to Morocco and also "burns" borders in order to film the impact of the men's departures.

"BURNING . . ."

Yasmine Kassari's Journey

Yasmine Kassari was born in 1970 in Jerada, in the northeastern region of Morocco bordering Algeria called l'Oriental, in the mines of which her father had worked until she was four years old, before he left the country. In her mid-teens, she joined her father in Paris, where she graduated from high school and studied at medical school for two years before she abruptly fell in love with the idea of becoming a filmmaker. This radical

change of curricular direction was not easy. "It was really a sudden decision. . . . But I knew nothing in cinema . . . I needed something poetic
and I also needed something concrete."[3] The Parisian cinema school,
FEMIS (École Nationale Supérieure des Métiers de l'Image et du Son),
demanded the equivalent of "two years at university level in everything
except medical studies," she claimed.[4] Hence she moved to Brussels to
study at the INSAS (Institut National Supérieur des Arts du Spectacle
et de Techniques de Diffusion/National Institute for the Arts of Show
Business and Broadcasting Technique), from which she graduated in
1997. While a student at the INSAS, Kassari started to work for a production company in Brussels, Les Films de la Drève, founded in 1973
by Jean-Jacques Andrien. At first an intern, over time she became an
assistant and a coproducer to her mentor and co-filmmaker Andrien.[5]
This allowed her to produce her first films: *Chiens errants/Stray Dogs*
(Belgium, 1995), a moving, spare 7-minute short on what happens when
wandering dogs are shot by the police in a village; *Lynda & Nadia* (Belgium, 2002), a 15-minute short showing one day in the life of two young
women, Belgian Lynda and Moroccan Nadia, as they commute to the
same workplace, work together, socialize over lunch, showing, all the
while, how and where they fit in their surrounding society; and *Quand
les hommes pleurent . . . /When Men Cry . . .* (Belgium, 2000), a remarkable
57-minute long documentary on the community of illegal immigrants in
Spain who followed their dreams for a better future, only to find themselves virtually trapped in Spain, some of them unemployed and yearning to go home but without the means to do so, and all of them surviving
in squalid accommodation. "One understands that we are not dealing
with one film on men and another one on women, but with a social, economic and political context that turns them into hostages," says Kassari.[6]
The tone is always restrained, delicate, and it is in the silences, the sad
smiles, or the fleeting glances that the emotions of the protagonists are
captured. In each of her previous films, Kassari meticulously observes
how various individuals "fit" or not in their surroundings, and how they
negotiate their roles in society accordingly. When she looks at diasporic
subjects, she shows how the men who have braved the dangers of the
sea to help their families survive at home have, literally, been stopped
in their tracks; or how a young woman is condemned to the same daily

routine organized around her work schedule in order to secure a thin margin of agency in her otherwise tedious life, caught as she is between two cultural systems. Paradoxically enough, Kassari's cinema does not describe any excitement in the journey of the immigrants, but, rather how they are forced into stasis in the so-called host country.

However, she resists successfully any such stasis in her own life. She established, for instance, her own production company based in Morocco, Les Coquelicots de l'Oriental (The Poppies of the Oriental), named for her native region where she spent long summers as a child. Les Coquelicots doubles up as a distribution company from which Kassari maps out the itineraries of film screenings in the rural towns and villages across Morocco, ensuring that films are widely seen beyond the few large urban centers.[7]

In this, Kassari appears to embody the very notion of the transnational director, going back and forth between Belgium and Morocco and having a producing setup in both countries. But there is more to her nomadic form of filmmaking and, indeed, to her nomadic life. She also has lived off and on in Australia for the past decade or so, cowriting and coproducing a feature film project for Andrien. "Yasmine spends several months there, between Adelaide and the red earth outback where she lives in immersion with the Walpiri aborigene community. 'I even have a totemic name, Numbjimpa,' she reveals with a smile."[8] "Immersion" is the rule for Kassari, who spent over a month with Moroccan immigrants in Spain in order to shoot her documentary *Quand les hommes pleurent... /When Men Cry....* Similarly, in order to film her first fiction film, she returned to the Taourirt region: "A few years later, after having scouted a village of the Beni Chbel tribe in the region of Taourirt for the set of *The Sleeping Child,* Yasmine went back, with her family and her production director, to spend six months in the same house as Zeinab, the fallen bride of the film. 'So as to give my scenario a reality check,' she remembers."[9] Kassari's freedom of movement stands in stark contrast to its absence in the intense close-ups of her films. Yet, her return to Morocco, to the region in which she was born, did not conclude any Odyssey in the Homeric sense of the term. Although she took detours (via Australia no less!) before temporarily settling in Morocco to shoot her film, Kassari's "return" was one only in form: *The Sleeping Child* is closer to the intimate exploration of a (re)discovered territory by one who is empathetically a participant-observer than the return of a daughter to her native land.

"Burning" Filmmaking

Before an analysis of the reverberations of the term "burning" in the film on the political level of gender, I wish to quickly sketch out how the central theme of the film affects – indeed determines – the very making of the film itself. For venturing beyond borders is not the sole province of the diegetic characters in the history of this particular work. In fact, the entire film project blurs boundaries, be they geopolitical, economic, musical, or narrative.

Yasmine Kassari financed her film through a mix of national and international coproductions. Her Moroccan sources of funding, outside her private production company Les Coquelicots de l'Oriental, illustrate the latest trends in state-sponsored Moroccan film production: she secured support from the Moroccan National Cinematography Center Aid Fund and from the Moroccan TV channel 2M, reflecting the recent government policy to link television and cinema production more closely.[10] "Recent policy developments include the announcement, in 2005, that the two existing Moroccan television stations would each increase their commitment to films so that a total of some 30 films per year – television and feature films – would be produced or co-produced with the stations' financial aid, thus enabling television to become a main workplace for film professionals and add to the corpus of Moroccan films."[11] She also designed a diverse and complex financing package for this film that reached across the Mediterranean and across several European and institutional borders. Hence, when a private company, Les Films de la Drève in Belgium, supported the film, so did a Belgian TV channel, RTBF, as did various state institutions: the National Cinema Center of Francophone Belgium (Centre du Cinéma et de l'Audiovisuel de la Communauté Française de Belgique), and both the French and the Belgian foreign ministries, as well as the French-based aid to francophone film institution Fonds Francophone de Production Audiovisuelle du Sud (Francophone Audiovisual Production Fund for the South). The financial montage resulting from all these institutions at home and abroad attests, in itself, to the director's will and ability to cross borders and proceed boldly from the local to the national, from the national to the international, from the South to the North.

Furthermore, the nostalgic ambiance of the musical soundtrack comes from a CD titled *The Doudouk beyond Borders* (released in 1999) by *duduk* player Lévon Minassian, an Armenian refugee in Marseille, France. The *duduk,* or *doudouk,* is a reed instrument found mostly in the regions of the Caucasus and the Middle East. Minassian uses it to play a type of refugee music that laments the absent, faraway mother country. His innovative music lies at the intersection of various musical cultures, as it harmonizes a felicitous mix of traditional pieces, played on the *duduk* and on Armenian, Algerian, Turkish, or South Indian instruments such as the *'ud,* the *ney* flute, the piano, the violin, the *tenpur* and various percussion instruments. Influenced by his experience with Peter Gabriel and Afro-Celtic sounds, Minassian weaves in and out of various musical traditions on this album. The resulting pieces have the haunting quality of musical airs both familiar and alien, again playing on the notion of possible bridges between what is close-by and what is distant.

The casting also reflects a desire to blur boundaries in its mix of actors. First of all, the only professional actress in the film is Rachida Brakni, a French woman of Algerian descent with an impressive theater and film career (she used to play the classical French repertoire for the Comédie Française, for instance, and was awarded a Molière in 2002, before she embarked on more varied and international theater, cinema, and TV roles). For her role as Halima in *The Sleeping Child,* she had to learn to speak Amazigh (Berber) phonetically.[12] All the other roles are played by nonactors, including the role of Zeinab, played by Mounia Osfour, a draughtswoman who had accompanied her younger brother to the casting.[13] Kassari sees herself as a painter looking for faces and authentic expressions. In that, she reminds us of Pontecorvo wanting to give faces to the Algerian Revolution, and of Djebar and Bachir-Chouikh in his wake (see chapters 1 and 3 respectively): the aim of her film is also to project on-screen the faces and voices of hitherto unrepresented (or underrepresented) women and men from l'Oriental.

Kassari also wrote the script of her film and, as we shall see below, crosses boundaries between narrative genres to produce a transmodern filmic story that supersedes them all. Doing so, she also mixes various media (in particular, she imports videos into her film) to tell a story that crosses borders between genres, countries – indeed continents, and gender.

". . . AFFECTS THE BODY . . ."

Film Synopsis

The Sleeping Child opens up with a shot from the point of view of a bride whose gaze pierces the translucent white veil that covers her face. The woman is motionless, and can see only the other women allowed into her room: the cloistered world of women living in a remote hamlet as their men plan to migrate and find a job abroad and send money back home.

What follows is the story of a community of women in the Taourirt region of western Morocco, whose husbands and sons leave for Europe. The narrative circles around two sisters: Zeinab (Mounia Osfour), the young bride who consummates her wedding the night before her groom, Hassan (Driss Abessamie), leaves for Spain; and Halima, her beautiful sister (Rachida Brakni), whose husband Ahmed (Mimoun Abdessamie) is another of the departing men.

Zeinab now lives with her husband's mother and grandmother (Grandma). She discovers she is pregnant and her mother-in-law decides to put the baby to "sleep" (see below). Meanwhile, Halima, who lives with her daughter Siham (Nermine Elhaggar), finds herself pregnant as well. The village people – and her in-laws in particular – believe Amziane (the only young man left in the area) is the father, and they beat up her and Amziane (Issa Abdessamie).

Meanwhile, the very occasional news the women receive from their husbands is through an infrequent videotape sent to them. In the first, Ahmed, Halima's husband, refuses to speak; in the second, we learn that he has left his companions and disappeared. Halima interprets his behavior as a consequence of nasty rumors about her and Amziane. She decides to ask for a divorce and leaves the hamlet and Siham behind, taking the baby boy with her.

The Sleeping Child

The title refers to an old belief in the Maghreb: when a father is absent (either because he has emigrated or died), a pregnant mother can decide to put the baby she is carrying to sleep and wait for the return of her husband or other more auspicious circumstances to wake the fetus. The latter will then resume its gestation and eventually be born. This legend allows women to resort to magic and sacred rituals, which may involve a *marabout* (a holy man endowed with magical healing powers) to exert control over their wombs.

The myth of the *ragued,* as the baby sleeping in utero is known, receives several interpretations. Sociologist Jamal Khalil explains it as follows: "Putting a baby to sleep means to delay, via white witchcraft methods (e.g. swallowed potions or amulets worn around the waist), the arrival of a child when the mother – or both parents – do not wish it to be born in the immediate future.... When a mother is not ready to have a child, she puts it 'in hibernation' and thus feels that she can control the moment of its birth."[14] This belief in the ability to delay the timing of birth is not unique to Morocco; it is still active all over the Maghreb, across social classes, and can be traced back to pre-Islamic times. Such elasticity in the time of gestation even has a legal aura, since it seems to be supported by article 154, for instance, of the present-day Moroccan Code de la Famille/Moudawana (Family Code, February 3, 2004).[15]

Psychoanalysts read the story of the *ragued* in different ways. Amal Chabach, psychoanalyst and sexologist, sees in it the symptom of a psychosis of women who might "suffer from other gastric or organic ailments and really think they are pregnant for years and years."[16] Psychoanalyst Malek Chebel reads the myth of the *ragued* as the expression of a pregnant woman's anxieties run amok:

> At some point in the development of the embryo, the mother will feel the little being kick her, in a universe still dominated by the warm, nurturing amniotic waters. If this manifestation does not appear soon, the mother will share her worries with her close relatives or friends and start to hallucinate around what

the custom has significantly enough termed the "sleeping" child (*bou mergoûd*[17]).
It is obviously an obsessive fear on the part of all mothers. Fantasizing around
this silent being who does not wake up to the maternal desire is abundant. The
uterus refuses to please. . . . The therapist's arsenal, under the circumstances, is
the only recourse and the only possible way is to wake the fetus up before it is
too late. Yet beliefs die hard: many women will naively tell you that the sleeping
child can remain in the maternal womb for over two years, with no trouble, and
will resume its gestation at the most unexpected time.[18]

The sleeping child, then, signals both a deeply rooted fear of one's in-
adequacy as a mother (the anguish of not being in control of one's ges-
tating child) and a desire to exert control over one's reproduction! In
the latter case, the interpretation of the mother's power over the timing
of her child-bearing has all sorts of implications for young widows or
lonely wives who are married to "burning husbands," for instance, as it
helps protect their honor when they are found pregnant a year, say, after
the husband has left. Kassari's film presents us with the sleeping child
story in its inception: a baby is put to sleep in its maternal womb on the
orders of a mother-in-law who considers that her grandchild should be
born only upon her son's return. In this case, putting a child to sleep is
a conscious, active decision made by a matriarch in order to cope both
economically and emotionally with the absence of the child's father. The
magical aura of it all still points to a survival stratagem in the hands of
women sanctioned by cultural traditions. At least, this is how Kassari
herself sees the *ragued*.

> I do not care whether the sleeping child is a myth or a fact. It is a social prac-
> tice, born from the adaptation of individuals to subterranean, secret realities
> constituted over time. Experiences accumulate, become sediments, and end up
> becoming crystallized in cultural ways. I wanted the sleeping child to appear
> in this film as a luminous point that sheds light on the situation of these women
> who have remained alone in the country, facing the absence of their men.[19]

Thus, while the film reflects the inscription of the myth in a cultural,
social, shared discourse as appropriated by women (as we shall see below), it never treats it as evidence of exoticism as has been suggested by
some critics.[20]

The "luminous point" of the myth, however, reverberates across
the narrative structure of the entire film, making the latter multifaceted and fluid. For the film presents a story that, while fictitious, none-

theless remains solidly anchored in the realistic world of today's rural Morocco, suddenly emptied of its men. In it, the contemporary, visible signs of modernity (e.g., the truck, the video recorder, the videotapes that are sent from Spain, the pack of contraceptive pills in Halima's house) are juxtaposed with signs of a lingering traditional, rural culture that reveres the *marabout*-healer and Grandma for their magical powers. The fictitious narrative resonates with ethnographic accents. The layers of narrative "truth" commingle here as the surface narrative activates a myth that then becomes one of its own vehicles: Zeinab becomes pregnant after her wedding night (one initial element in a causal chain of events). Her mother-in-law decides they cannot afford the newborn – a realistic twenty-first-century economic concern subsequent to the first chain of events. The baby is put to sleep, hence the activated myth now becomes part and parcel of the causal chain of events that constitutes the filmic narrative. Zeinab ends up not waking up the baby, a decision that now signifies her own agency in a narrative in which she has had none.

"Burning" Women – "Burning" Bodies

This film is in some ways reminiscent of Tunisian Moufida Tlatli's *Mawsim al rijel/La Saison des hommes/Season of Men* (2000): the latter portrays women on the island of Jerba waiting for the annual return of their husbands, gone to work in Tunis. Yet, the dangers of emigration are absent from Tlatli's film, and the return of the men to Jerba is like clockwork: as indicated in the title, there is such a thing as a season for the men's return and the monthly stay with their wives. Hence, although the waiting is described in similar terms (e.g., women's bodies start to express psychosomatic symptoms of their longing and solitude[21]), the anxiety of not knowing when or if the husbands will ever come back is absent from Tlatli's narrative. In Kassari's film, the "burning" of the husbands and sons also expresses itself in the bodies of the women, but it also prompts radical changes in the rural community of women and its culture. In the end, the women start "burning" hitherto unimaginable boundaries, and their transgressions redefine the contours and order of their rural culture.

The adventurous, mostly illiterate, husbands cross frontiers illegally out of desperation. When Hassan's mother tries to convince her son not to burn, and, with a large gesture of her arms, asks "What about all this land?" He responds, "There is nothing left in it." Here, the term "land" can be heard as both the impoverished earth from which the peasants eke a meager living and Morocco, the state that has failed its male youth and not provided them with the jobs, education, and employment that they need to support their families. Their women – wives, mothers, sisters – react to their departure in varying ways, seemingly along generational divides.

At first, the extra-diegetic viewer does not understand that Hassan's mother, a depressed figure emblematic of Morocco – the home country soon to be deserted, abandoned – is also responsible for tying Hassan down with his wedding just before the groom has to leave. It is Hassan's blind grandmother (the voice of female wisdom and history) who *sees* through everything and declares: "Why marry the day before you leave the country? Now we marry our sons to make sure they'll come back." These two characters are referred to as Grandma and Mother only, their anonymity stressing their emblematic functions further. Mother exerts her power in all sorts of ways, including the tricking of her son into marrying before he leaves, to ensure his return home. She is a powerful widowed matriarch whose rules are obeyed in the *douar* (village), especially in her son's absence. When she decides what is to become of her grandchild, Zeinab has no choice but to obey her, for instance. Yet, even this formidable character is beaten by the global phenomenon of illegal migration: distraught by her son's absence, she withers away into depression as she waits in vain for Hassan in the arid landscape she calls home (see figure 17), and eventually dies.

Meanwhile, her own mother, "Grandma," is a powerful, clairvoyant local figure: the embodiment of the traditional blind seer, she can read the future and decipher signs others cannot. For instance, she divines through a ritual staged like that of an ancient oracle that the men have made it to Spain. An oral historian of the women's community, she recounts how men and women worked together at constructing the *douar,* carrying each stone to build its walls, years ago, at a time when everyone was hopeful and shaping together a Moroccan future, instead of leaving

Morocco out of hopelessness. In the end, then, each woman has tradition-ally gendered responses and offers no real resistance to men's migration: one pines away into death; the other resigns herself to it and endures.

The younger women characters, on the other hand, respond to the situation with alternative forms of pragmatism. While they ache at see-ing their men leave, and yearn for news from them, they also take care of Grandma and of the children, milk the goats, feed the hens. The contrast-ing reactions are visually illustrated by recurring shots of the two older women seated and waiting, followed by scenes of Halima and Zeinab chatting and working together (and working hard!), supporting each other. And this initial image of their dynamic sisterly spirit gradually turns into an image of defiance.

Halima has a rebellious streak. She starts to break through danger-ous boundaries of proper behavior. An amorous wife, she is unhappy about her husband's absence and misses Ahmed extremely. One night she even expresses her sexual frustration by howling like a wolf. Once, she bathes in the river with Zeinab and does not immediately shy away from Amziane (the only young – and fetching – man left in the area) when he joins the women after their bath: although she does not sleep with him, the deed is done as far as the villagers are concerned. The child that she bears is then viewed as the fruit of adultery. Her in-laws punish her for her apparent breach in marital conduct. She is now seen as refus-ing to conform to the rules of honor. Eventually, once she understands her missing husband, Ahmed, no longer trusts or loves her, she decides to leave and ask for a divorce. In that, she breaks away from the *douar* and transgresses its rules of expected female conduct.

Meanwhile, "good sister" Zeinab, who obeys her mother-in-law's orders, and remains completely silent when Mother takes her to the *marabout* to put her child to sleep, ends up disobeying Mother's or-ders as well. After Mother dies, Zeinab wishes to awaken the baby. But Grandma tells her to get her husband's agreement first. By then, Zeinab has realized that videos are a tricky medium that can lead to disastrous misunderstandings. She then crosses spatial boundaries by getting a lift to the town of Taourirt with Grandma to pose for a group portrait at the photographer's studio. She is the first woman we see actually leaving the hamlet. After she has sent Hassan the photo with the latest news, she finally receives his answer: "Zeinab, wake the sleeper and never go back to Taourirt without my permission." Apprised of her first transgression (leaving home without her distant husband's permission), she consciously decides to transgress a second time: she throws away the talisman in the river. As a result, her baby will never be awakened, never be born. In doing so, she has become an agent of her own life and usurped her husband's authority.[22]

In the end, then, both sisters have chosen a path away from the pre-scribed rules and hierarchies of (male) power, in the absence of their burnt men. In this, they too burn bridges, burn frontiers of behavior, and end up modifying old patterns of marital relations. The "burning" of the wives of burnt men is expressed in several ways in the film: their emotional and sexual longing, their transgressions, their various acts of disobedience to the law and customs of the community as well as their husbands. In that, the emigration of men outside the community ricochets into a redefinition of territory as nonlocal (since half of the community is now displaced), reminiscent of Novak's contemporary notion of "after territory" (as applied to the virtual world of technology, in which there are similar splits and reconfigurations in a now globally dispersed community): "Territory: an area of limited political rights; contested ground of animal altruism and animal aggression, but also a device for limiting aggression; playground, mating ground, holy ground; area of jurisdiction, vital interest, prized resource. Terrestrials as we are, we find the notion of territory embedded within every concept we can utter, and in every concept territory figures ominously large." Our un-derstanding of territory is undergoing rapid and fundamental changes: within the scope of pragmatic experience both space and community are rapidly becoming nonlocal. At the level of advanced theories concerning the nature of space and time, we already live in an astonishingly different place than any other culture on earth has imagined. In either case, what Virilio calls the "big optics" of media communications at the speed of light result in a collapse of the horizon, divider of earth and heaven, or, to be more literal, demarcator of the borderline between the concrete and the abstract.[23]

Although the territory is now almost empty of its young and able men, and hence of its gendered power hierarchy, the patriarchal system is still maintained in place in the first part of the film by the matriarchs, the older generation. Hassan's mother acts as an avatar of her son when she makes decisions about Zeinab's *ragued,* and Ahmed's family beat up Halima and lock her up with the approval of Halima's mother. And yet, as the film progresses, Mother dies and the in-laws disappear from view, as if, literally, their stranglehold over the young women was weakening, had become irrelevant, was no longer part of the old territory as everyone knew it. By the end of the filmic narrative, the old territory has been deprived not only of its male resources, but also of its order and of what constituted it as territory. It has become a place in between the old territory and some other space *en devenir,* in becoming, forever evolving, that is abstract. Halima leaves it, and the *ragued* will not be born into such a space because its boundaries are unknown, strangely mysterious. (Here, the void left by the men within the familiar territory triggers a Freudian form of the *Unheimlich*/uncanny both similar and diametrically opposed to the violently invaded one that we saw in Bachir-Chouikh's *Rachida* – see chapter 3). *The Sleeping Child* thus explores much more than just the women's mere emotional response to the void(s) left by their "burning" husbands, for the women register the end of an era and witness the birth of an "after territory" that is in becoming. Yet they are no passive witnesses; rather, they start to adapt to the tectonic shift in their reality and start to actually (re)define active, female ways of gazing.

. . . AND REDIRECTS THE GAZE

Shot and Countershot ("Burning" Men and Burnt Women)

Yasmine Kassari's first fiction feature film follows her former 57-minute-long documentary *When Men Cry . . .* on clandestine Moroccan male immigrants who risk their lives crossing the sea in frail boats (or *bassines,* "buckets") in search of a better if uncertain future. In her synopsis of the film, she wrote:

> I first experienced clandestine emigration on the other side of the Western world: the side of absent fathers and of mothers left alone in the Moroccan rural land. On that side, we live in the grips of constant doubt, with fear in our guts, and end up telling ourselves: he will no longer come home, he will no longer

send money, the foreign country will swallow him up. It will swallow him up through its beauties: highways like ribbons, yoghurt with unrivaled hazelnut flavor and blonde, skinny, green-eyed girls.[24]

This statement was the only one in Kassari's synopsis that mentioned the women's experience of men "burning." At the time, her focus was to show men willing to leave their homes to join the ranks of "the modern form of slavery that has followed colonial slavery."[25] Yet, because of her initial experience of emigration on the Moroccan shores, she described her documentary as the male "countershot" of the female experience of waiting at home. No wonder, then, that she decided to film the female counterpart of her documentary a few years later. This time, the film was shot in Morocco (not in Spain), mostly taped women (as opposed to men), and took the perspective of the women left behind. Furthermore, *The Sleeping Child* is a fiction and not a documentary and explores various facets of the women's experience and world. But it also stages what Mohamed Bakrim aptly calls "an irruption of the real" within the space of the filmic fiction along a dynamic of countershots:

> Firstly, in the interplay between fiction and documentary, since the very construction of the film prolongs that debate: in *The Sleeping Child*, all attempts to stage become quickly neutralized by an irruption of the real in the temporality, in the actors' performance, in the decision to have people speak in their everyday language, Amazigh in particular. And then at the dramatic narrative level: the absence of men here responds to the absence of women in the documentary. They are the phantoms of the off-screen that haunt the social rituals, exchanges, and the bodies.[26]

The shot-countershot structure of both films taken as a dyad works at other levels of meaning: the poems on the loss of one's homeland, written and read by Mahmud Darwish in *When Men Cry . . . ,* also resonate with the fictitious women's plights in the second film: "Give birth to me, give birth to me, so I know in which land I shall die, so I know in which land I shall be born again."

Here questions of identity and ontology fuse into one: whose son am I if my father is away? And the easy answer (the son of adultery, for instance) provides no clue to the more profound existential doubt about one's belonging to a family, to a clan, to a land. In this regard, *The Sleeping Child* points to the representation of a state of being now unmoored from its original territory, which is in becoming, that is also symptomatic of transnational Moroccan cinema, which proudly reclaims the Berber and female identity as a double minority against the identity of the nation: "More precisely, I would like to propose that in the new transnational Moroccan cinema, the becoming-minoritarian of national cinema takes place through a 'becoming-woman' that can be read first and foremost in the body of the woman. This becoming-woman opens up national discourse from its traditional confinements and creates a possible future that is not yet fixed."[27] Hence, as Kassari films the pining women in their after-territory, she also suggests a political realignment of their identities, which no longer conform to the dominant (national) structure in which the national discourse and education, for instance, were arabicized. When men leave, she seems to be saying, the hitherto silenced minorities speak up in Amazigh and through female voices. For whom do they speak and to whom do they speak? And also, what does the world of emigration look like through the women's perspective? For it is clearly the womanly gaze on male emigration that is at stake in Kassari's second feature film, a gaze of longing but also a cinematic gaze that boldly faces the differed male one in an exchange of videos. In that regard, the women left behind burn new boundaries because of, and in the absence of, their men.

Women's Gazes

The film clearly locates women as the viewers and thus redefines the rules of the gazing game. Instead of having women be the object of male gazes, the tables are turned and men become the objects of expectant female gazes. Yet, the politics of the new gaze is not as simple as it might seem at first glance.

The film opens on a powerful image shot from Zeinab's standpoint: the bride is motionless and, to follow the rules of the wedding ritual, unable to move out of the room where she is sitting, a space for women and girls only. Condemned to immobility, her only possible act is to gaze through the pale gauze of her bridal veil, which softens everything around her.

Here, women are shown as petrified, motionless, powerless. Yet, as a countershot foreshadows, the film will also (and above all, perhaps) be about women looking at themselves, at what is going on in their own lives, at one another, and at their men. The traditional male gaze that is usually relayed by male intra-diegetic characters in films has been displaced here: it is about women and women's gazes only – "gazes" (plural) because the way to look and represent a gaze is complex and individual. Women characters are intra-diegetic viewers placed there to guide our extra-diegetic viewing. These relays constitute the first tangible evidence of an organization of the narrative along subjective, female gazes with which we are to identify. In this regard, the film seems to be addressing the spectator as female instead of (traditionally, goes the feminist argument) male. Yet, *The Sleeping Child* also seems to illustrate Teresa de Lauretis's notion of the radical shift at work in women's cinema: "Radical change requires a delineation and a better understanding of the difference of women from Woman, and that is to say as well, *the differences among women.*"[28] Indeed, the film is projecting images not of Woman but of a variety of women as social subjects in a rural region of Morocco. And it is addressing an audience constructed not as a monolithic Woman, but as heterogeneous and female. Again, this film seems to be a textbook illustration of de Lauretis's "aesthetic of reception":

> At any rate, as I see it, there has been a shift in women's cinema from an aesthetic centered on the text and *its* effects on the viewing or reading subject . . . to what may be called an aesthetic of reception, where the spectator is the primary concern – primary in the sense that it is there from the beginning, inscribed in the filmmaker's project and even in the very making of the film. An explicit concern with the audience is of course not new either in art or cinema, since Pirandello and Brecht in the former, and it is always conspicuously present in Hollywood and TV. What is new here, however, is the particular conception of the audience, which now is envisaged in its heterogeneity and otherness from the text.[29]

So who is this heterogeneous audience? Early on, some old gazing habits are reactivated, as we see the healer come to the rescue of the narrative. We learn that Zeinab the bride is still waiting for her husband to consummate her marriage, three days into the wedding ceremony. The healer from Taourirt is summoned to the village, where a ritual has to be performed on Zeinab (not on her husband). She is led to a room in which the holy man instructs her to step over long pieces of wood seven times while he recites verses from the Qur'an, to "untie" her, so that she will be receptive to her husband. She then has to be bathed in the water in which the ink of the verses written down on a piece of paper is dissolved. This scene is shot in the old style of the theater of the shadows: the camera turns away from the characters to face the wall on which the projected shadow of Zeinab can be seen disrobing and being bathed by sister Halima. The cinematic codes at work in this beautiful shot take the extra-diegetic audience back to a familiar, pre-cinematic mode of viewing that merges with the projection of the film on-screen. Here the screen (hijab) both points to the presence of the female body and protects it from the public eye.

Later in the narrative, we shall see the two sisters bathing in the river but also from very far (and with one nude actress doubling to boot), and therefore once again protected from the public eye, and thus still abiding by the local rules of propriety and gazing. The female body is not fetishized but appears in its blurry entirety.

Furthermore, the spoken languages are Berber and Arabic, and the subtitles are French (or English). The precise geography of the film is a hamlet in the area of l'Oriental, but there is – no pun really intended – no orientalism at stake, as the camera pans on a landscape emptied of its men, a landscape that is more and more desert-like by the minute. And the female characters are both looking and being looked at, inverting the dynamics of the gaze constantly in shot/countershot fashion, in the absence of the male gaze (with the one exception of Amziane's). Among the extra-diegetic viewers, some will recognize the geography of l'Oriental, some will be intimately familiar with the story of emigration, of the emptying of the landscape, while some will learn and absorb the new geography of the film. As the filmmaker takes her time in filming the gestures, the details of everyday life, and the wait for news from abroad, she gives her work a didactic *punctum* to alert viewers, whether they are local (from l'Oriental) or international. The means then to secure the audience of outsiders is through a transvergent device using the various gazing processes that enable identification with the emotions of the intra-diegetic viewers.

Looking at Burnt Men On-Screen

The news of the departed men arrives in the *douar* in the form of black-and-white videotapes. This means that it can be shared only in a particular, privileged household that has electricity and a TV and video player. The women thus congregate in someone's living room and share tea and pastries in order to watch together news of their men.

The first video-watching scene [39:40–41:54] opens with a shot of the seated women: we, the extra-diegetic viewers, are watching from the distance (and standpoint) of the TV set (see figure 18). This initial shot sustains the sense of an event of global proportions that we extra-diegetic viewers are in a position to appreciate: the men's world from the other continent is about to irrupt in the women's home, the *Heimlich*, the familiar. We are shown the women watching before we see the men and their shy messages on the TV screen (see figure 19). The intensity of the women's gazes matches their relief but also the oddity of the medium. Asynchronous representations of men have suddenly landed in their living space, highlighting the paradox of their situation: the familiarity of the men's faces and voices in the home and the spatial and temporal distance of their actual location. The shock of the absence/presence in the black-and-white images is acutely expressed by the stunned silence of the female gazers. The initial sense of connection brought about by the arrival of the tape and the lively feast quickly organized around its viewing transforms into muteness and astounded motionlessness (another powerful reminder of the fixed positions of the women waiting).

What takes place next on the screen within the screen begins a type of miscommunication that often occurs with love letters and distance. Ahmed's refusal to speak in front of the camera can be given multiple explanations (e.g., Halima's husband is ashamed of not having found a job; he is too shy to speak – and what could he say to his beloved in such a public forum anyway?), but, whatever impulse guided his behavior, his silence disappoints, indeed hurts, Halima ("the dreamer") who has been waiting for a sign from him for months. She cannot read him, since he avoids looking at her through the camera. There is no more dialogue between men and women – the alienation experienced by displaced men abroad is mirrored by the alienation experienced at home by women.

Here, the identities of the women characters (who are also the intra-
diegetic viewers) have been reconfigured by their men's exile so that
now they too are in exile. Their new state is masterfully projected on-
screen by Kassari, who in this regard outdoes most diasporic women
filmmakers of the 1980s and 1990s when they described their own physical and emotional form of exile in the host country, for Kassari locates
the women's exile right at home. In several ways, what the exilic cinema
of the diaspora imaged as cultural disembodiment abroad rings sadly
true at home in *The Sleeping Child*.

> While most Third World films assume the fundamental coherence of national
> identity, with the expulsion of the colonial intruder fully completing the process
> of national becoming, the postnationalist films call attention to the fault lines of
> gender, class, ethnicity, region, partition, migration, and exile. Many of the films
> explore the complex identities generated by exile – from one's own geography,
> from one's own history, from one's body – within innovative narrative strategies.
> Fragmented cinematic forms homologize cultural disembodiment.[30]

Via the video fragments, the simulacra of the men arrive but do not
quench any of the women's longing; quite the opposite. They highlight
the women's distance from their own territory as they knew it. What
could signify so differently in a media-obsessed American or European
culture (a piece of oxymoronic "TV reality" in which the speaker gets his
few minutes of stardom) becomes deflated, indeed turned on its head,
once it reaches the hamlet of the Taourirt region. As the mostly illiterate, modest men try to "talk" to the (also illiterate) wives and mothers
back home via videos, they do not seem to have the proper codes at their
disposal for such an asynchronous and public conversation. (Another
side effect of the structural violence of illiteracy is the lack of access to
the privacy of letters, hence of a chance for true "correspondence.") As
a result, there is no real communication. Here, when Kassari imports
videos into the *Heim*, it does not have the same function as it does in, say,
La Maison jaune/The Yellow House (Amor Hakkar, Algeria and France,
2008) in which Mouloud wants to show the video of his son, now dead,
to comfort his wife (in Hakkar's film, the video is seen as a remedy, as
the missing piece in a conversation the mother still desires to have with
her son). Neither does it correspond to the use of imported media in
Rachida (Yamina Bachir-Chouikh, see chapter 3) or embedded screens

in *Bedwin Hacker* (Nadia El Fani, see chapter 5). In *The Sleeping Child,* the medium further distances, further estranges, as is clearly shown in the second videotape scene.

When the second tape arrives [1:11:10–1:11:58], the festive, collective atmosphere that greeted the first one has disappeared altogether. Zeinab is the only viewer. There is no rejoicing. This time, Ahmed has left the black-and-white screen altogether, and Hassan reports his further absence, away from the men of the village. The attempt at communicating via videos fails miserably as asynchronicity has taken a turn for the worse:[31] Hassan is heard addressing his mother (who died, unbeknownst to him) and reporting that Ahmed has left the group, disappeared. The videotape takes on a new meaning as we watch Zeinab from the back as she keeps on staring at the screen, alone, too despondent to even turn off the set. The last, lingering shot is one of Zeinab's back against the blank, snowy, flickering screen. Even the video can only reflect absence, nothingness. There is no avoiding the worst possible explanation for Ahmed's absence: his refusal to be on-screen now indicates a more definitive separation, away from his wife, away from his community. The videotape, instead of bridging the gap between man and woman, widens it with crude cruelty (see figures 20 and 21).

CONCLUSION

Hence, on the narrative level, what appears at first as a technological aid to overcome separation and noncommunication ends up worsening the sense of exile. And yet, in a final and ironical twist, the videotapes that are sent as a means to communicate between men away from home and their wives and mothers at home invert the stereotypical gender politics of the gaze: instead of being the objects of their (desiring) gazes, women are now the gazers. Hence, what started as a film on "burning," on traversing dangerous territories, becomes a film on the reshuffling of gender roles: women are no longer passively awaiting signs of their men in the *douar;* they start making decisions without consulting them. In the end, Zeinab will not wake up her *ragued,* and this time it is her decision only.

Transmodern interconnectedness via TV or video across the globe fails the residents of Taourirt. The transvergent sense of barely differed (in the Derridian sense of the term: both deferred and displaced) and shared realities collapses in this filmic narrative. Yet, the narrative also addresses a transvergent, extra-diegetic audience able to decode the projection of a bifurcated world on the cinematic screen or hijab. While the hijab is represented in various guises in the film itself (e.g., Zeinab's bridal veil that colors her perception of the world, the videos coming from Europe and played on the family TV screen), the staged *mise en abyme* of the cinema screen offers a side reflection on the role and modes of filmic representations. In its various forms (from the shadow theater to video screens), the cinematic hijab always mediates the object of the extra-diegetic audience's gazes in provocative ways consonant with the female protagonists' provocative behavior in the filmic narrative. In the end, then, the cinematic screen becomes the medium of transgression.

7

Selma Baccar's Transvergent Spectatorship: *Flower of Oblivion* (Tunisia, 2006)

The site of Shahrazad's storytelling performance in *One Thousand and One Nights* is the Sultan's chamber. As we have seen before, her sister's presence in the liminal space between the realms of Eros and Thanatos – the nuptial bedroom is also the antechamber of Shahrazad's planned execution – is both a political and a survival stratagem, on the part of Shahrazad, who has enrolled her sister to help her resist the Sultan's death threat and impose Eros (life). Through it all, the sisterly dyad defines the tone of the storytelling in intimate terms that refer to a past, shared sisterly history, while each narrative is (over)heard by the less familiar figure of power.

Similarly, a Maghrebi woman director skillfully arranges her filmic tales, knowing the domestic forces in play: censorship, which is political – enforced by her nation's overbearing leader – and cultural. As a result, the filmmaker's cinematic discourse has to escape the watchful censor's radar, while still sharing secrets with the local viewers *and* telling a story whose interest transcends the frontiers of her nation. Fortunately, it is possible – indeed crucial – in cinema, through a semantic montage of off-screen and on-screen images, to say something by showing something else.[1] Just as Shahrazad could refer to familiar tales and allusions with sister Dunyazad unbeknownst to the Sultan, today's director can play with an off-screen shared reality and an on-screen fictitious narrative.

The multilayered narrative of Selma Beccar's *Khochkhach, Fleur d'oubli/Flower of Oblivion* (Tunisia, 2006) features an individual emblematic story (an opium-addicted woman interned in a French-directed psychiatric asylum in the 1940s remembers her past) that refers both to a crucial episode in the history of Tunisian consciousness (Moncef Bey's reign in a Vichy-ruled protectorate) and, of course, to present-day Tunisia. Dependence and independence resonate in both individual and collective ways in this portrayal of a woman negotiating her own path out of addiction.

Through the *mise en abyme* of its narrative, the film seems to also propose a way of telling a story that requires agile viewers to construct meaning across the various frames of the narrative, and even import information from a shared experience off-screen to complement what is offered on-screen. In that, it exemplifies a mode of viewing that qualifies as "transvergent," as the director sets, within the fictitious diegesis, a *mise en abyme* of spectatorship. By the latter, I mean that intra-diegetic spectators are planted in the narrative, and act as agents to extra-diegetic ones. (These characters on-screen are "agents" in all senses of the term: empowered with gazing authority, they are also representative as images or projections of viewers on-screen, and one could even say they spy for the viewer who is sitting off-screen!) It also stages a narrative gaze that leaps from the standpoint of one authority to that of another, refusing to adhere to any specific perspective for too long, but, rather, embracing them all serially. In that, *Khochkhach* constitutes a master class in spectatorial transvergence: the extra-diegetic spectator is invited to follow a gaze that changes standpoints within the filmic narrative, thus adopting a position as viewer that neither diverges from nor converges with the intra-diegetic perspectives on-screen, while at the same time producing meaning that relies on references shared off-screen.

SELMA BACCAR: A STUDY IN PIONEERING TUNISIAN "FEMINIST" CINEMA

Selma Baccar's career reads like a succession of groundbreaking steps for the women of her country. The first woman director and first woman producer in Tunisia, she has used her career to help other women filmmakers by producing their films.[2] Born in 1945, she is a product of the amateur cinema movement in Tunisia that was preponderant in the 1960s and 1970s. An avid cinephile from the start, Baccar was also part of the Hammam-Lif amateur cinema club, one of the most active and prolific clubs of the FTCA (Fédération Tunisienne des Cinéastes Amateurs/Tunisian Federation of Amateur Cinema Directors), created in 1962. The latter played a democratizing role in the development of Tunisian cinema, as it was independent of governmental aid, in contrast to the cinema establishment supported by the Tunisian authorities, which was seen as having a propaganda role contributing to the national discourse around the state of Tunisia.[3] Located outside the official national cinema, the FTCA was free to experiment in its forms and content. The FTCA started as a dissident move away from the establishment – an open, democratic association of amateurs eager to shoot documentaries and fiction films (usually shorts), with few technical means, nonprofessional actors, shoestring budgets, independent of the paths blessed by Habib Bourguiba, the leader of the country at the time. Tunisian cinema critic Hédi Khélil views the FTCA as an avant-garde think tank of the day, with an obvious political agenda:

> The avant-garde role played by a few Tunisian amateur directors was the product of a galvanizing social and political context, an intense associational life, and belief in causes and ideals in the 1960s and 1970s, a period marked by the repression of student protests, the dismantlement of Marxist circles on the left, and the serious blows struck at the unions. Amateur directors criticized, often derided, the personal power exercised by Habib Bourguiba . . . who monopolized the entire audiovisual sector for narcissistic, oligarchic purposes.[4]

The FTCA, paired with the FTCC (Fédération Tunisienne des Ciné-Clubs, created in 1949) constituted such fecund ground for film critique and production that soon, the amateurs had their own festival, starting in 1964 – the Amateur Film Festival of Kelibia, which remains very popular today.

Selma Baccar, an ardent FTCA member in Hammam-Lif, shot her first short film (10 minutes) in 1967, *L'éveil/The Awakening*, a portrayal of the daily problems faced by a young woman student who wants to be free from her parents' increasingly invasive authority. In 1969, Baccar was the leading actress in *Les Galériens/The Galley Slaves*, directed by a fellow member of the club, Hamadi Ghellala. The film suffered some delays and came out only in 1973. An Eisenstein-influenced piece, it depicted the humiliation of a miner paralyzed after an accident at work, whose wife (played by Baccar) had to resort to prostitution.[5]

The fate of her first full-length film, *Fatma 75* (1977, 60 min), the first feminist *documenteur* à la Varda[6] in Tunisia, embodies some of the contradictions inherent in the circumstances of film production in Tunisia at the time. Shot in time to celebrate the Year of the Woman, this film covered the history of women in Tunisia from the Carthaginian era to 1975, through a montage of evocations (e.g., Kahena, the Berber queen who successfully led her troops against the Muslim invasion of the Maghreb in the seventh century AD; Jelejel, Ibrahim Ibn el Aghleb's wife, who founded the first Qur'anic school for girls in the holy city of Kairouan) and interviews (e.g., with Bchira Ben Mrad, a leader of the Tunisian women's emancipation movement), so as to better explain three recent moments of women's consciousness and history. Three stages in Tunisian feminist consciousness are thus highlighted: (a) 1930–1938, a period that culminates in the creation of L'Union des Femmes Musulmanes Tunisiennes/the Association of Tunisian Muslim Women; (b) 1938–1952, in which the relationship between women's struggle and the struggle for independence is examined; (c) 1956–1975, showing the advancement of women's rights thanks to the laws passed by the Tunisian government. Although the film was partly funded by the government, and although its credits thanked Habib Bourguiba for his role in promoting women's equality through the Code du Statut Personnel,[7] it also showed that the condition of women in 1975 constituted "the logical end point of a long history"[8] (in which Tahar Haddad had played a leading role in the 1930s), and that in progressive Tunisia there was still ample room for improvement (for example, women did not have equal pay, and when applying for a passport, they needed their husband's authorization). Bourguiba was not pleased. The film was banned from screening after the information secretary of state decreed that some of the film's contents (e.g., a sequence on sex education in school) were unfit to be shown to the public;[9] its government copy remained in the vault of the Ministry of Culture's film collection until the ban was lifted just in time for a 2006 Selma Baccar retrospective in

Marseille. It did not, however, prevent a copy of *Fatma 75* from slipping out of the country and winning the Golden Ducat at the Mannheim Film Festival in 1977.

Her second feature film, *Habiba M'Sika/La Danse du feu/Dance of Fire,* released in 1995, was an inspired biopic of Habiba M'sika, a much-adored Tunisian star of the 1930s. The 115-minute-long film takes us to Tunis as well as (although mostly via interior scenes) Berlin and Paris. The tragic fate of the singer/dancer/actress (who was burned to death by a jealous lover) is depicted not as a study in victimhood but as the result of a passionate affair with life and the stage: "She chose her life. She lived it to the fullest, and it is this yearning for life that is significant. . . . The dance of fire is a dance of death. The performance of the dance foreshadows her death. She is like the moth that knows it is going to burn its wings if it comes too close to the light, but who cannot resist it." [10] Here too, then, Baccar is interested in (re)creating a formidable, independent woman character who was "outrageous" in the real sense of the term (extreme, hyperbolic) on and off the stage, that is, according to Box, "committing outrageous acts that cause genuine social awareness and change." [11] The film was generally well received and won two prizes at festivals. [12] And Baccar had achieved what she wanted most: to keep the memory of Habiba M'sika alive – just as she had resuscitated the long line of her foremothers in *Fatma 75.*

THE STORIES OF *KHOCHKHACH*

Baccar's Statement of Intent

"I was told the story of Zakia through snippets of whispers, the scandalized pursing of lips and the knowing laughter shared by several female members of my family," wrote Baccar in the statement of intent that accompanied the synopsis of *Khochkhach,* hinting at the historical and clandestine dimensions of her subject.

The title alludes to the dried opium buds used by women to brew "opium tea," a beverage given to new mothers to help them fall asleep and get over the pain endured during labor. According to Selma Baccar, this traditional administering of opium to mothers barely out of childbirth was most common in Tunis, not in the countryside. Crying babies were also given a spoonful to help them sleep and let their mothers rest. The practice was so widespread that it was part of the vocabulary in Tunis.

> Until a few years ago, we still used the word in the expression "*khochkhach* baby," to indicate that the baby had been given *khochkhach* to fall asleep. In fact some babies (but very few) died this way, having been inadvertently given an overdose by their mother. . . . Giving *khochkhach* to women was common. My mother drank *khochkhach* when she gave birth to us. So did my aunts. So did my grandmother. But they never became addicted to it. In fact, addiction to *khochkhach* was an extremely rare phenomenon.[13]

This rare phenomenon led Baccar to wonder under what circumstances a woman could become an addict.[14] The starting point of her enquiry was the pain endured during childbirth. She wondered what other aches – in both body and soul – that particular pain could echo or revive. She then elaborated a narrative around the utmost suffering that might lead a woman to seek comfort in *khochkhach*. "The worst possible bodily pain that can befall a woman, the pain that is felt deep within her body, is the pain of sexual frustration."[15] Yet this, I would contend, is only the starting point of her inquiry, not the sole purpose of the filmic narrative, a point often overlooked by critics (see Barlet, for instance[16]).

Synopsis

Khochkhach or the Flower of Oblivion is the story of Zakia, who is forcibly sent to a psychiatric asylum to cure her addiction to the opium tea she started to drink when she gave birth to her daughter, Meriem, some twenty years before. Her stay in the hospital constitutes a framing narrative that spans eight to nine months, in which the story of her life is embedded, narrated via flashbacks in a nonchronological order. The latter explain why she was brought to the hospital and what brought about her addiction.

The framing narrative of Zakia's stay in the insane asylum is itself "framed" by a telling episode of a larger narrative of Tunisian history: the short reign of Moncef Bey, most popular and beloved Bey, from June 19, 1942, to May 14, 1943. Baccar said she wished to film "an osmosis between Zakia's personal drama and the drama of Tunisia."[17]

Zakia is trapped in a marriage with Si Mokhtar, who does not desire her. Si Mokhtar became her husband to obey his mother, Lella Mannana, a fearsomely powerful matriarch who adores her son and has always wanted him to be a social success. Zakia lives in a beautiful house and leads a materially comfortable life while suffering a loveless existence with Si Mokhtar, under the iron rule of Lella Mannana. A wealthy crafts-man and merchant of chechias (or red fezzes) in one of the souks of Tu-nis, her husband is, however, a closeted gay man whose rare intercourse with his wife is a result of his mother's demand for a grandchild. When she gives birth to her daughter Meriem, Zakia tastes *khochkhach,* and becomes hopelessly addicted to the opium tea. Her dependence is such that, instead of ensuring that her daughter be a free woman, she ends up marrying her off to secure her supply of opium buds from Meriem's fa-ther-in-law's abundant orchards. Her solitude increases as her life comes undone: Lella Mannana dies; Meriem moves with her husband away from Tunis to Sfax; Si Mokhtar ends up leaving her (tellingly enough, to go to Mecca). She has become the butt of jokes and the object of inces-sant gossip in her extended family. We see her descent into hellish de-pendence (see figure 22) until, eventually, neighbors have her locked up.

While in the hospital, however, her life turns around: firstly, she becomes free from addiction; secondly, she finds herself at ease in the enclosed world of the insane and strikes up a meaningful friendship with Khemaïs, a patient who, like her, is burdened by a heavy past. In the end, she refuses to leave the hospital; she wishes to stay where she feels "free."

The matryoshka-doll structure of the narrative brings to mind Shah-razad's framed narratives as well as the very fabric of her tales, in which the intra-diegetic character comments, under the guise of fiction, on the extra-diegetic political situation. In *Khochkhach,* the whispers and cries of the insane, far from merely senseless, are revelatory about historical events and the world beyond the hospital walls.

The director carefully dates the film with a few details (a couple of radio broadcasts, seasonal events, etc.) planting the plot squarely in 1942–1943. At the time, Tunisia was "protected" by the Vichy govern-ment of France, which had signed a peace treaty with Hitler in 1941 in exchange for its (limited and collaborative) power. Meanwhile, the status of Tunisia as French protectorate meant that, at least officially, the Beylicale family reigned over the country. The Beys, "permitted" to remain on the throne by the French, had been complicit with the colonizer, as had the bulk of the aristocracy and ruling bourgeoisie in Tunis. That state of affairs changed, however, upon the death of Ahmed Pacha Bey II, with the advent of Moncef Bey, beloved by the people (and not just the "ruling" class) of Tunisia. Far from agreeing with the local French authorities, he supported de Gaulle's "fight for freedom" and heeded the call issued by the London Arabic radio. His enlightened, democratic vision was central to the inspiration for the Neo-Destour party, the party that fought for and eventually gained Tunisian independence in 1956. The French authorities ended up exiling Moncef Bey, first to Algeria, and then to France.

Framed Spectatorship

Khochkhach opens with lush views of a verdant Tunisian countryside traversed by a small road traveled by a single white vehicle. The soundtrack mixes both an extra-diegetic orchestral piece (whose lyrical accents echo classic Western film music) and intra-diegetic bird songs. No engine roar: the scene is one of quiet and beauty – a twentieth-century version of Eden perhaps. The white van keeps crossing the screen from right to left in its progress along the small road, at slightly closer range each time. Cut to a close-up on the small, rectangular rear window of the car: through the glass pane and the meshed wire behind it, Zakia's eyes are looking out. This pair of eyes framed by the window occupies the entire screen. We are looking in at someone looking out. Countershot (from the perspective of Zakia, now gazing inside the car in the opposite direction) on the back of a male nurse dressed in white, sitting in the front passenger seat. The same meshed wire separates the observer from the nurse. This time, we are located on the peering side of the meshed wire, as we learn that the encaged Zakia is in an ambulance, not a police car.

This opening sequence leads the viewer to expect the entire filmic narrative to be seen through the gaze of protagonist Zakia, an outlook on the world somewhat filtered or restricted by her seclusion. However, the second sequence – Zakia's arrival at the hospital – starts to complicate the position of the spectator by introducing a second, intra-diegetic authoritative viewer.

The arrival of the ambulance at the psychiatric hospital is shot from a high angle, through the intricate design of a wrought-iron balustrade high up on the roof or "terrace," above which the French flag is waving in the wind. In the next reverse (low-angle) shot, the French director of the asylum, standing under the flag, his arms resting on the balustrade, watches as the ambulance below him opens, and Zakia is forcefully pulled out of it. Here again, then, the inaugural shot of the hospital director presents him through another filter, parallel to the one that established Zakia's gazing position in the previous shot: the director's eye on the world is filtered by the imposing architecture of this French institution. He, too, will have a gaze restricted by his position. To underscore the French quality of his gaze, the camera lingers on a plaque on the wall that spells out the name of the French Red Cross psychiatric asylum. We are definitely on French territory.

Here, the vertical shot that reveals the all-seeing intra-diegetic viewer calls to mind Foucault's analysis of panopticism. In his essay, Foucault shows two forms of disciplinary space, devised to protect the city (the *polis,* society) from two different ills: leprosy and the plague. In the first instance, isolation was recommended; in the second, containment was very tightly organized in the plague-ridden city. Foucault translates these into two political dreams: "The first is that of pure community, the second that of a disciplined society."[18] The insane asylum in *Khoch-khach* seems to illustrate this double project: on the one hand, it exiles the insane from the *polis;* on the other, it exercises strict surveillance over the patients, along the Foucauldian analysis of disciplinary partitioning:

> They are different projects, then, but not incompatible ones. We see them coming slowly together, and it is the peculiarity of the nineteenth century that is applied to the space of exclusion of which the leper was the symbolic inhabitant (beggars, vagabonds, madmen and the disorderly formed the real population), the technique of power proper to disciplinary partitioning. Treat "lepers" as "plague victims," project the subtle segmentations of discipline onto the confused space of internment, combine it with the methods of analytical distribution proper to power, individualize the excluded, but use procedures of individualization to mark exclusion – this is what was operated regularly by disciplinary power from the beginning of the nineteenth century in the psychiatric asylum.[19]

Here the lepers are the insane, the addicted, the Tunisian nationalist insurgents, and they all need to be removed from the city (across the green countryside) to a place of exclusion, where they will be disciplined.

The entire disciplinary structure of the hospital is vertical, with the director watching and ordering his underlings from the altitude of his post atop the building. He does not speak, he points. Endowed with the authority of his position, he gestures to give precise, spatial orders: this patient needs to be removed from the courtyard, that one must be transferred there. Only an all-seeing power can exercise authority so wordlessly and efficiently. This way, the vertical spatial representation of the asylum hierarchy, with the all-seeing authority figure at the head of the pyramid, resembles Foucault's portrayal and analysis of Bentham's *Panopticon*, a central looming tower from which the watchman can survey prisoners in every single cell located on its periphery. Our introduction to this ominous, Godlike presence from the moment Zakia enters the asylum firmly sets the rules of the watching game. Her every action will be observed from high above. The French are monitoring the Tunisian "lepers" carefully.

How aware are the inmates of the gaze of authority? Foucault shows that they are conscious at all times of the possibility of being watched, of the constant threat of the eye of power on them. Therefore, they remain on the watch for the watcher who is visible but "unverifiable": "Visible: the inmate will constantly have before his eyes the tall outline of the central tower from which he is spied upon. Unverifiable: the inmate must never know whether he is looked at at any one moment; but he must be sure that he may always be so."[20] Not only are Zakia and Khemaïs aware of the constant possibility of surveillance, but they also play with that very possibility. In one scene, Zakia comes up to Khemaïs's window and asks for a cigarette. They both carefully look around; he then sends her one via a broken gutter pipe that runs along the wall from his window down to the courtyard. Zakia simply sits down next to the pipe's mouth to receive the cigarette and deftly takes it with one hand, in a gesture that, from afar, cannot be decoded as an act of disobedience, therefore as subversive. In this sequence, then, they both perform a small spectacle for the all-seeing eye, intended to deceive it. In other words, in order to survive as a couple (and as "free" agents within the confines of the asylum), Khemaïs and Zakia put on a show to fool the eyes of the intra-diegetic viewer (the director, the French authorities). The visual illusions they thus create on an individual level are attempts to cope with the dimension of spectacle in panopticism as described by Foucault:

> By the effect of backlighting, one can observe from the tower, standing out precisely against the light, the small, captive shadows in the cells of the periphery. They are like so many cages, so many small theaters, in which each actor is alone, perfectly individualized and perfectly visible. The panoptic mechanism arranges spatial unities that make it possible to see constantly and to recognize immediately. . . . Full lighting and the eye of a supervisor capture better than darkness, which ultimately protected. Visibility is a trap.[21]

In the play of power exerted in the system of the *Panopticon* – whose interlocking spaces here are both the psychiatric asylum and the colony – the victims become actors in a spectacle. They do not offer the viewer a frontal, collective "extravaganza," but rather a succession of disconnected, individual shows projected on a backlit screen. The visual imagery used by Foucault is strikingly reminiscent of both the shadow theater and the cinema in denoting what the three forms of spectacle have in common: a spectator's gaze always/already mediated by a screen. Here, the viewer is given to see the mere shadow of an unwilling actor, not the actor himself; the backlit screen of a performance at mid-distance, not its direct, full view.

Where does this subversion of gaze politics leave me, the extra-diegetic film spectator? Uncomfortably enough, I realize my position is fairly similar to that of the (conveniently anonymous) director's. As Christian Metz famously wrote: "The film is not exhibitionist. I watch it, but it doesn't watch me watching it. Nevertheless, it knows that I am watching it. But it doesn't want to know."[22] Likewise, the patients know but do not see that the hospital director is watching: they take precautions and stage a show for him only when doing something off-limits, like smoking cigarettes, but they can never watch him watching. Likewise, the patients do not want to know. Furthermore, Metz underlines the time divide between being seen and seeing (firstly, the actor on the set in the absence of an audience; secondly, the audience in the theater in the absence of the actor) to establish the asynchronous rules of the seeing game in cinema.[23] I see only what the institution of cinema has arranged for me to see: a story that has been concocted a while ago and that is now being projected in a different time and space. The "seen" on the flat screen cannot gaze back at me.

Back to the psychiatric asylum and its panopticism: here, the rules of the seeing game slightly differ. The divide between seeing and being seen is deployed in space and within a predetermined power structure that tellingly parallels the core and periphery situation of the colony (with France at the core and Tunisia on the periphery). "The panopticon is a machine for dissociating the see/being seen dyad: in the peripheric ring, one is totally seen, without ever seeing; in the central tower, one sees everything without ever being seen."[24] In other words, the framing device of spectatorship given at the beginning of the film establishes: (a) an intra-diegetic spectator as the power figure at the top of the watchtower catching glimpses of his unseeing patients, viewed as subjects to be redressed; (b) a parallel extra-diegetic spectator watching a photographic animation of unseeing actors putting on a show for her/him. This first framing device of spectatorship leads to another as we progress into the *mise en abyme* of the filmic narrative, for what I am given to see as extra-diegetic spectator is from an unstable position (unlike the intra-diegetic seer, who never switches position from his elevated power perch).

In the cigarette sequence, however, one might argue that something else is happening, for, instead of remaining passive objects of the authoritarian gaze, instead of remaining mere shadows on a preordained screen, Zakia and Khemaïs subvert their passive roles as surveyed objects to become directing agents of their spectacle. They thus also destabilize the vertical axis of the gazing power and the power hierarchy in place.

Transvergent Intra-diegetic Spectatorship

Framing has its own dynamics that keep on reproducing seemingly ad infinitum. Hence after that introduction to the authoritative viewer in the asylum, the film returns to the initial authoritative viewer, Zakia, as she undergoes a talking cure of sorts. The shift to her gaze provides a temporal change as we follow her retrospective self-discovery via a succession of informative flashbacks, although they are not immediately identified as such.

ZAKIA'S FLASHBACKS Zakia is introduced to us as an opium-tea addict required to remain in the hospital until she conquers the habit. Episodes of her long-term addiction start unfolding in flashbacks that give us access to her memory; in the first few moments of her incarceration in the asylum, we are permitted to observe only the clinical manifestations of her illness. At this point, our clinical observation of her parallels the authoritarian one of the hospital: we see her skin itch, we hear her moan for her tea. Her withdrawal symptoms are clearly violent. Her sense of self is shattered, as is her mind, as is her memory.

Flashbacks start invading her consciousness. The first one, whose recurrence throughout the narrative will visually punctuate the film, illustrates her addiction: she drops a cup of freshly poured opium tea. It shatters into a thousand pieces, the hot liquid spilled all over the kitchen floor. If flashbacks are supposed to give clues as to the identity of the protagonist, this one is hyperbolic, almost redundant: Zakia is overdefined by her addiction. There is no other character in the frame: she is alone with her *khochkhach*.

Zakia's second flashback is unsettling at first because it features a young woman whom the extra-diegetic viewer has not seen before (this is the only scene in which a different actress, Najoua Zouhir, plays the role of young Zakia) being penetrated by a man whose face in unseen. This sexual encounter looks violent, and denotes pain instead of pleasure. Cut to a shot of Si Mokhtar (the husband on top of the young woman) walking to his young male lover's bedroom, while his wife is spying on them in the hallway. Cut to a third, high-angle shot of a woman in a bathroom pouring water on herself. We see a body, not a face. She could be the young woman or the older protagonist (played by Tunisian film star Rabia Ben Abdallah). At this point in the story, Zakia receives her invasive memories without relating to them: she is a passive viewer seeing her own inner film starring a different "Zakia," whom she does not seem to recognize. However, after Khemaïs asks her what her name is and she is unable to remember, she "receives" another flashback: this time, she is drinking her very first cup of *khochkhach,* lovingly prepared by her own mother, who warns her not to fall asleep with newborn Meriem in her arms, for fear of smothering the baby. When she wakes up from her sleep/flashback, she smiles at the recognition of her name pronounced by her mother. She is finally starting to piece back together the scattered pieces of her past and her self.

The first flashback is interesting in that it questions the notion of spectatorship yet again: Zakia watches her other, past self without identifying it. Intra-diegetic spectator Zakia watches a traumatic episode of her past at such distance that she is unable to recognize the victim of the trauma as herself. The traditional introspective quality of the flashback is in question, as the eruption of the incomplete memory illustrates the schizophrenic-like quality of a split subject working through an episode of amnesia: the addict sees her former self as a separate entity who is not she. Here, the seeing/being seen dichotomy is reworked in time (present-day Zakia sees younger Zakia from the past) and in psychological terms: her suffering at the hands of a sexually inadequate husband has created a rift between her seen, former, passive self and her seeing, present one. It will take the recovery of her name via her mother (who thus asserts the preeminence of a matrilineal force) to will her to actively recover her identity. After her name resurfaces, her flashbacks will blur the representation of the seeing/being seen dichotomy as Zakia becomes the willing spectator of her own past drama. Now aware of being both the active seeing spectator and the seen performer of her past, she adds one more piece of information to the active reconstruction of her own narrative with each flashback. It is this call-and-response mode of spectatorship that interests me here because it points to an active participation in the production of meaning within the filmic narrative. If Zakia, a formidable intra-diegetic spectator who leads us through her own narrative across time and space, is trying to piece together her life and its meaning, I, the extra-diegetic spectator, am also trying to stitch together a meaning derived from two perspectives: Zakia's and the hospital director's.

But how can I do that amid so many shifting positionings? The answer might lie in the transvergent qualities attributable to both intra-diegetic spectators, a transvergence that might affect and engage the extra-diegetic one. "While convergence and divergence contain the hidden assumption that the true, in either a cultural or an objective sense, is a continuous landmass, transvergence recognizes true statements to be islands in an alien archipelago, sometimes only accessible by leaps, flights and voyages on vessels of artifice."[25] A transvergent form of intra-diegetic spectatorship can leap from one seeing subject to another in order to offer a multiple, kaleidoscopic view that in no way compromises the meaning of the narrative unfolding, but, rather, multiplies its resonances and gives it new shadings and ripples. The monopoly of one intra-diegetic seeing eye thus destroyed, the insider's point of view is always/already rubbing against (and completing) another insider's point of view. Deeply democratic (like the *nuba* musical form; see chapter 1) in its distribution of "viewing authority" to a variety of characters in *Khochkhach,* this construction of transvergent intra-diegetic spectatorship clearly subverts the panopticon-like original vertical structure of the seeing power. For power cannot penetrate into the chambers of Zakia's flashbacks; it can only spy on the shadow of Zakia the addict. The transvergent intra-diegetic spectator manages to further dethrone old models of seeing by interchanging the sites of seeing. Hence, the watchtower may also shift from one location to another, from one dimension to another.

THE TREE(S) IN THE COURTYARD The asylum building surrounds a central, square courtyard in which patients come to walk and breathe in fresh air. It is reminiscent of both a traditional Arab home and a European place of seclusion (as in Foucault's images of prisons, hospitals, and schools). In the middle of the enclosed yet open space: two old trees. It is against the bark of the massive trunks that Zakia confides to her friend Anissa, and that Zakia and Khemaïs talk. However, according to Baccar, these trees quickly became endowed with their own characteristics during the shooting of the film. "I called them 'Anissa's tree' and 'Khemaïs' tree.' They are the two poles of hope for Zakia in life. At first, she is in the shade of one, chatting away with Anissa; later, she is transferred to the other tree, right next to the first one, and that tree seems to be, in all regards, Khemaïs'. I never took Khemaïs to the other tree, although these two trees are so close."[26] Both trees constitute the locus where Zakia reveals herself to others, her words pouring out of her. They are thus symbolic of a force that sustains her as she is going through the pains of giving birth to her new self (the timeline of the framing narrative is almost that of a pregnancy). At the same time, the trees signal a new point of departure for the intra-diegetic gaze: this is the basis from which Zakia observes Khemaïs, and from which she excavates her own memory. Sitting at the base of the tree, Zakia the seer offers a perfect counterpoint to the director up on the balcony. She is in full view, in full light, and has taken center stage. During these moments when I, the extra-diegetic spectator, see through the eyes of Zakia, I see through eyes that do not belong to the French, patriarchal power. Zakia evades the system of the authoritarian gaze on at least two grounds: (1) she is willingly exposing herself as an object of the clinical, male director's gaze; and (2) she is simultaneously taking possession of the gazing power by turning her eyes onto Khemaïs, into the dark recesses of her own memory, and onto the snatches of narrative misery uttered by the insane surrounding her. Thanks to her, I, sitting outside the convolutions of the diegesis, am given access to a view of the insane different from the one imposed by the all-seeing eye of power perched high above. Her position next to the tree gives her gaze centrality in the most subversive way, since she sees from the heart (literally) of an asylum, a locus we could see as the most marginal possible, and yet this is where she and Khemaïs have taken center stage. The old margins and center have been reversed, hinting at the possibility of not only a fresh start for Zakia and Khemaïs, perhaps a new couple-hood, but also a new "order," a new "age" finally made possible for this unconventional two-some. As their discourse unfolds, they gradually recover their deepest sense of identity – as is illustrated by Khemaïs leading Zakia back to the name she has forgotten: "You will remember your name. We all do. We all have to." The ensuing recovery of her individual identity shows a possible way for individuals (male and female) to negotiate a passage from oblivion to agency. Projected against the backdrop of national history, it also shows a way for communities to recall the memory of their history prior to colonization (their identity), overcome their recent past, and prepare for a hopeful present and future; a way for a nation to advance boldly into independence.

Finally, the insane are no longer Foucault's "lepers" seen from afar but fellow victims, shot at eye level. Spatially, then, the gazing contest now takes place between two vertical positions: up above, on the asylum terrace (below the French flag flapping in the wind) on the margin of the building (see figure 23), and down below, at the foot of the tall, old trees in the middle of the courtyard (see figure 24). These two very different viewpoints and these two positions and modes of gazing relay two markedly different framed stories.

BACK TO THE ASYLUM DIRECTOR The director, as we have already seen, stands as the emblematic point of convergence of a national system and a local one: the French "protecting"/ruling over Tunisia and the powerful doctor directing/ruling over the insane (of Tunisia). He is the ultimate figure of power. He is a man of few words. Only once do we hear him speak, when Meriem comes to visit her mother and is received by the director in his office. The gaze here is unmistakably powerful and arrogantly (heterosexually) male. As his voice is speaking, we follow his gaze going up the beautiful legs of his listener, dressed in an elegant European suit.

> "Vous n'êtes pas sans ignorer, chère Madame, que dans notre établissement, nous nous évertuons à restituer nos malades sains de corps et d'esprit à leur famille, bien sûr, mais surtout à ce pays que nous chérissons tant." (You are aware, undoubtedly, dear Madam, that, in our institution, we strive to give our patients back healthy in mind and body to their families, of course, but above all, to this country that is so dear to us.)

A macho agent of the colonizing system, he delivers – in French, of course (the language of power) – a paternalistic, nationalistic speech to Zakia's first and only visitor, her daughter. In one sentence, he maps out the colonial political project: the Tunisian "lepers," the insurgents, the mad, must be brought back to order (health) and sustain what amounts to *his* country. The family/country is not really one in this type of colonizing discourse: the invoked "we," the French and the Tunisian, constitute a family so long as the French I/eye remains in its ruling position as father. Hence the need to correct the unruly children before handing them back to Tunisian society so that they will not rebel against the French "family" order.

Extra-diegetic Transvergent Spectatorship

In the end, what am I seeing from outside the screen? And why? How has my spectatorship become transvergent in my experience of the film?

In the preceding scene, I cannot but notice that the hospital director's gaze and words are brought upon Meriem, who looks like a supermodel recently escaped from a French magazine cover. He speaks only with the members of the Tunisian upper class, not the riffraff under his care. His gaze at Meriem's legs further underscores the orientalist feminization of the colony (or protectorate): Tunisia is a seductive woman to be possessed by France – which will "protect" its offspring. The lines of flight between both perspectives (Zakia's and the hospital director's) leave me scope to reconfigure a multiple story into my own understanding of the filmic narrative on several levels.

FRAMED: THE NATION AND ZAKIA   In this film, the cinematic *mise en abyme* of various narratives framed by the main story and the main space (a psychiatric asylum) points to an off-screen/on-screen retelling of Tunisian history. The time of the framing narrative is clear: it is the short reign of Moncef Bey.

Zakia's stay in the hospital is indirectly dated: she is institutionalized some time after the death of a ruling Bey. This corresponds to the death of Ahmed Pacha Bey II (the "Bey of the French") on June 14, 1942. The night she is driven to the hospital is dated in an indirect way: the heavy rain of that night corresponds to the annual *as salah an nouadir,* the last rain of summer that separates the grain from the hull. Said to "wash away tales and legends, it always happens in early September."[27] Toward the end of the film, Khemaïs's destructive rampage in his room appears as an act of desperation in reaction to the news he hears on the radio. Here, the film alludes to Moncef Bey being deposed by the French and taken into exile to the city of Laghouat in the Algerian Sahara. "He was the only enlightened King, the only nationalist King we had," says the director. "This is why I linked his deposition to Khemaïs' breakdown, to his breaking his plant and pot, to this shot that starts with the radio, the debris of the plant, where we are given to read the unfolding of historical events."[28]

Throughout the film, Khemaïs has been listening to the BBC radio in Arabic calling for North Africa to rally to the resistance movement to defeat the Nazi forces and their allies. At the time, the Tunisian protectorate was "governed" by Admiral Jean-Pierre Esteva, the Vichy government representative, as Résident Général de France en Tunisie. In the background of these embedded stories, the presence of the French authorities is clearly felt: the French decide whom to imprison, whom to call marginal or crazy, whom to depose and silence. Yet the French are also unable to understand the forms of "Tunisian" madness in the asylum, a madness that they themselves have caused. For instance, we see various patients traumatized by World War I: a man marching as if to the trenches, a woman still waiting for her lover or fiancé to return from the war.

THE REBELLION SCENE: TRANSVERGENCE AS A FORM OF RE-BELLION One sequence in particular pulls the strands of the national and the personal narratives together and further exemplifies what transvergent spectatorship can mean, as the extra-diegetic viewer imports off-screen information to fill in the semantic gaps in the framed diegesis on-screen.

This scene [24:07–28:00] resonates on several levels for a Tunisian audience as it alludes to several stories outside the frame of the film, each leading to another, much like a Chinese box opening up to reveal another one. Here, the rebellion of the mad patients in the hospital has a telling soundtrack, and takes the notion of "madness" one notch further on the scale of dissonance and dissidence.

The scene starts at the center of the courtyard with Zakia and her confidante Anissa. It is the end of recess and the nurses are ordering the patients to get back inside the building. Zakia wants to visit Khemaïs, and a nurse tries to prevent her from doing so with a demeaning remark. Anissa starts a fight with the nurse. The individual confrontation escalates into a general melee. Nurses start to forcibly remove patients, and in particular Zakia. Khemaïs, who has always stayed clear of trouble and crowds, witnesses the scene from his window and comes down to the arena to free Zakia. He is a big, strong man. It will take two male nurses to immobilize him and take him to an isolated cell. Meanwhile, the patients are led up the stairs to a refectory, where they refuse to eat their meal.

Several things happen in this scene, visually and in the soundtrack. First of all, we are given diverse perspectives: when the inmates rebel against the authorities, the French director is seen briefly, shot from a low angle, giving silent orders with his arms, as usual, seen from the standpoint of the patients; when the latter are forced to go up the stairs to the refectory, they are shot from a high angle (we are back to the French authorities' standpoint); when Khemaïs is dragged to his cell, he is shot from a high angle as well.

But then, something is dissonant with the soundtrack: while the patients are climbing up the stairs, one of them is heard quoting in Arabic from Tunisian poet Chebbi's famous poem that inspired the nationalist anthem (today's Tunisian national anthem):

> When some day a people wants to live,
> Destiny can only respond,
> The shadows of gloom can only dissipate,
> Chains can only be broken.[29]

Here, the mad are really the political rebels, the ones that need to be imprisoned by the French authorities before they break out of dependence. They are people who are not understood by the authorities: they sing the anthem of liberation and nothing happens because they have been branded mad and the director does not understand them. To the extra-diegetic viewer, the careless deafness of the French authorities to the language of those they have subjugated is the sign of their coming downfall. The rebellion of the mad is a precursor to the successful struggle for Tunisian independence. It makes the entire scene reverberate with the power of history.

There is more. Once the inmates are seated around tables at the refectory, they start a hunger strike in protest against what has happened to Khemaïs, and we hear the nurses bark *"Mange!"* (Eat!) in French, as they try to force them to eat, to no avail (except for Anissa, the instigator of the rebellion, who has worked up an appetite!). Why present a hunger strike of insane Tunisian patients in a French psychiatric asylum in the 1940s? Such a scene may resonate loudly off the screen for a contemporary extra-diegetic viewer in Tunisia and elsewhere. In today's prisons throughout the world, where political inmates are tortured, some desperate prisoners start hunger strikes as a last resort in order to attract the attention of the foreign media to their plight. Human Rights Watch notes that it is the only right left to them.[30] Although such cases never appear in the muzzled press of Tunisia, the information is relayed through the grapevine, and Tunisians are aware of such cases. That particular scene thus acquires an eerie quality of realism in its possible commentary on today's situation beyond the fictitious screen. It also highlights the "audacious and brave" quality of the film, which was noted by only one commentator, Tunisian critic and academic Abdelfattah Fakhfakh.[31]

Hence, to a transvergent extra-diegetic spectator, *Khochkhach* is not a film strictly about an opium-addict forced to kick the habit, or a filmic pun about a *dépendante* trying to reach *indépendance*. Taking leaps of flight within the film and outside its frame, the spectator can merge together the various layers of meaning and view the film as an allegory about the sad state of Tunisia then and now – about the pent-up dreams of independence and freedom of expression and the brutality of the authorities. If the second or third messages are never explicitly stated, they are simply understood by alert audiences accustomed to narratives that are framed by and/or alluding to a shared world off-screen. The film also proposes a fresh panoptic view of Tunisian history before and after Moncef Bey, from an ambiguous space of confinement from which it symbolically reimagines the nation, not as a woman (as the colonizer used to), but as the unifying love of a nascent egalitarian couple.

CONCLUSION

The construction of meaning in *Khochkhach* via the call-and-response of the intra-diegetic spectator or agent on-screen and the spectator off-screen relates to several important elements in the cinema of Maghrebi women directors. This positioning of the extra-diegetic spectator is empowering on two levels.

Firstly, the fact that she is provided with several intra-diegetic viewing agents providing her with various perspectives allows her multiple points of entry into the narrative and an appreciation of the fleeting nature of "authority." One voice is heard, then another. One gaze is as valid as another. Hence, as we have seen, the gaze of power, once de-railed by the gaze of the powerless, not only empowers Zakia-the-intra-diegetic-gazer, but also me, the extra-diegetic gazer who can see the same situation from the privileged angle of not one but two vantage points. Furthermore, as the direction of the intra-diegetic gaze shifts, I am also taught an unsettling yet democratic gazing rule: the gazing game is never securely moored; it is always in becoming, always in motion. That very aspect is visible in other films such as *Red Satin* (see chapter 4), in which we see Lilia dance but also watch Lilia's audience and fellow musician through her eyes; or *Marock* (by Marrakchi, 2006), in which the Jewish community looks at the Muslim one and vice versa; and Tlatli's final montage in *Season of Men* (2000), the entire meaning of which relies on a multiple intra-diegetic gaze and an extra-diegetic viewer in the know.

Secondly, because, as a transvergent spectator, I gather meaning from beyond the screen to supplement what cannot be said/shown on-screen, I am empowered as an interlocutor in semantic dialogue with the filmmaker. In this new position, I enjoy egalitarian privileges of sorts and am called upon to respond to the clues disseminated by the direc-tor. This too seems to be one of the characteristics of Maghrebi women's films, as they whisper half-secrets in the audience's ear. I am thinking in particular of Nadia El Fani's *Bedwin Hacker* (see chapter 5), which builds its plot on her audience's shared knowledge of both the French and the Tunisian governments (whether in legal matters of immigration or in matters of surveillance) or Kassari's *Sleeping Child* (see chapter 6), whose title alone hints at Maghrebi stories around fatherless pregnan-cies. In all ways, then, establishing a transvergent form of spectatorship is a means of empowering the viewer in the movie theater – as well as her agent on-screen.

17. Mother pining away, waiting for her son's return. (*L'Enfant endormi/ The Sleeping Child*. Dir. Yasmine Kassari. Morocco, 2004).

18. Women gathered to watch their "burnt" men's video. (*L'Enfant endormi/ The Sleeping Child*. Dir. Yasmine Kassari. Morocco, 2004).

19. Women watchers watched. (*L'Enfant endormi/*
The Sleeping Child. Dir. Yasmine Kassari. Morocco, 2004).

20. Zeinab watching Hassan alone. (*L'Enfant endormi/*
The Sleeping Child. Dir. Yasmine Kassari. Morocco, 2004).

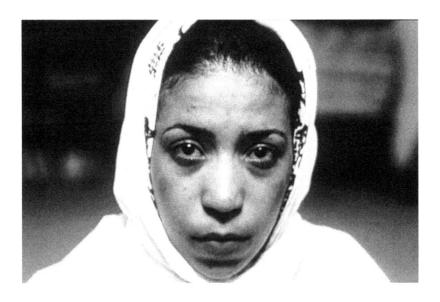

21. Zeinab facing the cruelty of absence. (*L'Enfant endormi/
The Sleeping Child*. Dir. Yasmine Kassari. Morocco, 2004).

22. Zakia drinking her opium tea. (*Khochkhach/Fleur d'oubli/
Flower of Oblivion*. Dir. Selma Baccar. Tunisia, 2006).

23. The French director's authoritarian gaze. (*Khochkhach/ Fleur d'oubli/Flower of Oblivion*. Dir. Selma Baccar. Tunisia, 2006).

24. Khemaïs and Zakia's gaze now center stage. (*Khochkhach/ Fleur d'oubli/Flower of Oblivion*. Dir. Selma Baccar. Tunisia, 2006).

25. Selma Baccar at work. Photography: Walid Harbaoui.
© Abdelaziz Ben Mlouka, CTV Services, Tunis.

Coda

Films by Maghrebi women are exceedingly diverse in both form and content. Gathering them under the singular, reductive label of "Maghrebi women's cinema" does not do justice to the array of their nuances and idiosyncratic styles. Nonetheless, we observed similar trends and patterns in the films we examined, which unite the directors beyond the geographical and cultural site from which they operate. These include a dialogical practice very similar to the ones highlighted by the two Mediterranean storytellers, Echo and Shahrazad; a transnational feminist worldview and agenda; and mobile patterns of transvergence.

This study is structured in three steps that retrace – along a loosely chronological axis – the cinematic pattern of delivery, as it examines: (1) the storyteller/film director's narrative devices; (2) the performance of the tale (with its play on the cinematic hijab on which the narrative is performed and projected); (3) the transvergent audience that receives and responds to the filmic tale. Through it all, modern-day directors recycle and adapt ancient narrative devices to their transmodern reality. The first act of the book, in which Echo and Shahrazad are reinterpreted by Djebar and Benlyazid in their films (*The Nuba* and *Door to the Sky*), has firmly established that the structures of storytelling away from the male (narcissistic) center of power endure. Echo's words, which the nymph steals from Narcissus and then manipulates, linger long after her corporeal obliteration from the landscape. The self-absorbed male power figure is unable to erase them. Shahrazad's narrative *mise en abyme* allows today's filmmakers to inject politics in their films, and talk to both the sultan and Dunyazad.

Dunyazad is the primary witness of everything, once she has been invited on the first night into the sultan's chamber at her sister's request.[1] The storytelling rests on Dunyazad's cooperation. She asks and her sister responds. Yet, Suzanne Gauch tells us, there is more to this relationship: "The often overlooked relationship of the two sisters is fraught with complexities, for without [Dunyazad]'s convenient, prearranged prompting, Shahrazad would never have had occasion to deploy the power of her stories. [Dunyazad]'s discreet presence, her disembodied voice from beneath the bed, effectively legitimates Shahrazad's voice."[2] The "disembodied voice" of the sister resembles the one of Echo, as it responds to and helps fashion Shahrazad's narrative. In a cinematic context, Dunyazad's incorporeal voice serves as a useful metaphor for two phenomena: the asynchronous relationship between filmmaking and film screening, as well as the mode of construction of meaning specific to film viewing. The viewers in a movie theater see the film long after it has been made, and thus they respond to the director's film projection in a delayed fashion; while she makes her film, the director has to imagine and stage their future responses, their disembodied voices that will respond to and complete its performance at the time of projection. The audience sees the film and then mentally brings together clues taken from the referential space off-screen shared with the tale-teller. Here the prompt comes after the time of the storytelling, but the director still relies on that prompt for the performance of the film to achieve full meaning.

Hence the mythical Shahrazad/Dunyazad dyad mirrors the contemporary director/viewer dyad. A transnational feminist reading of these films has allowed us to see a set of not only shared narrative structures, shared filmic aesthetics, but also what de Lauretis calls women's "aesthetics of reception" across borders. In that regard, women directors are clearly whispering to their female audience. Such revelatory cinema may backfire at times, when the directors (who often commute between the Maghreb and Europe) face an extra layer of culturally enforced resis-

tance from their audience at home.[3] Yet women directors (like participant observers born in the culture they represent), given their intimate
knowledge of women's interiors and language, are the only ones in a
position to project women's hushed, private secrets. If the revelation is
at first deemed obscene (in the original sense of the term: off-stage, away
from the proscenium), it endures nonetheless and becomes recognized
at an institutional level – *Satin Rouge*, for instance, became the official
Tunisian film shown at Tunisian embassies in the United States and
Europe over the next few years following its release.

In this study, the critique of transvergence yields useful readings as it
highlights how Maghrebi women's cinema subscribes to no fixed regime
of truth, meanders along one path (e.g., Western or Egyptian cinema)
only to later veer away from it, and is both allusive and transgressive.
Such transvergent cinema produces an *allo*-self, that is, generates an
"other" both on-screen and within the extra-diegetic viewer during the
screening. It is this flexible, mobile interplay in between various systems,
audiences, and levels of consciousness that creates a cinema forever in
becoming, and a cinema that is, in the end, politically charged and effectively so. In this, the women's films are not alone: the cinema by both
men and women in the Maghreb is defiant in what it projects for all
to see. "The current trends in Maghrebi cinemas seem to encompass
documenting the various forms of resistance, breaking through barriers,
daring to represent oneself differently, ducking the growing control of
the fundamentalists, calling for a greater respect for women."[4] According
to Olivier Barlet, these cinemas speak to young Maghrebi viewers, north
and south of the Mediterranean, eager to see images of their dreams of
an individual fate along a Western narrative model and also to recognize their treasured cultural roots. I would add that the cinemas of the
Maghreb address a plural, transvergent audience, and that – whether
authored by male or female directors – they function on the basis of
various shared sets of references that the active viewer is required to
decode. In their attempt to tell a dissident story despite the various levels
of censorship enforced by each government, Maghrebi directors, rather
than flashing their intended meaning, point to its direction. They remain
suggestively silent instead of shouting. The careful detours elaborated by
these filmmakers are meant to both thinly veil and denounce political

forms of oppression. This "cinema of intervention" requires a Dunyazad in each of the viewers to work toward the production of meaning rather than receive it passively and directly. It is a political cinema that requires extra-diegetic viewers to meet the director off-screen and produce meaning conjointly.[5]

I would contend that Maghrebi women directors' "intervention cinema" is even bolder than that of their male peers because they point to a history of women either hitherto untold or only recently whispered – as illustrated by Djebar's *Nuba* staging the narratives of women freedom fighters in Algeria, or Djamila Sahraoui's *Barakat/Enough* (2006) on the same theme as Bachir-Chouikh's *Rachida*. Yet, women also represent life narratives that were hushed,[6] and seem to construct portraits of women seen from beneath the cinematic hijab and then projected on its backlit surface. The dimension of these films is political not only on a macro level but also on the personal, intimate level of the everyday life and conditions of women in the Maghreb. During the time of the screening, I, the viewer, experience an intensely political and personal adventure, or, as Noureddine Saïl describes with the elegance of utter simplicity, a new order: "A film puts life in order. It lines up my gaze with its own ordering gaze."[7] For the time of the screening at least, someone's outlook on life comingles with mine and leaves some of its images to be stored in my memory for later contemplation.

And yet, I cannot help but see the fragility of this audacious, innovative, rich cinema, and fear for its future, given the current drastic changes in film-viewing practices, reception, and conservation. These days, in the Maghreb as everywhere else, film viewing has become an increasingly solitary practice: viewers watch a DVD (whether pirated or not) at home, most often in a fragmentary fashion (the screening is interrupted by other people in the household needing immediate attention or the phone ringing), and often alone. The consumption of film now tends to be individual rather than the collective feast it used to be in the twentieth century. As a result, the discussions, the intense, collective, often political debates engendered by cinema in cafés or in the *ciné* clubs of yore are vanishing. If the art of filmmaking has evolved, so has the art of viewing. How are films that are not shared by alert cinephiles remembered?

Who, then, discusses these films today and from where? In Europe and in the United States, for instance, the practice of film reviewing seems to have altered its goal: it promotes, it heralds, the film ahead of its release, instead of accompanying the film on its journey and probing the filmmaker's gaze. In the Maghreb, a few articles appear in the press when a film first comes out, and film criticism suddenly erupts in a couple of unlikely places. For instance, in Morocco, when *Marock* (Leïla Marrakchi, 2005) or *Casanegra* (Nour Eddine Lakhmari, 2008) came out, the Parliament took upon itself to critique the films and issued strong warnings against them. Fortunately, Moroccan film critics quickly took up the challenge of dislodging film critical discourse out of the sphere of the power in place: they organized roundtables and panels in various venues in order to reinstate film criticism as an art and a discourse (away from an up or down vote by representatives in the Parliament), and have been successful so far.

Furthermore, we are in the midst of a far-reaching digital revolution that lowers the cost of film production dramatically and allows for a greater flexibility in filming. Yet, as Noureddine Saïl warned: "Digital cinema will not save our memory."[8] Indeed, a negative can last, if not forever, at least for a very long time, when stored properly, but the lifespan of a digital film, right now, lies somewhere between ten and twenty years. What, then, will remain twenty years from now of the films we are fortunate enough to be able to see today? Who will shoot in a digital format and who won't? Whose filmic memory is the world committed to sustain? The support (and support system) of this cinematic production has such fragile, blind spots that we need to remain alert and devise careful ways to intervene as viewers and critics in the North and in the South, to ensure that this cinema thrives now and will survive later. For we and others after us, here and elsewhere, have still a lot to learn from its gifted directors and their enthralling stories.

Theirs is a cinema that addresses simultaneously local, regional, and global alert viewers. If I follow the transvergent detours along the paths walked by these filmmakers, even I, from my distant seat in Paris or Baltimore, am able to glimpse some of the episodes of dissidence offered on-, and off-, screen. As the film unrolls, the director educates me, and turns me into one of her alert responders. I then keep waiting

for the next tale, the next lesson in storytelling and filmmaking. I fleetingly become Dunyazad by occupying a similar space, in the dark room
of a picture house, invisible yet present; by learning from the voice of
the scholar entertainer the secrets of ancient woman's storytelling; by
heeding the urgent tone with which she unmutes the suppressed cries of
the oppressed as she talks, night after night, to the self-absorbed tyrant;
by following the whimsical arabesques of her film on a screen she has
peacefully occupied.

Political and Cinematic Chronology

SOURCES CONSULTED

"Algeria: Women in Public Life." *United Nations Development Programme/ Programme on Governance in the Arab Region*. http://gender.pogar .org/countries/country.asp?cid=1. Accessed 03/06/2009.

Charrad, Mounira M. *States and Women's Rights*. Berkeley: University of California Press, 2001.

"Country Profile: Algeria." *BBC News*. http://news.bbc.co.uk/2/hi/middle_ east/country_profiles/790556.stm. Accessed 02/27/2009.

"Country Profile: Morocco." *BBC News*. http://news.bbc.co.uk/2/hi/middle_ east/country_profiles/791867.stm. Accessed 02/27/2009.

"Country Profile: Tunisia." *BBC News*. http://news.bbc.co.uk/2/hi/middle_ east/country_profiles/791969.stm. Accessed 02/27/2009.

"Morocco: Women in Public Life." *United Nations Development Programme / Programme on Governance in the Arab Region*. http://gender.pogar.org/ countries/coutry.asp?cid=12. Accessed 03/06/2009.

"Personal Status Code – Tunisia." *International Labor Organization*. http://www .ilo.org/public/english/employment/ gems/eeo/law/tunisia/eeo-psc.htm. Accessed 03/06/2009.

Hillauer, Rebecca. *Encyclopedia of Arab Women Filmmakers*. Cairo: American University in Cairo Press, 2005.

Stora, Benjamin. *Algeria: A Short History*. Trans. Jane Marie Todd. Ithaca, N.Y.: Cornell University Press, 2001.

Tartter, Jean R. "Government and Politics." In *Tunisia: A Country Study*, ed. Harold D. Nelson. Washington, D.C.: American University Press, 1986.

Appendix A Table follows

(Key: s=short; d=documentary; f=feature film)

Compiled by Florence Martin and Anndal Narayanan.

YEAR	MOROCCO	ALGERIA	TUNISIA
1956	Independence.		Independence.
	Sultan Mohammed V regains the throne after returning from exile.		Code of Personal Status instituted.
1957	Family Law instituted by series of decrees, 1957–1958.		Habib Bourguiba (Destourian Socialist Party) becomes first president.
1961	Sultan Mohammed V dies. His son Hassan II ascends to the throne.		
1962		Independence.	
		Ahmed Ben Bella (National Liberation Front, FLN) invested as first president.	
1965		Ben Bella arrested in coup.	
		Houari Boumédienne (head of National People's Army) leads government by revolutionary decree.	
1974		*The Nuba of the Women at Mount Chenoua*, A. Djebar. (f)	
1975			Bourguiba proclaimed president for life.
1976			*Fatma 75*, S. Baccar. (f)
			To Serve You, N. Ben Mabrouk. (d)
1979	*Identity of Women*, F. Benlyazid. (s)	Chadli Bendjedid (FLN) elected president.	
		Zerda or the Songs of Oblivion, A. Djebar. (f)	
1980		*Houria*, D. Sahraoui. (s)	

YEAR	MOROCCO	ALGERIA	TUNISIA
1981	*Aicha*, F. Benlyazid. (s)		
1982	*The Ember*, F. Bourquia. (f)		*The Ember*, F. Bourquia. (f)
1984		Code of Personal Status instituted.	
1985			*In the Land of Tarayoun*, S. Baccar. (s) *The Golden Fleece*. S. Baccar. (s)
1987			Bourguiba impeached on basis of senility. Zine El Abidine Ben Ali becomes president.
1988	*A Door to the Sky*, F. Benlyazid. (f)		*The Trace*, N. Ben Mabrouk. (f) *Three Characters in Search of a Theater*, K. Bornaz. (f)
1990		*Years in the Aurès Mountains*, D. Sahraoui. (s)	
1991			*In Search of Shaima*, N. Mabrouk. (s)
1992		*Chadli forced from office by army coup. Civil war begins.* *First Name Marianne*, D. Sahraoui. (s)	*The Gaze of the Seagull*, K. Bornaz. (f) *Fifty-fifty, my love*, N. El Fani. (f)
1993	*Aminata Traoré: A Woman of the Sahel*, F. Benlyazid. (d)	*Fatima and the Sea*, N. Cherabi. (s) *Fatima Almaria*. N. Cherabi. (s)	Code of Personal Status is amended.
1994	*Contraband*, F. Benlyazid. (d)	*Female Devils*, H. Zinai Koudil. (f)	*Give me a Tanit*, N. El Fani. (s) *Silences of the Palace*, M. Tlatli. (f) *The Dance of Fire*, S. Baccar. (f)

YEAR	MOROCCO	ALGERIA	TUNISIA
1995	On the Terrace, F. Benlyazid. (s)	General Liamine Zéroual elected president (FLN) in first election after coup.	The Bouquet, R. Amari. (f)
	Five Films for a Hundred Years, F. Benlyazid. (s)	The Other Half of Allah's Heaven, D. Sahraoui. (d)	
1996	200 Dirhams, L. Marrakchi. (s)		The Secret of Crafts, S. Baccar. (d)
			Wedding Nights in Tunis, K. Bornaz. (s)
1997	In My Father's House, F. Jebli Ouazzani. (f)	The Exiled Man in Bougie, N. Cherabi. (s)	The Lost Thread, K. Bornaz. (f)
			Women in Our Memory, S. Baccar. (d)
1998	Fishing in Morocco: Between Tradition and Modernity, F. Benlyazid. (d)	Algeria: Life in Spite of It All, D. Sahraoui. (s)	April, R. Amari. (s)
			As Long As There Is Film, N. El Fani. (s)
			El medfoun, K. Bornaz. (s)
1999	Hassan II dies. His son Mohammed VI ascends to the throne. The "years of lead" end.	President Zéroual cuts term short. Abdelaziz Bouteflika (FLN) elected president.	
	The Wiles of Women, F. Benlyazid. (f)		
	Salam, S. El Bouhati. (s)		
2000	Lost Horizon, L. Marrakchi. (s)	Tele-projects Mission, D. Sahraoui. (s)	Code of Personal Status is amended a second time.
	When Men Cry, Y. Kassari. (f)		One Evening in July, R. Amari. (s)
	Naïvety Wins, F. Benlyazid. (s)		The Season of Men, M. Tlatli. (f)
2001	El Boukma, F. Benlyazid. (s)	Algeria, Life Goes On, D. Sahraoui. (d)	

Primary Filmography

NB: *The following selection of directors reflects a desire to reference not only women's cinema in the Maghreb but also the "accented cinema" by women directors born in the Maghreb and residing in Europe. This is by no means an exhaustive filmography: it highlights women filmmakers who either have made – or are currently in the process of making – at least one feature fiction film, for which details are given below, or are directors of at least one long documentary. Hence, many talented Maghrebi directors who have made shorts exclusively do not appear below.*

AMARI, RAJA (1971–), TUNISIA

Al Dowaha/Les secrets/Secrets **(91 min), Tunisia, 2009**
Selection at the Mostra, Venice, 2009
Grand Prix, Arte Mare Mediterranean Cultures and Film Festival, Bastia
Best Feature Film, Milano Festival 2010
Director and Script: Raja Amari
Cinematography: Renato Berta
Sound: Patrick Becker
Music: Philippe Héritier
Editing: Pauline Dairou
Cast: Hafsia Herzi, Sondos Belhassen, Wassila Dari, Rim el Benna, Dhafer L'Abidine, et al.

Production: Nomadis Images – Dora Bouchoucha (Tunisia)/Les Films d'Ici – Serge Lalou (France)/AKKA Films – Nicolas Wadimoff (Switzerland); and Ministery of Culture, RTT, Fonds Sud Cinéma, CNC, Canal + (France), et al. (Tunisia and France)

'Ala khoutta al nessyan/Sur les traces de l'oubli/Seekers of Oblivion **(documentary, 52 min), Egypt and Tunisia, 2004**

Al sitar al asmar/Satin Rouge/Red Satin **(100 min), Tunisia and France, 2002**
Best African Film, Montreal World Film Festival, 2002
New Director Showcase Award, Seattle International Film Festival, 2002
Prize of the City of Torino, and Special Mention for Best Script, Torino International Festival of Young Cinema, 2002
Director and Script: Raja Amari
Cinematography: Diane Baratier
Sound: Frédéric de Ravignan
Editing: Pauline Dairou
Cast: Hiam Abbas, Hend el Fahem, Maher Kamoun, Monia Hichri, et al.
Production: Nomadis Images, ANPA, ADR Productions, Arte France Cinéma, Canal +, CNC (Tunisia and France)

Un Soir de Juillet/One Evening in July (26 min), Tunisia, 2000

Avril/April (35 min), Tunisia, 1998

Le Bouquet/The Bouquet (short), France, 1995

BACCAR, SELMA (1945–), TUNISIA

Kamanja Salama (TV film series), Tunisia, 2007

Layali el bidh (TV film), Tunisia, 2007

Khochkhach/Fleur d'oubli/Flower of Oblivion (107 min), Tunisia and Morocco, 2005
Director and Script: Selma Baccar
Best Actress Award for Rabia Ben Abdallah, Rotterdam International Film Festival, 2006,
Best Actress Award for Rabia Ben Abdallah, Institut du Monde Arabe Film Festival, Paris and Marseille, 2006,
Best Actress Award for Rabia Ben Abdallah and Silver Award for Best Film, Valencia Mediterranean Film Festival, 2006
Best Actress Award for Rabia Ben Abdallah and Audience Award for Best Feature Film, Rabat International Film Festival, 2007
Amina Award for Rabia Ben Abdallah, Montreal "Vues d'Afrique" International Film Festival, 2007
Cinematography: Andreas Sinanos
Sound: Hechémi Joulak
Music: Rabii Zaouri
Editing: Karim Hammouda and Kéhna Attaia
Cast: Rabia Ben Abdallah, Alaeddine Ayouh, Raouf Ben Amor, Leila Chebbi, Hend el Fehem, et al.
Production: CTV (Tunis)

Assrar âailya (TV Ramadan sitcom), Tunisia, 2006

Nouassi Wâateb (TV Ramadan sitcom), Tunisia, 2006

Chaâbane fi Romdhane (TV sitcom), Tunisia, 2005

Chaara el hob (TV series), 2005

(With Kutaiba al Janabi) *Le train/The Train* (docudrama, 26 min), UK, Iraq, and Tunisia, 2004

Raconte-moi le planning (Tell Me about Planning) (docudrama, 26 min), Tunisia, 2004

Farhat Amor/ Joie d'une vie (Joy of one life) (TV Ramadan sitcom), Tunisia, 2002

Femmes dans notre mémoire/Women in our Memory (a TV series of 15 docudramas), Tunisia, 1997

Le Secret des métiers/The Secret of Crafts (a TV series of 24 documentaries), Tunisia, 1996

Habiba M'sika/La Danse du feu/The Dance of Fire (124 min), Tunisia/Algeria/France, 1994
ACTT Award, Namur International Francophone Film Festival,1995
Jury's Special Prize, Montreal "Vues d'Afrique" International Film Festival, 1996
Director: Selma Baccar
Script: Saïda Ben Mahmoud
Cinematography: Allel Yahiaoui
Sound: Faouzi Thabet
Music: Hamadi Ben Othman
Editing: Moufida Tlatli
Cast: Souad Amidou, Nejob Belkadhi, Feodor Atkine, et al.
Production: Phenicea Films, Intermedia Productions, Canal Horizon, ERTT, CAAIC, Auramax, Eurofilms, Euroma Films (Tunisia, Algeria, and France)

L'Histoire des coutumes (The history of customs) (fiction), Tunisia, 1985

De la Toison au fil d'or/The Golden Fleece (documentary, 16 min), Tunisia, 1985

Au Pays de Tarayoun/In the Land of Tarayoun (51 min), Tunisia, 1985

Fatma 75 (docudrama, 60 min), Tunisia, 1976
Director: Selma Baccar
Script: Samir Ayadi and Selma Baccar
Cinematography: Allel Yahiaoui
Sound: Faouzi Thabet
Cast: Jalila Baccar, Fatma Ben Ali, Halima Daoud, Hédi Daoud, Abdellatif Hamrouni, Jemil Joudi, Abdelmajid Lakhal, Mouna Nourreddine
Production: SATPEC (Tunisia)

Najet Mabaoujet/ Le Crépuscule (Dawn), Tunisia, 1968

BACHIR-CHOUIKH, YAMINA (1954–), ALGERIA

Hier . . . Aujourd'hui et demain/Yesterday . . . Today and Tomorrow (documentary, 102 min), Algeria, 2010

Louisa Sid Ammi (documentary, 26 min), Algeria, 2003

Rachida (100 min), France and Algeria, 2002
Audience Award and Golden Unicorn for Best Feature Film, Amiens International Film Festival, 2002
Satyajit Ray Award, London International Film Festival, 2002
Cinema of the South Award, Marrakech International Film Festival, 2002
Golden Bayard (for Best Francophone Film) and Youth Jury Award – Special Mention, Namur International Film Festival, 2002
Award for Best First Feature, Mexico International Contemporary Film Festival, 2004
Director and Script: Yamina Bachir-Chouikh

Cinematography: Mustapha Belmihoub
Sound: Rachid Bouaffia, Martin Boisseau
Music: Anne-Olga de Pass
Editing: Cécile Andreotti and Yamina Bachir-Chouikh
Cast: Ibtissem Djouadi, Bahia Rachedi, Rachida Messaoui En, Hamid Remas, et al.
Production: Arte France Cinéma, Ciel Production, Ciné-Sud Promotion/ Thierry Lenouvel, GAN Cinema Foundation, French Ministry of Culture, Canal + (France)

BEDJAOUI, AMAL (1963–), FRANCE AND ALGERIA

Un fils/A Son (58 min), France, 2003
Director: Amal Bedjaoui
Script: Amal Bedjaoui and Isabelle Pichaud
Cinematography: Nara Keo Kosal
Sound: François Groult, Jérôme Harlay, Pascal Lesaulnier, Olivier Marlangeon
Music: Matthieu Charter
Editing: Gwen Mallauran
Cast: Mohamed Hicham, Hamou Graïa, Isabelle Pichaud, Aurélien Recoing et al.
Production: ML Productions (France)

Suite Saturnienne/Saturnine Suite (doc on digital video, 15 min), France, 1999

Shoot Me Angel (9 min), France, 1995
New York Film Academy Scholarship Award

Une Vue imprenable/Look Out (15 min), France, 1993

BENLYAZID, FARIDA (1948–), MOROCCO

Casanayda/Casa, ça bouge/Casa Is Rocking (documentary, 52 min), Morocco, 2007

La vida perra de Juanita Narboni/ Juanita de Tanger/The Wretched Life of

Juanita Narboni (101 min), **Morocco
and Spain, 2005**
Award for Best Second Role for Salima
 Ben Moumen, Tangier National Film
 Festival, 2005
Award for Best Script, Salé International
 Women's Film Festival, 2006
Director: Farida Benlyazid
Script: Ángel Vázquez (novel) and Ge-
 rardo Bellod (adaptation)
Cinematography: José Luis Alcaine
Music: Jorge Arriagada
Sound: José Luis Alcaine Bartolomé
Editing: Pablo G. Plant
Cast: Mariola Fuentes, Nadia Alami,
 Francisco Algora, Saad el Fassi, et al.
Production: Tingitiana Films, ZAP Pro-
 ducciones SL (Morocco and Spain)

Casa ya Casa/Casablanca, Casablanca
(90 min), Morocco, 2002
Director: Farida Benlyazid
Script: Farida Benlyazid and Ahmed
 Boulane
Cinematography: Serge Palatsi
Music: Hamza Abderrazik
Editing: Alla Sahbi
Cast: Younès Megri, Rachid el Ouali, Mo-
 hamed Razine, et al.
Production: Tingitiana Films,
 RTM, Waka Films (Morocco and
 Switzerland)

El Boukma (film for TV), **Morocco, 2001**

Nia Taghleb/La naïveté l'emporte/
Naivity Wins (film for TV), **Morocco,
2000**

Keid Ensa/Ruses de Femmes, ou le conte
de la fille au basilic/The Wiles of Women
**(90 min), Morocco, Switzerland,
Tunisia, France, 1999**
Best Feature Film, 6th International Fes-
 tival of Marrakech, 1999
Audience Award, Ferney Voltaire Film
 Festival, 1999
Audience Award, Milano International
 Film Festival, 1999

Prize of the City of Setúbal for the Best
 Upcoming Actress, Samia Akarriou,
 Festróia-Troia Film Festival, 1999
Director and Script: Farida Benlyazid
Cinematography: Serge Plasti
Music: Mohamed Charraf
Sound: Faouzi Thabet
Editing: Kathéna Attia
Cast: Samira Akariou, Rachid el Quali,
 Amina Alaoui, et al.
Production: Tingitiana Films, Waka
 Films, Touza Productions, Cephéide
 Productions (Morocco, France, Tuni-
 sia, and Switzerland)

La pêche au Maroc entre tradition et
modernité (**Fishing in Morocco
between Tradition and Modernity)
(TV documentary), Morocco, 1998**

Cinq films pour cent ans/Five Films
for a Hundred Years (**one episode in a
collective), Morocco, 1995**
Mention, Montreal Film Festival

Sur la terrasse/On the Terrace (15 min),
Morocco, 1995

Contra Bande (documentary),
Morocco, 1994

Aminata Traoré une femme du Sahel/
Aminata Traoré, a Woman of the Sahel
(**documentary, 26 min**), **1993**

Bab al sama maftouh/ Une Porte sur
le ciel/ A Door to the Sky (**100 min),
France/Tunisia/Morocco, 1988**
A.C.C.T. Award, Namur International
 Francophone Film Festival, 1988
Bronze Annaba, Journées Ciné-
 matographiques d'Annaba, 1988
Bronze Tanit for Best Feature Film,
 Journées Cinématographiques de
 Carthage, 1988
Best Scenario Award, Meknès Film Festi-
 val, 1988
Director and Script: Farida Benlyazid
Cinematography: George Barsky
Music: Anouar Brahem

Editing: Moufida Tlatli
Cast: Chaabia Laadraoui Zakia Tahri, Eva St Paul, et al.
Production: France Media, SATPEC, CCM (France, Morocco, and Tunisia)

Aicha, Morocco and Germany, 1981

Identités de Femme/Women's Identities (TV documentary, 16 min) **France, 1979**

BEN MABROUK, NÉJIA
(1949–), TUNISIA

Fi al bahti'an Shaïma/A la Recherche de Shaima/In Search of Shaima (video documentary, 13 min, part of collective work, *Harb al halig . . . wa ba'da?/La Guerre du Golf . . . et après?/The Gulf War . . . Then What?* 1991

Al-Sâma/La Trace/The Trace (90 min), **Tunisia/Belgium/Germany, 1988**
Caligari Prize, International Forum of New Cinema, Berlin International Film Festival, 1988
Director and Script: Néjia Ben Mabrouk
Cinematography: Marc-André Batigne
Music: François Gaudard
Sound: Faouzi Thabet
Editing: Moufida Tlatli
Cast: Fatma Khemiri, Mouna Noureddine, Basma Tajine, et al.
Production: SATPEC, No Money Company, ZDF (Tunisia, Belgium, and Germany)

Pour vous servir/To Serve You (documentary), **1976**

BORNAZ, KALTHOUM
(1945–), TUNISIA

Shtar m'haba/L'Autre moitié du ciel/The Other Half of the Sky (93 min), **Tunisia/ France/Morocco, 2008**
Cinema in Movement Award, San Sebastian, 2006
Director and Script: Kalthoum Bornaz

Dialogues: Mohamed-Raja Farhat
Cinematography: Julio Ribeyro
Music: Alla and Mamdouh Bahri
Sound: David Rit
Editing: Isabelle Ratheri and Arbi Ben Ali
Cast: Younes Ferhi, Sana Kassous, Mourad Meherzi, Fethi Messelmani, et al.
Production: Les Films de la Mouette, CCM, Mille et Une Productions (Tunisia)

El Medfoun/La Forêt d'el Medfoun (10 min), **Tunisia, 1998**

Keswa, al khayt al dayya/Keswa, le fil perdu/Keswa, the Lost Thread (100 min), **Tunisia/France/ Morocco, 1997**
Director and Script: Kalthoum Bornaz
Cinematography: Claude Bennys
Music: Anouar Brahem
Editing: Kalthoum Bornaz
Cast: Rim Turki, Lotfi Achour, et al.
Production: Les Films de la Mouette, Morgane Productions (Tunisia and France)

Laylt 'urs fi tunis/Nuit de noces à Tunis/ Wedding Nights in Tunis (video, 27 min, for ARTE), **France, 1996**

Regard de mouette/The Gaze of the Seagull (35 min), **Tunisia, 1992**

Trois Personnages en quête d'un théâtre/ Three Characters in Search of a Theater (42 min), **Tunisia, 1988**

Couleurs Fertiles (Fertile Colors), **Tunisia, 1984**

BOUCHÂALA-TAHIRI, ZAKIA
(1963–), MOROCCO AND FRANCE

(with Ahmed Bouchâala) *Belleville Tour* (Belleville Tower) (film for TV, 90 min), **France, 2008**

Number One (109 min), **Morocco, 2007**
Director: Zakia Tahri and Leighton Pierce

Script: Zakia Tahiri
Cinematography: Pascale Granel
Music: Djamel Laroussi
Sound: Vivien Mergot
Editing: Sarah Turoche
Cast: Khadija Assad, Nezha Rahile, Aziz Saâdallah, et al.
Production: Made in Morocco Films

(with Ahmed Bouchâala) *Pour l'amour de Dieu* (For the Love of God) (film for TV, Arte), France, 2004

Origine contrôlée/Made in France (2001)
First Film Prize, Florence France Film Festival, 2000
Audience Award and Critics' Award, Alpe d'Huez International Comedy Film Festival, 2001
Directing Prize and 2M Prize, Tetouan International Mediterranean Film Festival, Tetouan, 2001
21st Century Director's Award, New-York/Avignon Transatlantic Crossroads of French and American Independent Cinema, 2001
Directors: Ahmed Bouchâala and Zakia Bouchâala-Tahiri
Script: Ahmed Bouchâala
Cinematography: Yves Cape
Sound: Frédéric Dubois, Laurent Lafran, Joël Rangon et al.
Music: Serge Perathoner and Jannick Top
Editing: Roland Baubeau
Cast: Patrick Ligardes, Atmen Kelif, Ronit Elkabetz, El Kebir, Alexia Stresi, François Lépine, Jean-Luc Possaz, Isabelle Sadoyan, Karim Belkhadra, et al.
Production: Blue Films, Deluxe Productions, M6 Films, New Mark, Rhône-Alpes Cinéma (France)

EL BOUHATI, SOUAD (1962–), MOROCCO AND FRANCE

Française/French Girl (84 min), France and Morocco, 2008

Best Actress Muhr Award for Hafsia Herzi, Dubai International Film Festival, 2008
Director and Script: Souad el Bouhati
Cinematography: Florian Boucher and Olivier Chabon
Music: Patrice Gomis
Editing: Josiane Zardoya
Cast: Hafsia Herzi, Farida Khelfa, Maher Kamoun, Alexandra Martinez, et al.
Production: Canal+, France 2 Cinéma, Irène Production, Jem Productions (France)

Salam (31 min), France and Morocco, 1999
National Competition Grand Prize, Special Award from the International Jury, Acting Award for Benaïssa Ahaouri, mentions from both youth juries, Clermont-Ferrand Short Film Festival, 2000
Arte Prize, Brest Short Film Festival, 2000
Lutin for Best Fiction Film, Paris, 2000
Lutin for Best Direction, Paris, 2000
Kodak Prize, Cannes International Film Festival, 2000

BOURQUIA, FARIDA (1948–), MOROCCO

Deux Femmes sur la route/Women's Road (90 min), Morocco, 2007
Director: Farida Bourquia
Script: Youssef Fadel
Cinematography: Kamal Derkaoui
Music: Younes Megri
Sound: Patric Mondez
Editing: Marcella Figuero
Cast: Aicha Mahmah, Mouna Fettou, Bachir Ouakine, Mohamed Bastaoul et al.
Production: Espace Production (Morocco)

Al jamra/La Braise/The Ember (104 min), Morocco, 1982
Director: Farida Bourquia

Script: Mahmoud Migri
Cinematography: Houcine el Khattabi
Music: Abdelghani al Yousfi
Editing: Larbi Ben Zouina
Cast: Hamid Zoughi, Rachida Machnoua, Mustapha Zaari, et al.

CHAMKHI, SONIA (1968–), TUNISIA

L'Art du mezoued (documentary video, 52 min), Tunisia 2010

Wara el Blayek/Borderline (26 min), Tunisia, 2007

Making of La vie est un songe (Life Is a Dream) [by Hacen Mouathan] (video, 52 min), Tunisia, 2009

Nesma wa Rih/Normal (20 min), Tunisia, 2002

Douz, la porte du Sahara (Douz, the Gate of the Sahara Desert) (video documentary, 38 min), Tunisia, 2003

CHERABI, NADIA (1954–), ALGERIA

Wara el mir'at/L'Envers du miroir/ The Other Side of the Mirror (105 min), Algeria, 2007
Director: Nadia Cherabi-Labidi
Script: Sid Ali and Nadia Cherabi
Cinematography: Smaïl Lakhdar-Hamina
Music: Redwan Nassri
Sound: Kamel Mekesser
Editing: Ali Leylane
Cast: Rachid Farès, Nassima Shems, Abdelhamid Rabia, Kamel Rouini, et al.
Production: Procom International, Télévision Algérienne (ENTV) and the Algerian Ministry of Culture (Algeria)

L'Exilé de Bougie/The Exiled Man in Bougie (19 min), Algeria and Portugal, 1997

Fatima Almaria (22 min), Algeria, 1993

Fatima al hawata/Fatima et la mer/Fatima and the Sea (22 min), Algeria, 1993

DJEBAR, ASSIA (1936–), ALGERIA

Al zerda/La Zerda ou les chants de l'oubli/Zerda or the Songs of Oblivion (documentary, 60 min), Algeria, 1982
Director: Assia Djebar
Script: Assia Djebar, Malek Alloula
Music: Ahmed Essyad
Editing: Nichole Schlemmer
Production: Radiotélévision Algérienne (Algeria)

Nuba nisa al djebel Shnua/La Nouba des Femmes du Mont Chenoua/The Nuba of the Women of Mount Chenoua (115 min), Algeria, 1978
Venice Biennal International Critic Prize (1979)
Director and Script: Assia Djebar
Cinematography: Ahemd Sedjane, Cherif Abboun
Music: Béla Bartók, traditional Algerian music
Editing: Nichole Schlemmer, Areski Haddadi
Cast: Noweir Sawsan, Mohamed Haymour et al.
Production: Radiotélévision Algérienne (Algeria)

EL FANI, NADIA (1958–), TUNISIA

Ouled Lenine (documentary, 82 min), Tunisia, 2007

Bedwin Hacker (103 min), Tunisia, 2002
Director and Script: Nadia El Fani
Cinematography: Habib Azouz, Stéphane Cazes, Sofiane el Fani
Music: Milton Edouard
Editing: Juliette Hautbois, Claude Reznik
Cast: Sonia Hamza, Muriel Solvay, Tomer Sisley et al.
Production: Canal + Horizons, Soread-2M, Z'Yeux Noirs Movies (Tunisia and France)

Tant qu'il y aura de la pelloche/As Long as There Is Film (3 min), Tunisia, 1998

Tanitez-moi/Give Me a Tanit (22 min), Tunisia, 1993

Al nisf bil nisf ya hobbi/Fifit fifty, mon amour/Fifty-fifty, My Love (20 min), Tunisia, 1992

Pour le plaisir/For Pleasure (35 min), France and Tunisia, 1990

FERCHIOU, SOPHIE (1931–) TUNISIA

Paroles sculptées (Sculpted Words) (35 min), Tunisia, 2005

Stambali (documentary video, 35 min), Tunisia, 1996

L'Imnarja (Imnarja Feast) (documentary, 40 min), Tunisia, 1980

Les Ménagères de l'agriculture (The Farming Housewives) (documentary, 35 min), Tunisia, 1978

La Pêche traditionnelle en Tunisie (Traditional Fishing in Tunisia) (documentary, 40 min), Tunisia, 1977

Gallala/Guellala: A Potters' Village in Tunisia (documentary, 35 min) Tunisia, 1975

Mariage Sabrya (Sabrya Wedding) (ethnographic documentary, 50 min), 1974

Zarda/Zarda: A Nomadic Tribe's Feast Days (documentary, 40 min), Tunisia, 1971

Chechia (documentary, 35 min), Tunisia, 1966

GÉNINI, IZZA (1942–), MOROCCO

Nuba d'or et de lumière/Sprees of Gold and Light (documentary, 80 min), Morocco and France, 2007

Cyberstories (beta documentary, 28 min), France, 2001

Al tubul/Tambour battant/With Drums Beating (beta, 52 min), France and Morocco, 1999

La Route du cédrat/Citron, Fruit of Splendor (documentary, 26 min), France and Morocco, 1997

Pour le Plaisir des yeux/For the Eye's Delight (T V documentary, 50 min), France and Morocco, 1997

Retourner à Oulad Moumen/Return to Oulad Moumen (video documentary, 49 min), France and Morocco,1994

Maroc: corps et âmes/Morocco, Body and Soul (a series of eleven 26-minute documentary films on Moroccan secular and sacred music: *Aita, Lutes and Delights, Gnawas, Malhoune, Rhythms of Marrakesh, Songs for a Shabbat, Embroidered Canticles, Vibrations in the High Atlas, Weddings in the Atlas, Moussem*), France and Morocco, 1987–1992

JEBLI OUAZZANI, FATIMA (1959–), MOROCCO AND NETHERLANDS

Halima's Paradise (best screenplay, Sundance Film Festival, 2001), film still in project at time of writing

Sinned Again/10 Geboden – Het was weet zondig (50 min), Netherlands, 2000

Fi bayt abi/In het huis van mijn vader/In My Father's House (documentary, 67 min), Netherlands, 1997
Golden Calf Award, Netherlands Film Festival, 1998
Golden Spire Award, San Francisco Film Festival, 1998
Iris Prize, Best European Documentary, 1999

Vorbij de jaren van Onschuld (Innocence) (documentary, 17 min), Netherlands, 1993

De Kleine Hélène/The Little Hélène (29 min), Netherlands, 1992

Het dode vlees (The Flesh of the Dead) (10 min), Netherlands, 1990

Forbidden Love (15 min), Netherlands, 1988

Schape-ogen (Sheep's Eyes) (15 min), Netherlands, 1988

Het maagdenvlies (The Maidenhead) (docudrama), Netherlands, 1987

KASSARI, YASMINE (1970–), MOROCCO

L'Enfant endormi/The Sleeping Child (95 min), Morocco and Belgium, 2004 (among over 40 prizes –) Best European Film Award, Mostra, Venice

Great Amber 2004 and Best Actress Award, Koszalin International Film Festival, 2004

Audience's Award, Namur Francophone Festival, 2005

Audience's Award and Best Actress Award, Premiers Plans Festival, Angers, 2005

Provincia di Milano Prize, 15th African, Asian and Latin American Film Festival, Milan, 2005

Silver Astor to the Best Director and Best Cinematography Award, Mar del Plata International Film Festival, 2005

Best Feature Film Award, Montreal "Vues d'Afrique" Festival, 2005

ACID Selection, Cannes Festival

Best Film Award, International Women's Film Festival, Barcelona, 2005

FIPRESCI Prize, Fribourg International Film Festival, 2005

Griot de Viento for best feature film, Tarifa African Film Festival, 2005

Best Film Award, Valdivia International Film Festival, 2005

Parajanov Prize, Tbilisi International Film Festival, 2005

Director and Script: Yasmine Kassari

Camera : Yorgos Arvanitis

Music: Koussan Achod, Armand Amar, (performance by Lévon and Roselyne Minassian)

Editing: Susana Rossberg

Cast: Mounia Osfour, Rachida Brakni, Nermine El Haggar, Fatma Abdessamie et al.

Production: Les Films de la Drève, Les Coquelicots de l'Oriental, Radio-Télévision Belge Francophone (RTBF), Spread 2M (Belgium and Morocco)

'Andama yabki al rijal . . . /Quand les hommes pleurent . . . /When Men Cry . . . (documentary, 57 min), Belgium, 2000

Lynda & Nadia (15 min), Belgium, 2002

Kilab mutasharrida/Chiens errants/ Wandering Dogs (7 min), Belgium, 1995

Le Feutre noir (short) 1994

KILANI, LEILA (1970–), MOROCCO AND FRANCE

Sur la planche (fiction feature film), Morocco, in production at time of writing

Nos Lieux interdits/Our Forbidden Places (documentary, 102 min), France and Morocco, 2009

First Prize for Best Documentary, FESPACO, Ouagadougou, 2009

Zad Moultaka/Passages (documentary, 52 min), France, 2004

FIPA Award, Biarritz, France

Tanger, le rêve des brûleurs/Tangiers, The Burners' Dream (TV documentary video, 53 min), France, 2002

First Work Prize and Documentary Prize, Ouagadougou FESPACO, 2003

Golden Tanit for video, Tunis Journées Cinématographiques de Carthage, 2004

KRIM, RACHIDA (1955–), ALGERIA

Trois Visas pour un charter/Three Visas, One Charter Plane, **France, in production at time of writing**

Pas si simple (Not That Simple) (TV film, 93 min), **France, 2008**

Permis d'aimer (Licence to Love) (TV film, 99 min), **France, 2005**

Houria (TV series on AIDS), **Algeria, 1997**

Imra'a safira/La Femme dévoilée (The Unveiled Woman) (27 min), **Algeria, 1998**

Sous les pieds des femmes (Beneath the Feet of Women) (85 min), **Algeria and France, 1997**
CICAE Award, Namur International Francophone Film Festival, 1997
SACD Award, Avignon Film Festival, 1998
Director: Rachida Krim
Script: Rachida Krim and Catherine Labruyère Colas
Cinematography: Bernard Cavalié
Music: Alexandre Desplat
Cast: Claudia Cardinale, Fejria Deliba, Yorgo Voyagis, Nadia Farès et al.
Production: Clara Films (France)

Al fatha (The Feast) (18 min), **Algeria and France, 1992**

MARRAKCHI, LAÏLA (1978–), MOROCCO

Marock (103 min), **Morocco and France, 2005**
"Un certain regard," Cannes International Film Festival, 2005
Director and Script: Laïla Marrakchi
Cinematography: Maxime Alexandre
Sound: Pierre André
Editing: Pascale Fenouillet

Cast: Morjana Alaoui, Mathieu Boujenah, Razika Simozrag, Fatym Layachi, Assad Bouab, Rachid Benhaissan, et al.
Production: Lazennec (France)

Momo Mambo (7 min), **France, 2003**

200 Dirham/200 Dirhams (15 min), **Morocco and France, 2002**
Diploma of Merit, Tampere International Short Film Festival, 2003

L'Horizon perdu/Lost Horizon (12 min), **Morocco and France, 2000**
Cipputi Award and Prize of the City of Torino, Torino International Festival of Young Cinema, 2000

MESBAHI, IMANE (1964–), MOROCCO

Le Paradis des pauvres/Paradise of the Poor (100 min), **Morocco, 2002**
Director: Image Mesbahi
Script: Abdellah Mesbahi
Cinematography: Abdelkrim Derkaoui
Sound: Najib Chlih and Karim Ronda
Editing: Ahmed Bouanani and Abdellatif Raïs
Cast: Jil Jilalla, Touria Jabrane, Abdellah Lamrani, Aïcha Sajid, Slaheddine Benmoussa et al.
Production: Maya Films, Morocco

Traces sur l'eau (Traces on Water), **Morocco, 1983**

Une Femme dans le tourbillon de la vie (Woman in the Whirl of Life), **Morocco, 1980s**

Une Femme mal à l'aise (Uneasy Woman), **Morocco, 1980s**

NEJJAR, NARJISS (1971–), MOROCCO

L'Amante du Rif (The Lover from the Rif), **France and Morocco, in postproduction at time of writing (2011)**

Terminus des anges (Angels' Last Stop)
(105 min), Morocco, 2010
Directors and Script: Narjiss Nejjar, Mo-
hamed Mouftakir, and Hicham Lasri
Cinematography: Xavier Castro
Sound: Karim Ronda
Editing: Julien Fouré
Cast: Sanaa Akroud, Nadia Niazi, Salah
Bensalem, Bouchra Ahrich, Driss
Roukh, et al.
Production: LA Prod (Morocco)

Wake up, Morocco (110 min), Morocco
and France, 2006
Director and Script: Narjiss Nejjar
Cinematography: Stefano Paradiso
Music: Sophia Charai
Sound: Zacharie Naciri
Editing: Cristel Aubert
Cast: Hassan Skalli, Fatim-Zahra Ibrahi-
mi, Raouia, Qassem Benhayoun, Leila
Slimani, Siham Assif, et al.
Production: Jbila Méditerranée Produc-
tions, Terre Sud Films (Morocco and
France)

Les Hirondelles reviennent toujours
(Swallows Always Return) (film for
TV), Morocco, 2008

*Al ouyoune al jaffa/Les Yeux secs/Cry No
More* (116 min), France/Morocco, 2003
Golden Bayard for Best screenplay,
Namur Film Festival, 2003
Award for Best Screenplay, Marrakech
Festival, 2003
Grand Prize of the Jury, Rabat Interna-
tional Film Festival, 2003
Best Feature Film, National Film Festival
of Morocco, 2003
Best Actress, National Film Festival of
Morocco, 2003
Best Costumes, National Film Festival of
Morocco, 2003
Francophonia Award, Paris Film Festival,
2004
Director and Script: Narjiss Nejjar
Cinematography: Denis Gravouil

Music: Guy-Roger Duvert
Sound: Laurent Benaïm
Editing: Emmanuelle Pencalet
Cast: Siham Assif, Khalid Benchagra,
Rafika Belhaj, Raouia, et al.
Production: Jbila Méditerranée Produc-
tion, Soread-2M, Terre Sud Films
(Morocco and France)

Le Miroir du fou (The Fool's Mirror) (63
min), Morocco, 2001

Le Septième ciel (Seventh Heaven) (35
min), France and Morocco, 2001

SAHRAOUI, DJAMILA (1950–),
ALGERIA AND FRANCE

Ouardia avait deux enfants, Algeria
and France, in production at time of
writing

Barakat/Enough (105 min), Algeria and
France, 2006
Oumaru Ganda Prize for best first film,
Best Screenplay (shared with Cécile
Vargaftig), Best Music, Ouagadougou,
FESPACO 2007
Director: Djamila Sahraoui
Script: Djamila Sahraoui and Cécile
Vargaftig
Cinematography: Katell Djian and
Raphaël O'Byrne
Music: Alla
Sound: Olivier Scwob
Editing: Catherine Gouze
Cast: Rachida Brakni, Fettouma Boua-
mari, Zahir Bouzrar, et al.
Production: Les Films d'Ici, BL Prod,
Nomadis Images, Arte France Cinéma,
ENTV (Algeria, France, and Tunisia)

*Et les arbres poussent en Kabylie/Trees
Grow Too in Kabylia* (86 min), France,
2003

*Al jaza'ir al hayah musta'mirra/Algérie,
la vie toujours/Algeria, Life Goes on*
(documentary, 53 min), France, 2001

Opération Télé-cités/Tele-projects Mission (**T V documentary, 26 min), France, 2000**

Algérie, la vie quand même/Algeria: Life in Spite of It All (**52 min), France, 1998**

Silver Dove, Leipzig D O K Festival, 1999

Nisf khalq allah/La Moitié du ciel d'Allah/ The Other Half of Allah's Heaven (**documentary, 52 min), France, 1995**

Ismaha Maryan/Prénom Mariaan/ First Name Marianne (**documentary, 26 min), France, 1992**

Avoir 2000 ans dans les Aurès/Years in the Aures Mountains (**26 min), Algeria, 1990**

Houria (**26 min), France, 1980**

TLATLI, MOUFIDA (1947–), TUNISIA

Le Jardin intérieur (**The Patio), France and Tunisia, in production at time of writing**

Nadia wa Sarra/Nadia and Sarra (**91 min), France and Tunisia, 2004**
Director: Moufida Tlatli
Script: Moufida Tlatli and Hélène Couturier
Cinematography: Alain Levent
Sound: Faouzi Thabet
Editing: Ariane Boeglin
Cast: Hiam Abbas, Dorra Zarrouk, Hichem Rostom, Néjia Ouerghi, et al.
Production: Arte France Cinéma, Ciné-tévé (France and Tunisia)

Mawsim al rijel/La Saison des hommes/ The Season of Men (**124 min), Tunisia/ Morocco/France, 2000**
Best Actress Award, Namur International Film Festival, 2000
Grand Prize, Institut du Monde Arabe, Paris, 2000

Special Mention for Caméra d'Or, Cannes Festival, 2000
Feature Film First Prize, Toronto International Festival of Women's Cinema, 2001
Best Screenplay (shared with Nouri Bouzid), Köln Mediterranean Film Festival, 2001
Director and Script: Moufida Tlatli
Cinematography: Yousssef Ben Youssef
Music: Anouar Brahem
Sound: Faouzi Thabet
Editing: Isabelle Devenick
Cast: Rabiah Ben Abdallah, Ghalia Ben Ali, Hend Sabri,
Production: Les Films du Losange, Maghreb Films Carthage (France and Tunisia)

Samt al qusur/Les silences du palais/ Silences of the Palace (**124 min), Tunisia/France, 1993**
Golden Tanit, Tunis Journées Cinématographiques de Carthage, 1994
Golden Camera – Special Mention, Cannes International Film Festival, 1994
FIPRESCI Award, Toronto International Film Festival, 1994
Golden Tulip, Istanbul International Film Festival, 1995
Satyajit Ray Award, San Francisco International Film Festival, 1995
Sutherland Trophy, British Film Institute Awards, 1995
Director and Script: Moufida Tlatli
Cinematography: Youssef Ben Youssef
Music: Anouar Brahem
Sound: Faouzi Thabet
Editing: Moufida Tlatli
Cast: Ghalia Lacroix, Hend Sabri, Amel Hedhili, Fatma Ben Saïdane, et al.
Production: Cinétéléfilm, Magfilm, Mat Films (France and Tunisia)

ZINAÏ-KOUDIL, HAFSA
(1951–), ALGERIA

Al shaytan imra'a/Le Démon au féminin/
Female Devils (**90 min**), **Algeria, 1994**
Director and Script: Hafsa Zinaï-Koudil
Cinematography: Ahmed Messaad

Music: Safi Boutella
Sound: Ali Moulahcène
Editing: A Cherigui
Cast: Djamila Haddadi, Ahmed Benaissa,
   Fatima Berber et al.
Production: Etablissement National de
   Productions Audiovisuelles (Algeria)

Appendix C

Selected Filmography of Hiam Abbas (chapter 4)

AS ACTOR

Romance in the Dark (Rie Rasmussen, France, in postproduction at the time of writing)

Peace after Marriage (Bandar Albuliwi and Ghazi Albuliwi, U.S., in postproduction at the time of writing, 2011)

The Promise (Peter Kosminsky, UK, TV miniseries, in postproduction at the time of writing)

Habibti (Nour Wazzi, UK, 2010)

Miral (Julian Schnab, U.S., 2010)

I Am Slave (Gabriel Range, UK and Kenya, 2010)

The Limits of Control (Jim Jarmusch, U.S., 2009)

Espions/Spies (Nicholas Saada, France and UK, 2009)

Amreeka/America (Cherien Dabis, U.S., Canada, and Kuwait, 2009)

Chaque jour est une fête/Everyday Is a Holiday (Dima el Horr, Lebanon, 2009)

Clichés (Nadine Naous, Lebanon, 2009)

Persécutions/Persecutions (Patrice Chéreau, France, 2009)

Human Zoo (Rie Rasmussen, France, 2009)

Al mor wa al rumman/Pomegranates and Myrrh (Najwa Najjar, Palestine and Germany, 2008)

L'Aube du monde/Dawn of the World (Abbas Fahdel, France and Germany, 2008)

Etz Lemon/ Shajarat limon/Lemon Tree (Eran Riklis, Israel, 2008)
Best Actress Award, Asia Pacific Screen Awards, 2008
Best Actress Award, Awards of the Israeli Film Academy, 2008
Best Actress (shared with Rona Lipaz-Michael), Cinefan Festival of Asian and Arab Cinema, 2008

Un Roman policier/A Police Romance (Stéphanie Duvivier, France, 2008)

La Fabrique des sentiments/ The Feelings Factory (Jean-Marc Moutout, France, 2008)

The Visitor (Thomas McCarthy, U.S., 2008)

Hitnatkoot/Disengagement (Amos Gitaï, Israel, 2008)

Dialogue avec mon jardinier/ Dialogue with My Gardener (Jean Becker, France, 2007)

Disengagement (Amos Gitaï, Israel, 2007)

The Nativity Story (Catherine Hardwicke, U.S., 2006)

Munich (Steven Spielberg, U.S., 2006)

Free Zone (Amos Gitaï, Israel, 2006)

Nadia & Sarra (Moufida Tlatli, Tunisia and France, 2006)

Paradise Now (Hany Abou Assad, Palestine, 2005)

Le Démon de midi/The Demon Stirs (Marie-Pascale Osterrieth, France, 2005)

Ha-Kala Ha-Surit/The Syrian Bride (Eran Riklis, Israel, France, and Germany, 2004)

Baba el shams/La porte du soleil/ The Door to the Sun (Yousry Nasrallah, France, Egypt, Morocco, Belgium, 2004)

Pierre & Farid (Michel Favart, France, TV, 2003)

Red Satin/Satin rouge (Raja Amari, Tunisia, 2002)

Fais-moi des vacances/We Need a Vacation (Didier Bivel, France, 2002)

Aime ton père/A Loving Father (Jacob Berger, France, 2002)

L'Ange de goudron/Tar Angel (Denis Chouinard, Canada, 2001)

Ligne 208 (Bernard Dumont, France, 2001)

Ali, Rabiaa et les autres/Ali, Rabiaa and the Others (Ahmed Boulane, Morocco, 2001)

Mix-cité (Cristophe Lepêtre, France, TV, 2000)

Vivre au paradis/Living in Paradise (Bourlem Guerdjou, France and Algeria, 1998)

Raddem (Danielle Arbid, France and Lebanon, 1998)

Haïfa (Rashid Masharawi, Palestine, 1996)

Chacun cherche son chat/When the Cat's Away (Cédric Klapisch, France, 1996)

La nuit miraculeuse/The Miraculous Night (Ariane Mnouchkine, France, TV, 1989)

AS DIRECTOR

The Inheritance/L'Héritage (Israel and France, in preproduction at the time of writing, 2012)

La Danse éternelle/The Eternal Dance (26 min, France, 2003)

El Khobs/Le Pain/Bread (18 min, France, 2001)

Notes

OVERTURE

1. See, for example, Barlet, *African Cinemas;* Diawara, *African Cinema;* Givanni, *Symbolic Narratives/African Cinema;* Gugler, *African Film.*

2. See Dönmez-Colin, *The Cinema of North Africa and the Middle East,* or Nicosia, *Il Cinema Arabo,* for instance.

3. See Laviosa, *Visions of Struggle in Women's Filmmaking in the Mediterranean.*

4. Dönmez-Colin, *The Cinema of North Africa and the Middle East,* 1.

5. I am even tempted to follow in the footsteps of Malek Chebel's literal typographical questioning of the hyphenated adjective, as he alludes to one of the common traits uniting Maghrebi nations: "the history of an ('Arabo-Muslim'?) civilization" characterized by three elements: language, religion, and history. See Chebel, *La Formation de l'identité politique,* passim.

6. "Le problème dans 'le cinéma maghrébin' est aussi l'adjectif. Il suppose acquise une identité que ce cinéma n'a pas (encore), l'adjectif, comme le substantif dont il dérive désignent moins une réalité qu'ils n'expriment un souhait. Maghreb, au sens littéral, recouvre le mot arabe ainsi translitéré: l'Occident (du monde arabe). En réalité, le Maghreb est construit sur le déni de l'expression coloniale 'Afrique du Nord'. Le Nord (de l'Afrique) devint l'Occident (du monde arabe) et, revanche soft de l'histoire, ce qui a appartenu au tiers-monde fait désormais partie du Sud. Cet embarras sémantique en dit long sur la situation. La force frénétique de la revendication de l'arabité souligne a contrario l'influence de la culture française et plus généralement occidentale. Elle ne l'efface pas" (Chikhaoui, "Maghreb: de l'épopée au regard intime," 25).

7. "En cherchant à créer un cinéma maghrébin, on cherchait à préserver les pays du Maghreb de l'influence du nationalisme arabo-musulman à visée indépendantiste" (Benali, *Le Cinéma colonial du Maghreb,* 337).

8. Woodhull, "Postcolonial Thought and Culture in Francophone North Africa," 213.

9. Camps, *Des Rives de la Méditerranée aux marges méridionales du Sahara,* 62.

10. These languages are numerous, for instance: Tachelhit or Chleuh, Tamazight, and Tarifit in Morocco; Kvayelith or Kabyle, Chenoui, Chaouï in

Algeria; Chelha in Tunisia; Tuareg across the Sahara across national borders.

11. Stora, "Constantine, la Jérusalem du Maghreb."

12. For instance, the Jewish population in Tunisia decreased from 100,000 at the beginning of the 20th century to 2,000 in 2005. See Ridha Kéfi, "Au Pays du dialogue interreligieux," *Jeune Afrique,* June 4th, 2005.

13. In her film, *La Petite Jérusalem/Little Jerusalem* (France, 2005), the character of the Tunisian Jewish mother is seen fumigating her daughter's bed, then hiding a Hamza under it in order to deliver Laura from a hex.

14. Caillé, "Le Maroc, l'Algérie et la Tunisie des réalisatrices ou la construction du Maghreb dans un contexte postcolonial," 271.

15. Shohat, *Taboo Memories,* 291.

16. Other women filmmakers produced documentaries early on, notably Sophie Ferchiou and Nejia Ben Mabrouk in Tunisia. See Primary Filmography (appendix B).

17. Armes, *Postcolonial Images,* 179–180.

18. Ibid., 55–56.

19. See Martin, "Tunisia," 214–217.

20. See Armes, *African Filmmaking North and South of the Sahara,* 56–57.

21. The big (and complicating) cofunder of Maghrebi cinema has remained France, through its self-serving Francophonie union. As Armes describes it, France used to back African films (of which Maghrebi films were a subset) if the latter catered to a French, then a European, vision of what an African film should look like. However, the whole scheme of funding has evolved over the years, and although there still is a sizable amount of money flowing north to south irrigating film production in the Maghreb, the institutions and the structure of the commissions that review screenplays to be funded

have changed significantly over the past fifteen years or so and seem more nuanced in their approach. Armes, *African Filmmaking,* 56–57.

22. This debate was recently revived along gender lines at the Cinémas du Maghreb Colloquium in St. Denis, France (April 2010), when Nadia El Fani and Amal Bedjaoui denounced the French and European Aid Commissions as wanting to see "more hammams, more Arabic folklore" and "less Maghrebi faces" while Abdellatif Ben Ammar talked about "the dramatic quality of the scenario."

23. See the "Save Cinemas in Morocco" website: http://www.savecinemas inmarocco.com/actualite-du-cinema-marocain/actions-de-sensibilisation/il-etait-une-fois-les-cinemas-au-maroc/.

24. Hammadi Gueroum, roundtable "L'État des lieux du cinema maghrébin depuis les indépendances," at Cinema in the Maghreb AIMS conference, Tunis. May 2008.

25. Our corpus excludes Yamina Benguigui, for instance, born in France from Algerian immigrant parents, who is viewed not as a diasporic director but as French (she also finances her films in France).

26. Although, abroad, it is sometimes further complicated by the outlier positions of some directors of Maghrebi descent in Europe, whose gaze remains firmly fixed on their community of origin, such as French directors Yamina Benguigui and Karin Albou, for instance. Yamina Benguigui directed: *Aïcha* (TV film, 90 min, 2009); *Changer de regard – Portrait No 5*/Changing Perspectives – Portrait No 5 (documentary, 3 min, 2007); *Les Défricheurs* (documentary, 104 min, 2006); *Le Plafond de verre*/The Glass Ceiling (documentary, 52 min, 2004); *Aïcha, Mohamed, Chaïb . . . Engagés pour la France*/Aïcha, Mohamed, Chaïb . . . French Recruits (documentary, 52 min, 2003), *Inch 'allah Dimanche/Inch'Allah Sunday* (98

min, 2001); *Pimprenelle* in *Pas d'histoires!/ Don't Make Trouble!* (4.20 min, 2001); *Le Jardin parfumé/*The Perfumed Garden (documentary, 52 min, 2000); *Mémoires d'immigrés, l'héritage maghrébin/ Immigrant Memories* (documentary, 160 min, 1997); *Femmes d'Islam/*Women in Islam (documentary, 160 min, 1994).

Karin Albou directed: *Corps de Dame/* Lady's Body (3 min, 2009); *Le Chant des mariées/ The Wedding Song* (130 min, 2007); *La Petite Jérusalem/Little Jerusalem* (96 min, 2004); *Aïd el kebir/*The Feast (36 min, 1999).

27. See Moura, "La Francophonie littéraire."

28. Shohat and Stam, *Multiculturalism, Postcoloniality, and Transnational Media,* 14.

29. Ibid., 15.

30. See Bhabha, *The Location of Culture,* 4.

31. Foucault, "Discourse on Language," 216–237.

32. Novak, "Speciation, Transvergence, Allogenesis," 66.

33. Rosa María Rodríguez Magda, *El Modelo Frankenstein* (Madrid: Tecnos, 1997), 82. Translation on: http://transmodern-theory.blogspot.com/.

34. Higbee and Lim, "Concepts of Transnational Cinema," 10.

35. Lazreg, *The Eloquence of Silence,* 12.

36. Kaplan et al., *Between Woman and Nation,* 7.

37. Shohat, *Taboo Memories,* 298.

38. Anderson, *Imagined Communities.*

39. Mohanty, "Cartographies of Struggle," 4.

40. Schipper, *Imagining Insiders,* 180.

41. *Beyond Borders: Arab Feminists Talk about Their Lives East and West,* a documentary made by Jennifer Kanawa (Canada, 1999), follows a group of Arab feminists on a tour of North America four years after the end of the (first) Gulf War. We hear about the various difficulties they meet in Algeria (in the middle of its terror

years), Jordan, Sudan, Egypt, Lebanon, Syria, Morocco, etc. They all speak Arabic, some French, others English. They compare notes among themselves and open up dialogue with women from the North, allowing for wide-ranging multicultural exchanges by and for women.

42. Naficy, *An Accented Cinema,* 19.

43. This point raised by Naficy is debatable: if Hollywood is not meant to officially defend an ideology, at the very least it endorses a legalistic, consumerist, capitalistic "American way of life" steeped in Judeo-Christian morals.

44. Naficy, *An Accented Cinema,* 23.

45. Ibid., 25.

46. "The inscription of these visual and vocal accents transforms the act of spectatorship, from just watching to watching *and* literally reading the screen." Ibid., 25.

47. Tarr, *Reframing Difference,* 190.

48. Higbee and Lim, "Concepts of Transnational Cinema," 13.

49. "La culture est aussi une possibilité qu'a un individu ou un groupe d'individus de créer, de juger, de critiquer, de penser et de communiquer. La transculturalité récupère l'aspect critique de toute culture pour en déterminer à la fois d'une façon transversale et transcendante ce qui peut être universel et constituer par là un corpus critique et toujours renouvelable de valeurs communes à toute l'humanité. . . . Les cultures ne dialoguent pas et il est inutile de trouver un ordre dialogique entre les cultures. Il y a plutôt une 'rencontre' des cultures, rencontre qui peut se faire dans l'ordre de l'hospitalité, de l'étrangeté et de l'extériorité, mais aussi, dans l'ordre de l'hostilité et du désir de 'consommation' et de destruction" (Triki, "Transculturalité et convivialité").

50. See volume 7, no. 1, 2007.

51. Marcos Novak, describing his work, in *The World Technology Network,* http://www.wtn.net/2004/bio212.html.

52. Deleuze and Guattari use the concept of rhizome in opposition to the vertical, hierarchical structure of a tree. Once deployed, the notion of rhizome indicates a system of multiple connection points, absence of hierarchy, flexibility: "Unlike the graphic arts, drawing or photography, unlike tracings, the rhizome pertains to a map that must be produced, constructed, a map that is always detachable, connectable, reversible, modifiable, and has multiple entranceways and exits and its own lines of flight" (Deleuze and Guattari, *A Thousand Plateaus*, 21.

53. Higbee, "Beyond the (trans-)national," 87.

54. Novak, "Speciation, Transvergence, Allogenesis," 66.

55. Martin, "Transvergence and Cultural Detours," 127.

56. See Novak, "Trans Terra Form."

57. Braudel, *Les Mémoires de la Méditerranée*.

58. Cf. El Haggar, *La Méditerranée des femmes*.

59. Ovid. 1925. *Metamorphoses*. Trans. Frank Justus Miller. London & New York: Putnam: 151.

60.

Hic stupet, utque aciem partes dimittit in omnis,
Voce "veni!" Magna clamat: vocat illa vocantem.
Respicit et rursus nullo veniente "quid" inquit
"Me fugis?" et totidiem, quot dixit, verba recepit.
Perstat et alternae deceptus imagine vocis
"huc coeamus" ait, nullique lientius umquam
Responsura sono "coeamus" rettulit Echo.

Ibid. (*Metamorphoses*, Book III): 150–151.

61.

Vox tantumque atque ossa supersunt:
Vox manet, ossa ferunt lapidis traxisse figuram.
Inde latet silvis nulloque in monte videtur,
Omnibus auditur ; sonus est qui vivit in illa.

Ibid. (Book III, l. 399–401): 152–153.

62. Spivak, "Can the Subaltern Speak?" 271–313.

63. Omri, *Nationalism, Islam and World Literature*, 65.

64. The receptive sultan, although quite narcissistic, is, nevertheless, antithetical to the solipsistic Narcissus, who wants no distraction from his own reflection.

65. Gates, *The Signifying Monkey*.

66. Burton, *The Arabian Nights*, 22.

67. As Tunisian filmmaker Nouri Bouzid states, "The power of cinema lies in its ability to convey at once what is on-screen and what is off-screen" (Bouzid and Barlet, "La Leçon de cinéma de Nouri Bouzid").

68. Mernissi, *Woman's Rebellion and Islamic Memory*, 156.

69. Shafik, *Arab Cinema*, 67.

70. "Celles représentant des êtres vivants ayant un souffle vital (*rûh*), donc les êtres humains et les animaux" (Naef, *Y a-t-il une "question de l'image" en Islam?* 13).

71. Bouhdiba, *La Sexualité en Islam*, 255.

72. "La protestation politique s'est glissée en Tunisie derrière le personnage qui dans des représentations mémorables s'est attaqué au buste de la belle Marianne et à une carte de géographie stylisée représentant la France. René Millet, résident général de France en Tunisie à l'époque, l'interdit. Mais Karakouz vit encore et prospère en Orient" (ibid.).

73. "The preponderance of Europeans among Karagöz' victims suggests that the performances conveyed a political message, which at times became a thorn in the ruler's flesh. In Algeria in 1843, the French authorities banned the native shadow plays for being subversive; they were thus condemned to extinction." Shafik, *Arab Cinema*, 76.

74. Dönmez-Colin, *The Cinema of North Africa and the Middle East*, 5.

75. See Fanon, "Chapitre I: L'Algérie se dévoile," in *L'an V de la révolution algérienne*.

76. "Le vêtement, loin de remplir sa fonction sociale de 'pudeur', exacerbe les rapports entre ce qu'il masque, le corps, et le voyeur. Le 'pudique', ou ce qui se donne comme tel dans le vêtement, crée donc son 'public' et le vêtement se nourrit de son propre dépassement : l'érotisme" (Chebel, Malek, *L'Esprit de Sérail*, 148).

77. "Tout le paradoxe du voile tient à cette impossibilité principale de nier une érogénéité qu'il installe admirablement. 'Installer' est même trop faible et apte à rendre compte de cette véritable 'offre contrariée' qui est le propre de la séduction au Maghreb" (ibid., 155).

78. "Le voile est à considérer comme ce vêtement dont l'objectif essentiel est d'empêcher que la femme ne soit vue et, simultanément, de lui donner, à elle, la possibilité de regarder les autres" (ibid., 154).

79. "Il n'est donc pas étonnant que le personnage de l'aveugle ait alimenté d'une façon significative la mythologie amoureuse des anciens Arabes. L'aveugle est tantôt musicien, tantôt messager, puisqu'il se charge souvent de la transmission du verbe de l'amant à son amante" (ibid., 155–156). It comes as no surprise, then, that the character of the blind man fed the amorous mythology of ancient Arabs so significantly. The blind man is either a musician or a messenger, since he is in charge of transmitting words from the lover to his beloved.

80. In that, it resembles the paradoxical position of epistolary literature that is written within the private sphere and then finds itself published, an object of consumption for the public.

81. Marks, *The Skin of the Film*, 129.

82. See, for instance: Hochberg, "National Allegories and the Emergence of Female Voice in Moufida Tlatli's *Les Silences du palais*"; Mulvey, "Moving Bodies"; Sherzer, "Remembrance of Things Past"; Gauch, *Liberating Shahrazad*.

1. ASSIA DJEBAR'S TRANSVERGENT *NUBA*

1. The famous Senegalese director Ousmane Sembène was a novelist before he started shooting films. At first he wrote novels and novellas in French. Then he decided to reach a wider audience at home and turned to film at age forty. He also adapted some of his earlier work published in French to the screen (e.g., *Le mandat* published in French in 1965, and turned into *Manda bi/Le mandat*, a film in Wolof in 1968), and later still, shot films in Wolof first before he wrote their French literary adaptations (e.g., *Guelwaar*, the film, in 1992; and *Guelwaar*, the novel in French, Paris: Présence Africaine, 1996).

2. "Fin des années 70 dans les villes d'Algérie, dans les salles obscures, c'était un public presque exclusivement masculin. Or, les femmes de tous âges, de tous niveaux regardaient en majorité la télévision. Ainsi *La Nouba des Femmes du Mont Chénoua* fut une production de la télévision algérienne, originellement – alors qu'en fait, il mérite surtout d'être vu sur grand écran." Salhi, "Assia Djebar Speaking," 177.

3. "Le film est diffusé une seule fois dans l'émission 'Téléciné Club' que je produisais alors. . . . Le lendemain, la presse (militante autoproclamée) et les milieux spécialisés autour de l'Alhambra persiflaient et se moquaient. Peu de temps après, je montrais le film à Carlo Lizzani, grand cinéaste du néoréalisme italien et nouveau président du Festival de Venise. Enthousiaste, il sélectionne l'œuvre qui, en septembre 1979, remporte le prix de la critique, en réalité le

seul décerné cette année-là par les journalistes. Dans la salle, enfin, un public italien sublime et artiste jusqu'au bout des ongles." [The film was broadcast once only in the program 'Téléciné Club' that I was producing at the time.... The next day, the (self-proclaimed militant) press and the inner circles around the Alhambra were deriding and mocking the film. Shortly thereafter, I showed the film to Carlo Lizzari, the great director of Italian neo-realism and new president of the Venice Festival. He was so enthusiastic he selected the piece and, in September 1979, the film was awarded the Critics' prize, which, that year, was the only prize given out by journalists. In the theatre, it finally found a thoroughly artistically minded, sublime, Italian public.] Bedjaoui, "Assia Djebar, l'immortelle."

4. "Comme toi je ne peux rien voir, ni le bourreau, ni le martyr. Seulement le ciel et le pourpre de l'aube. Une aube rouge au-dessus du sang de mon frère." Quoted in Cheniki, "Théâtre algérien, Itinéraires et tendances."

5. Aresu, "(D)écrire, entendre l'écran," 216.

6. See Donadey, *Recasting Postcolonialism,* chapter 3, 43–62.

7. Djebar is quoted by Zimra at the end of a session on *The Nuba* as saying: "La narration ne doit pas raconter l'histoire mais l'interrompre: c'est-à-dire, la suspendre, la surprendre à tout prix" (Zimra, "Sounding off the Absent Body," 108).

8. See Khannous, "The Subaltern Speaks."

9. "Il ne suffit pas de faire des films ou d'écrire des livres pour évacuer les passages douloureux de l'Histoire: c'est plus compliqué que cela. Le problème de tous les films qui ont été réalisés depuis la fin de la guerre d'Algérie, c'est qu'ils ont été faits pour des publics qui ne se mélangent jamais. On peut voir des films pour les pieds-noirs, des films pour les Algériens, ou pour les Harkis. Mais il n'y a pas de vision d'ensemble. De ce fait, les mémoires ne se mélangent pas: quand on réalise un film, c'est un film pour soi-même ou sa propre 'communauté'. Cela crée un perpétuel sentiment d'absence, qui vient du fait de la non-rencontre des mémoires." [One cannot simply make films or write books to evacuate the painful passages of History: it is far more complicated. The problem with all the films that have been produced since the end of the Algerian war, is that they were made for audiences that would never mix. One can see films for *pieds-noirs,* films for the Algerian, or for Harkis. But there is never an overview. As a result, memories do not mix: people make films for themselves or their communities. This creates a perpetual feeling of absence, due to the non-meeting of memories.] Stora, *La Gangrène et l'oubli,* 252.

10. Harkis (from *harka* حركة: "war party") were Algerian natives enrolled by the French army as auxiliaries during the war. They are doubly victimized: Algeria considered them traitors, collaborationists after the war, and France has not treated them as veterans. Some of the Harki families were "repatriated" to France, lodged in camps for a long time, and could not mix with other immigrant groups. Often, according to Fatima Benasci-Lancou (*Fille de Harki/Daughter of a Harki*), families in Algeria would send one or more sons to the FLN and one or more sons to become Harkis, so the family would survive, no matter what the outcome of the war would be.

11. "It is a strategy especially embraced by women writers, for whom self-portraiture (the autobiographical genre) is transformed into a piecing together of a collective history. In a context in which one's history has been written by the hegemonic dominant, anamnesis becomes a

way of resisting the occlusions created by official history, of recovering the traces of another, submerged history in order to create a countermemory" (Donadey, "Between Amnesia and Anamnesis," 111–112).

12. She drives a Mehari (the Citroën off-roader in the 1970s). "Mehari" is also the name of the Northern African dromedary of yore.

13. Benidir, *Inititaion à la musique arabo-musulmane,* 80.

14. Bensmaïa,"La Nouba des femmes du Mont Chenoua," 162.

15. Some of the collected Algerian folk music material inspired the second movement of his String Quartet No. 2, composed in 1917.

16. Salhi, "Assia Djebar Speaking," 177.

17. Béla Bartók, "The Influence of Peasant Music on Modern Music" (1931), in *Béla Bartók Essays,* ed. Benjamin Suchoff (London: Faber & Faber, 1976), 344.

18. Malkmus and Armes, *Arab and African Filmmaking,* 141.

19. "Ces noubas existent, comme culture collective, depuis quatre siècles ... C'est un film sur la campagne, or la nouba est une forme citadine, c'est une ancienne musique de cour! A l'intérieur du film, j'ai utilisé des musiques très diverses. Autant au niveau de l'image, c'est un film régionaliste, autant sur le plan du son, il y a des morceaux de toutes les campagnes d'Algérie. Il y a eu volonté d'alterner, de rapprocher. Il y a de la flûte de la région de Sétif, de la musique touareg, qui était utilisées pour les choses anciennes. J'ai essayé d'avoir une bande-son qui illustre la réalité sonore algérienne, à la fois dans le passé et dans l'espace." Ben Salama, Léon, and Martineau."J'ai recherché un langage musical," 107.

20. "Dans une époque où l'Algérie était complètement cernée, les gens isolés dans des coins perdus exprimaient leur désarroi par un son de flûte" (ibid., 109).

21. "Contrairement à ce à quoi on pourrait s'attendre, bien qu'il y ait autant de morceaux musicaux que de séries narratives ou documentaires, il n'existe ici aussi aucune correspondance terme à terme entre telle série narrative ou documentaire et telle série musicale. La musique ne suit pas l'image, elle ne 'l'illustre' pas. ... Ainsi, contrairement à ce à quoi on pourrait s'attendre, la musique ne vient pas suppléer le manque de continuité et la dissémination des unités visuelles et dramatiques." [Unlike what one could expect, although there are as many musical pieces as narrative or documentary series, there is no exact correspondence between this narrative or documentary series and that musical series. The music does not imitate the picture, it does not "illustrate" it. .... Hence, unlike what one could expect, the music does not fill the lack of continuity nor complement the dissemination of visual and dramatic units.] Ibid., 173.

22. Ibid., 200.

23. Novak, "Speciation, Transvergence, Allogenesis," 67.

24. See Niang, *Littérature et cinéma en Afrique francophone.*

25. "Quand la présence acousmatique est celle d'une voix, et surtout quand cette voix n'a pas été visualisée – quand on ne peut mettre encore sur elle un visage, on a donc un être d'une espèce particulière, sorte d'ombre parlante et agissante à laquelle nous donnons le nom d'acousmêtre, c'est-à-dire acousmatique." [When the acousmatic presence is the one of a voice, and above all when this voice has not been visually located – when you cannot put a face on it, then we are faced with a being of a particular kind, a kind of talking and acting shadow to which we give the name of *acousmêtre,* i.e., acousmatic.] Chion, *La Voix au cinéma,* 32.

26. Zimra, "Sounding off the Absent Body," 112.

27. Lazreg, *The Eloquence of Silence*, 172.

28. Calle-Gruber, *Assia Djebar ou la résistance de l'écriture*, 214–215.

29. "Ici, on a fini de (se) raconter des histoires pour commencer à écrire un peu de notre historie compliquée. On est passé du monde clos du conte à l'univers fragmentaire et ouvert de l'Histoire." Bensmaïa, "Une rhétorique trop souvent codée," 61.

30. This is a recurring theme in narratives by *mujahidat*. Djamila Boupacha volunteers the following information: "Men and women in the movement can share a room without molesting each other in any way. We have a private tribunal of our own for dealing with those who fail to respect this rule." Halimi, *Djamila Boupacha*, 54.

31. "Dans cet espace très habituellement unaire, parfois (mais, hélas, rarement) un 'détail' m'attire. Je sens que sa seule présence change ma lecture, que c'est une nouvelle photo que je regarde, marquée à mes yeux d'une valeur supérieure. Ce 'détail' est le *punctum* (ce qui me point)." [In the most often unary space of the photograph, sometimes (but, alas, rarely so), I am attracted by one 'detail.' I feel that its mere presence changes my viewing, that what I am looking at is a new photo, endowed to my eyes with a superior value. This 'detail' is the *punctum* (that which points in me).] Barthes, *La Chambre claire*, 71.

32. Bensmaïa, "Une rhétorique trop souvent codée," 172.

33. Martin, "History 'Re-lit.'"

34. Ramanathan, *Feminist Auteurs*, 99.

2. FARIDA BENLYAZID'S INITIATION NARRATIVE

1. "C'est notamment moi qui ai écrit 'Une Porte dur le ciel' qui, tout en n'étant pas autobiographique, s'inspire de ma quête spirituelle. Cette expérience a été une grande aventure." Farida Benlyazid, interview, *Citadine*, April 1999, 37.

2. The film was selected in the following festivals: Los Angeles and Washington, D.C. (United States), Montreal (Canada), Rimini and Bologna (Italy), Alexandria (Egypt), Valencia (Spain), Tunis (Tunisia), Angers (France). It was broadcast on Maghrebi T V channels – 2M International (Morocco) and Canal Horizon (Tunisia) – and on European channels – R F O (Radio France Outremer), C F I (Canal France International), T V 5 International (France), and Z D F (Zweites Deutsches Fernsehen, Germany).

3. Benlyazid, "Le Cinéma au féminin," 224.

4. "On entendait du flamenco, à Noël les Espagnols sortaient et tout le monde faisait la fête. A Pourim les enfants juifs se promenaient dans les maisons et offraient des gateaux. A l'école, on avait des fêtes musulmanes, chrétiennes et pour les fêtes israélites il était permis de s'absenter. C'est cette identité multiple, ces différentes religions voisinant dans la convivialité que j'aimerais retrouver dans le monde maintenant." Farida Benlyazid, quoted in Hamid Aïdouni, "L'œuvre au feminine, éloge au cinéma," in Benlyazid et al., *L'Oeuvre Cinématographique de Farida Belyazid*, 28.

5. Ibid., 222.

6. Ibid.

7. Smail Salhi, "Maghrebi Women Filmmakers and the Challenge of Modernity," 67.

8. Lamrini, *Les Puissants de Casablanca*.

9. "Keid Ensa qui veut dire en arabe 'la ruse des femmes' est un conte d'origine andalouse dont on retrouve la trace dans le théâtre de marionettes de Federico Garcia Lorca" Farida Benlyazid, *"Keid Ensa*: Note of intent," in Keid Ensa Press Dossier, 1999.

10. Vázquez, *La vida perra de Juanita Narboni.*

11. Quoted in Simarski, "North African Film through North African Eyes," 1–2.

12. See Bouchta Farqzaid, "Codes et cinéma dans 'Une porte sur le ciel,'" in Benlyazid et al., *L'Oeuvre Cinématographique de Farida Belyazid,* 17.

13. Jacquemond, *Conscience of the Nation,* 185.

14. This chapter expands on an earlier work of mine. See Martin, *"Bab al-Sama Maftouh."*

15. Deeb, *An Enchanted Modern,* 70.

16. "Des érudits comme Iqbal reprennent, au début du siècle, le même thème et sont d'avis que les générations actuelles ont non seulement le droit mais le devoir d'exercer l'ijtihad ou le jugement indépendant, si elles veulent que l'islam soit adapté au monde moderne." [Scholars like Iqbal take up the same theme again at the beginning of the century and think that today's generations have the right as well as the duty to pursue itjihad or independent critical thinking, if they want to adapt Islam to the modern world.] Azadeh Niknam, "Le statut de la chariah en Iran: de l'islamisme au postislamisme," *Esprit,* August 2001, http://www.esprit.presse.fr/archive/review/article.php?code=9054.

17. De Franceschi, "Entre la maison et la ville, la lutte pour l'espace social," 63.

18. "Je me suis réfugiée dans l'atelier de ma mère pour t'écrire. Mon père est mort et je n'ai même pas pleuré. Je me sens étrangère. Tu me manques. Tout est si absurde. J'ai la tête qui vacille. Je me sens coupable: pourquoi? De quoi? Je bois et cela ne me fait aucun effet."

19. See Martin, *"Bab al-Sama Maftouh,"* 128.

20. Fischer, *Cinematernity,* 30.

21. Ibid., 224.

22. See Bourget, "Traditions orales et littéraires dans Une Porte sur le ciel de Farida Benlyazid," 755.

23. Benlyazid, "The Gate of Heaven Is Open," 298.

24. Renard, *Seven Doors to Islam: Spirituality and the Religious Life of Muslims,* 54.

25. Ibid., 160–161.

26. See Martin, *"Bab al-Sama Maftouh,"* 126.

27. Novak, "Speciation, Transvergence, Allogenesis," 67.

28. Karl Marx, "Introduction to A Contribution to the Critique of Hegel's Philosophy of Right," in *Marx's Critique of Hegel's Philosophy of Right,* ed. Joseph O'Malley (Cambridge: Cambridge University Press, 1970), i. [First published in *Deutsch-Französische Jahrbücher* (Paris, February 1844).]

29. Martin, *"Bab al-Sama Maftouh,"* 126–127.

30. Ibn 'Arabî, "Shaykh al-Akbar Sidi Muhyiddin Ibn Arabi al-'Hatimi al-Andalusi (d. 636/1221)," http://www.dar-sirr.com/Ibn-Arabi.html.

31. Ibn 'Arabî, excerpt from "The One Alone," http://www.nonduality.com/ibn.htm.

3. YAMINA BACHIR-CHOUIKH'S TRANSVERGENT ECHOES

1. Armes, *Postcolonial Images,* 55.

2. Ibid., 56.

3. Hillauer, *Encyclopedia of Arab Women Filmmakers,* 264.

4. "Après 1992, le cinéma algérien affronte directement un double péril: le marteau islamiste, qui pèse de tout son poids par le chantage au scénario, les menaces et les intimidations sur les comédiens et les techniciens, les tentatives d'assassinat sur les cinéastes (Djamel Fezzaz est grièvement blessé le 6 février 1995); et l'enclume étatique, des gouvernements qui ne favorisent pas la diffusion de films qui leur déplaisent pendant les années infernales" (Stora, *La Guerre invisible,* 88).

5. Merzak Allouache directed, among other successful films: *Omar Gatlato*

(1976), *A Love in Paris* (1987), *Bab El Oued City* (1994), *Chouchou* (2003), *Harragas* (2009).

6. Yamina Bachir-Chouikh, interviewed by Christophe Carrière, "Pour l'honneur de l'Algérie," *L'Express*, January 2, 2003.

7. "C'est néanmoins un événement: la chaîne nationale passe la bande-annonce à longueur de journée, tous les murs d'Alger sont couverts d'affiches" (ibid.).

8. "Lors de la première projection à Alger, le 20 décembre (La Croix du 31 décembre 2002), une partie des spectateurs ont pleuré. Plusieurs ont retrouvé des moments de vie qui furent leurs – notamment les scènes de funérailles" (Méreuze, "Chronique algérienne des années de peur").

9. Yamina Bachir-Chouikh, interview, http://www.diplomatie.france.gouv .fr/fr/actions-france_830/cinema_886

10. See Stora, *La Guerre invisible.*

11. Ibid., 115.

12. Ibid., 84–92. He discusses six films, three French and three Algerian. The French films are: Dominique Cabrera's *L'autre côté de la mer* (1996), Rachida Krim's *Sous les pieds des femmes* (1997), and Alexandre Arcady's *Là-bas, mon pays* (2000); the Algerian ones are Merzak Allouache's *Bab El Oued City* (1994), Hafsa Zinaï Koudil's *Le démon au féminin* (1995), and Abderrahmane Bouguermouh's *La Colline oubliée* (1997).

13. Hadj-Moussa, "Marginality and Ordinary Memory," 189.

14. Novak, "Speciation, Transvergence, Allogenesis," 67.

15. Ibid., 68.

16. "Lorsque j'ai commencé à écrire, j'ai pensé images, mouvements, bande-son. Et je me disais que, sans montrer forcément l'état de siège et la terreur, je pouvais les suggérer par des bruits: les ambulances, les rafales de balles . . ." (Charpentier, "'Dire la violence, toutes les violences'").

17. For instance:

"*Rachida* est un hommage à toutes ces victimes sans visage. Je voulais raconter le désarroi des citoyens ordinaires." (*Rachida* is an homage to all these faceless victims. I wanted to tell the hopelessness of ordinary citizens.) Leclère, "Elle filme la peur."

"Images showing the situation in Algeria were rare, and even those that existed were never shown. Victims did not have a name or a face." Yamina Bachir-Chouikh, interview, Paris, October 2002, trans. Anna Bernstein (New York City, March 2004), Global Film Initiative DVD bonus (with *Rachida*).

"There were Algerians dying, and they had no faces. I wanted to talk about the human dimension of this violence and give it a face." Quoted in Ganley, "Algerians Transform Nation's Agony into Art," E16.

18. "For me the physical resemblance of the person that we choose is more important, than their ability or cleverness. Of course, if I find an actor that is very good and resembles what we want, I am happy. However, I prefer losing hour after hour, because with a non-professional you do lose a lot of time, if he has the right face. For me it is like a painter who has to have the right imagined colors. This is decisive. So in preparing for *The Battle for Algiers* we went around Italy and France until we found the faces that corresponded to those we were after." Gillo Pontecorvo, "Stay Close to Reality," interview by Maria Esposito, June 9, 2004, *World Socialist Web Site*, http://www.wsws.org/ articles/2004/jun2004/pont-j09.shtml.

19. Hillauer, *Encyclopedia of Arab Women Filmmakers*, 278.

20. See Djebar, *Oran, langue morte,* and *The Tongue's Blood Never Runs Dry.*

21. Martin, "History 'Re-lit.'"

22. Djebar, *The Tongue's Blood Never Runs Dry*, 112.

23. Ibid., 113.

24. Ibid., 117.

25. Ibid., 121.

26. Ibid., 122.

27. Ibid., 123.

28. Ibid., 124.

29. Ibid., 124.

30. Ibid., 125.

31. Ibid., 100.

32. Hadj-Moussa, "Marginality and Ordinary Memory,"195.

33. "The film makes us want the women to complete their task, if not out of conscious political sympathy, then through the specific protocols of cinematic identification: scale (close-up shots individualize the women); off-screen sound (the sexist comments of the French soldiers heard as if from the women's aural perspective); and especially point-of-view editing. By the time the women plant the bombs, spectatorial identification is so complete that it is not derailed even by close shots of the bombers' potential victims." Stam, "Fanon, Algeria, and the Cinema," 29.

34. Bachir-Chouikh, interviewed by Patrick Simonin, *L'Invité*, TV5, January 10, 2003.

35. See Patricia Geesey's article on the writings of Algerian women at that time, "Violent Days: Algerian Women Writers and the Civil Crisis."

36. "Il fallait, à un moment donné, se regarder et donner l'image de soi qui n'est pas l'image qu'on donne de nous ... J'avais envie de me regarder et de donner l'image de nous-mêmes, parce qu'on est toujours raconté par les autres, dit par les autres. Et nous mêmes, on a peur des miroirs" (ibid.).

37. Fanon, "Algeria Unveiled."

38. Mohamed Harbi quoted in Stam, "Fanon, Algeria and the Cinema," 31.

39. "Tout est dans les voiles, pour moi, dans ce film: les voiles qui séparent l'intérieur de l'extérieur ou les hommes des femmes pendant la cérémonie du mariage. Et ces étoffes sont tour à tour symboles de bonheur, d'interdit ou de deuil. Cela ne se discerne pas forcément, mais cela fait partie de mon regard, de ma culture" (Charpentier, "'Dire la violence, toutes les violences'").

40. "Dans cette scène où les femmes enlèvent leurs foulards pour en recouvrir la jeune fille violée, il y a comme un défi aux intégristes, ceux-là mêmes qui leur défendent de montrer leur chevelure et qui ont enlevé et violé la jeune fille. Les voiles dont elles la recouvrent ont les couleurs de la vie, c'est comme si elles la protégeaient, en la transformant en un petit jardin" (ibid.).

41. See Hadj-Moussa, *Le Corps, l'histoire, le territoire*, ch. 10.

42. See Barthes, "L'Effet de réel."

4. RAJA AMARI'S SCREEN OF THE HAPTIC

1. Burton, *The Arabian Nights*, 726.

2. FEMIS stands for Fédération Européenne pour les Métiers de l'Image et du Son (European Federation for Audio and Visual Professions). Its administrative name, however, is École Nationale Supérieure des Métiers de l'Image et du Son, since it follows the highly selective format of the French Grandes Écoles.

3. *Cinécrits* is published in Tunis under the aegis of the ATPCC (Association tunisienne pour la promotion de la critique cinématographique), with an editorial board composed of academics (in French literature and cinema) including Tahar Chikhaoui, professor and cinema critic in Tunis.

4. *Avril* was awarded the following:

Winner Special Jury Prize – Milan Film Festival

Winner Special Jury Prize – Tunis Short Films Festival (Tunisia)

Winner Best Cinematography Award – International Short Film Festival, Larissa (Greece)

5. *Mama Africa,* produced by Zimmedia, gathered six 26-minute-long films from as many different directors from the entire continent: Raja Amari (Tunisia), Fanta Regina Nacro (Burkina Faso), Ngozi Onwhura (Nigeria), Zulfah Otto-Sallies (South Africa), Bridget Pickering (Namibia), Ingrid Sinclair (Zimbabwe). It is now available on DVD (Wellspring, 2002).

6. Raja Amari in an interview in the Press dossier for *Les Secrets:* 5.

7. "La sexualité chez elles est reléguée au rang d'une réalité obscène (d'où les secrets, les mystères et les prohibitions jusqu'à l'absurde et le stupide)." Chamkhi, "Films de cinéastes femmes tunisiennes."

8. Ibid.

9. Raja Amari, interviewed by Indiewire, "Self-Empowerment by Way of the Midriff; Raja Amari's *Satin Rouge,*" *Indiewire,* http://www.indiewire.com/article/interview_self-empowerment_by_way_of_the_midriff_raja_amaris_satin_rouge/.

10. Sotinel, "Productrice, réalisatice et actrice face aux préjugés."

11. See Martin, "*Satin Rouge* de Raja Amari," 63.

12. "After using the French actress, Juliette Berto, for the lead in his first feature, Abdellatif Ben Ammar chose an Algerian actress (Dalila Ramès) and a Lebanese actress (Yasmine Khat) for the key roles in his masterpiece, *Aziza.* Similarly, Taïeb Louhichi, after choosing an Italian, Despina Tomazini, to play the Bedouin matriarch in *Shadow of the Earth,* cast a Roumanian actress, Anka Nicolaï, as the dream embodiment of Arab beauty in his adaptation of the classic tale of Leila and Majnun, *Leila My Reason.*" Armes, *African Film-Making North and South of the Sahara,* 177–178.

13. Raja Amari, quoted in Brigitte Baudin, "Raja Amari, la danse libératoire," *Le Figaro,* April 24, 2002.

14. See Martin, "*Satin Rouge* de Raja Amari," 60–61.

15. I am indebted to Susan Hayward for this insight.

16. Silverman, *The Acoustic Mirror,* 27–28.

17. Deleuze and Guattari, *A Thousand Plateaus,* 492.

18. Marks, *Touch,* xvi.

19. See chapter 5, "Clothes, Power and the Modern *Femme Fatale,*" in Bruzzi, *Undressing Cinema.*

20. Marks, *Touch,* 3.

21. Ibid., 13.

22. Ibid., 18.

23. Habib Bourguiba prohibited women from wearing the veil in public spaces on October 11, 1986. However, in October 2007, the law was annulled after a veiled teacher won a lawsuit engaged after she was excluded from her school in Hammam-Lif (in accordance with the law) in 2002.

24. Macleod, *Accommodating Protest.*

25. Novak, "Trans Terra Form."

26. See Rodríguez Magda, "Globalization as Transmodern Totality."

5. NADIA EL FANI'S MULTIPLE SCREENS

This chapter is an adapted, enriched version of my article "Transvergence and Cultural Detours: Nadia El Fani's *Bedwin Hacker* (2002)," *Studies in French Cinema* 7, no. 2 (2007): 119–129.

1. Gabous, *Silence, Elles tournent!* 123.

2. "Ces glissements identitaires sont liés à des facteurs d'histoire et de géographie, mais ils ne sont pas sans rapport avec les transformations du statut même du cinéma, devenu un élément dans un tout cyberculturel. L'errance des personnages, la présence lancinante de la matérialité du monde extérieur, la traversée des frontières sont l'expression de ce mouvement" (Chikhaoui, "Maghreb," 36).

3. "Bedwin Hacker, de Nadia El Fani, 2003, en donne une expression explicite où

se posent de façon frontale la question de la double appartenance et du déplacement dans l'espace, et, sur le mode de la provocation, la nécessité de repenser l'identité de la femme et de la nation à la faveur de la transformation cyberculturelle" (ibid.).

4. See "La saga des sans-papiers," *Libération,* August 23, 2006.

5. Novak, "Speciation, Transvergence, Allogenesis," 65.

6. Freud, "The 'Uncanny'"; Arthur Rimbaud, "Lettre à Georges Izambard" [Letter to Georges Izambard], May 13, 1871, in *Le silence qui parle,* http://lesilence quiparle.unblog.fr/2009/05/12/je-est-un-autre-arthur-rimbaud/; Nietzsche, *Die Götzen-Dämmerung.*

7. Novak, "Speciation, Transvergence, Allogenesis," 66.

8. Deleuze and Guattari, *A Thousand Plateaus,* 95–139.

9. Novak, "Speciation, Transvergence, Allogenesis," 66.

10. "L'idée m'est venue d'une pirate informatique, pour une prise de parole. J'avais envie de dire qu'au Sud de la Méditerranée on trouve des esprits libres. Nos images ne sont pas diffusées au Nord et il en ressort un malentendu terrible qui fait croire aux gens qu'on est des arriérés et qu'on ne vit pas en 2002." Barlet, "A propos de *Bedwin Hacker.*"

11. "Kalt représente la liberté: elle avait le choix de 'devenir quelqu'un' dans cette société française mais a préféré une société où elle n'est pas libre, ce qui est en fait le summum de la liberté. Julia est celle qui essaye de contenir la liberté des autres et Chams est celui qui, comme la plupart des gens, croit qu'il est libre mais se trompe tout le temps." Ibid.

12. "La vocation unificatrice et 'clôturante' de l'identité collective, c'est-à-dire socioculturelle, et son opposition radicale à toute forme de subjectivité et de singularité individuelle." Chamkhi, *Cinéma tunisien nouveau,* 8.

13. Mernissi, *Women's Rebellion and Islamic Memory,* 16.

14. "Ce que tu appelles *'métissage,'* je préfère l'appeler *'synthèse.'* C'est la synthèse qui consiste à dire qu'après tout, nous avons une culture populaire qui est d'une richesse inouïe et qui était, curieusement, très cohérente avant l'indépendance. Grâce à cet acquis, je peux, en tant que cinéphile, arriver à voler à l'Ociddent sa modernité dans le cinéma et arriver à donner au citoyen tunisien un miroir aimable de lui-même et de sa propre culture. Une Tunisie bonne à aimer, mais pas une Tunisie simpliste, caricaturale, crédule, ou folklorique." Khelil, *Le Parcours et la trace,* 145.

6. YASMINE KASSARI'S "BURNING" SCREENS

1. The slang term *brûler* (burning) has been explained to me in two ways: (1) it is what drivers do when they go through a red light (*brûler un feu rouge*), thus going forth when the law says not to do so; (2) it refers to the documents that are burnt or disposed of before the migrants leave, so as not to be forced back to their original country if they are arrested on their way to or in Europe.

2. "Bouchara Khalili is a Franco-Moroccan artist. She was born in Casablanca in 1975. Her videos explore the Mediterranean space that she sees as a Nomadic territory and a wandering labyrinth. In her videos, she explores the plastic and conceptual relationships which maintain physical, imaginary and mental geography. Her work attempts to disturb the limits between cinema and graphics, fiction and documentary, trials and experiments. Her videos have been shown at numerous festivals, exhibitions and biennales. Bouchra Khalili studied cinema at the Sorbonne Nouvelle and has a degree from the Ecole Nationale Supérieure d'Art in Paris-Cergy." "Catalogue," *Rencontres In-*

ternationales, http://www.art-action.org/ proposition/catalogue/detail_cat.php?co deoeuvre=S26782&lang=en&qui=reali& oeuvre=S26782.

Selective filmography for Bouchra Khalili (1975–), Morocco and France:

> *Anya (Des Histoires vraies/Straight Stories – Part II)* (experimental documentary video, 12 min), France, 2008.
> *Des Histoires vraies/Straight Stories – Part I* (experimental video, 10.06 min), Morocco and France, 2006.
> *Napoli Centrale* (experimental fiction video, 8.15 min), France, 2002.

3. "C'était vraiment un coup de tête. . . . Mais je ne connaissais pas le cinéma. . . Il me fallait quelque chose de poétique, et il me fallait aussi quelque chose de concret." Yasmine Kassari, interviewed in *Maroc annonces,* 2005, http://www.marocannonces .com/index.php?page=actualite_cinema& debut=10&numero=37.

4. Ibid.

5. Jean-Jacques Andrien's filmography includes:

> *Le fils d'Amr est mort/Amr's Son Is Dead,* Belgium, 1971, Pardo d'Oro at the Locarno Film Festival.
> *Le Grand Paysage d'Alexis Droeven / Alexis Droeven's Wide Landscape,* Belgium, 1981, First Prize at the Aurillac Film Festival.
> *Mémoires/Memoirs,* Belgium, 1985, International Film Festival, Mannheim-Heidelberg.
> *Australia,* Belgium, 1989, Best Photography Award, Venice Film Festival.

6. "On comprend alors qu'il ne s'agit pas d'un film sur les hommes et d'un autre sur les femmes, mais d'un contexte social, économique et politique qui en fait des otages" (Yasmine Kassari, quoted in Maréchaux, "Portrait").

7. Ibid.

8. "Yasmine y passe plusieurs mois par an, entre Adelaïde et l'outback de terre rouge, où elle vit en immersion avec le groupe aborigène Walpiri. 'J'ai même un nom totémique, Numbijimpa,' dévoile-t-elle, amusée" (ibid.).

9. "Quelques années plus tard, après des repérages dans un village de la tribu Béni Chebel, dans la région Taourirt, pour les décors de L'Enfant endormi, Yasmine revient y passer six mois, avec sa famille et sa directrice de production, dans la même maison que celle de Zeinab, mariée déchue dans le film. 'Pour confronter mon scénario à la réalité', se rappelle-t-elle" (ibid.).

10. See Dwyer, "Moroccan Cinema and the Promotion of Culture," 279–280.

11. Ibid., 279.

12. In that, she reminds us of Palestinian actress Hiam Abbas, who had to learn the inflections and lexicon of Tunisian dialect in order to play the role of Lilia in *Red Satin* (see chapter 5).

13. Maréchaux, "Portrait."

14. "Endormir un bébé consiste à retarder, via le recours à la sorcellerieblanche (ndlr : lotions à ingurgiter et autres talismans portés autour de la taille), l'arrivée d'un enfant quand la mère – ou les deux parents – n'en souhaitent pas la naissance dans l'immédiat. . . . Quand la mère n'est pas prête à avoir un enfant, elle le 'met en hibernation,' se donnant ainsi l'impression de contrôler le moment de la naissance." Jamal Khalil, quoted in Elaji, "Société."

15. Article 154: "La filiation paternelle de l'enfant est établie par les rapports conjugaux (Al Firach): 1) si cet enfant est né au moins dans les six mois qui suivent la date de conclusion du mariage et à condition que la possibilité de rapports conjugaux entre les époux soit plausible, que l'acte de mariage soit valide ou vicié; 2) si l'enfant est né durant l'année qui suit la date de la séparation." (The paternal affiliation of the child is established by marital intercourse [*Al Firach*]: 1) if the child is born at least within 6 months following the consummation of the marriage and

under the condition that the possibility of marital intercourse between spouses is plausible, whether the marriage contract be valid or not; 2) if the child is born during the year that follows the date of separation.) http://www.justice.gov.ma/MOUDAWANA/Codefamille.pdf.

16. Amal Chabach, quoted in Elaji, "Société."

17. *Bou mergoud* is the Berber term for the sleeping child, the age-old belief being still active in the Berber regions across Algeria, Morocco, and Tunisia in particular.

18. "A un moment donné du développement de l'embryon, la mère va ressentir les coups donnés par le petit être, dans un univers encore dominé par les eaux amniotiques chaleureuses et nourricières. Si cette manifestation n'apparaît pas rapidement, la mère s'inquiète auprès de ses proches parents ou amies et commence à halluciner ce que la coutume a consacré sous le terme significatif de l'enfant 'endormi' (bou mergoûd). C'est évidemment une hantise qui poursuit toutes les mères. La fantasmatisation autour de cet être silencieux qui ne se réveille pas au désir maternel est abondante. L'utérus refuse de 'plaire.' . . . L'arsenal du thérapeute est dans ces circonstances, le seul recours, la seule voie possible: réveiller le fœtus avant qu'il ne soit trop tard. Pourtant les croyances sont tenaces: de nombreuses femmes vous diront très naïvement que l'enfant endormi peut rester dans le corps maternel pendant plus de deux années, sans souffrir d'aucun trouble et sera gesté au moment où il sera le moins attendu. L'absence du mari pendant une certaine période, excédant la période normale des neuf mois biologiques, peut être secondaire du point de vue de la puissance de la preuve, d'un adultère possible." Chebel, *Le Corps en Islam*, 51–52.

19. "Peu m'importe si l'endormi est un mythe ou une réalité. Il s'agit d'une pratique sociale née de l'adaptation des individus à des réalités souterraines et secrètes qui se sont constituées à travers le temps. Des expériences qui s'accumulent, sédimentent et finissent par se cristalliser en manières culturelles. J'ai voulu que l'endormi agisse dans ce film comme un point lumineux qui éclaire la situation de ces femmes restées seules au pays, face à l'absence de leurs hommes" (Yasmine Kassari, quoted by Olivier Barlet, "*Enfant endormi (L')* Yasmine Kassari").

20. See Orlando, *Francophone Voices of the "New" Morocco in Film and Print*, 194.

21. See Martin, "Silence and Scream."

22. In that she follows the tradition of the *nushuz* described by Fatima Mernissi in *Dreams of Trespass*.

23. Novak, "Trans Terra Form."

24. "L'émigration clandestine, je l'ai d'abord vécue de l'autre côté de l'Occident. Du côté des pères absents et des mères restées seules dans la ruralité marocaine. De ce côté, nous vivons le doute permanent et la peur au ventre, et nous en arrivons à nous dire: qu'il nous oublie, qu'il ne revienne plus, qu'il n'envoie plus d'argent, que la terre étrangère "l'avale." Qu'elle l'avale par ce qu'elle a de beau : les rubans d'autoroutes, les yaourts au goût de noisette incomparable et les filles blondes et maigres aux yeux verts" (Kassari, "Note de présentation avant tournage").

25. "A l'esclavagisme colonialiste succède un esclavagisme moderne" (ibid.).

26. "D'abord, dans le jeu de la fiction et du documentaire puisque le film prolonge ce débat dans sa construction même: toute velléité de mise en scène dans L'enfant endormi est vite neutralisée par une irruption du réel dans la temporalité, le jeu des acteurs, le recours au parler quotidien des gens, l'amazigh en particulier. Contre-champ à un niveau dramaturgique, ensuite, puisque aux femmes absentes dans le film documentaire répond ici l'absence des hommes. Ils sont

les fantômes du hors champ qui hantent le rituel social, les échanges et le corps" (Bakrim, "Poétique hors-champ").

27. Pisters, "Refusal of Reproduction," 77.

28. De Lauretis, *Technologies of Gender*, 136.

29. Ibid., 141.

30. Shohat, *Taboo Memories*, 308.

31. Between the two video-viewing scenes, there is a video-shooting one, as Zeinab and Halima get ahold of a camcorder and film each other sending messages to their respective husbands [55:39–57:26]. Each performance is extremely brief: Zeinab catches Hassan up on the progress of the crop, and Halima asks Ahmed what the matter is with him. Halima has arranged herself beautifully, is wearing lovely earrings, in a clear effort to stage her appearance (unlike all the other characters we see on tape). Yet the women's attempt at communicating with their husbands is disastrous.

7. SELMA BACCAR'S TRANSVERGENT SPECTATORSHIP

1. As Tunisian filmmaker Nouri Bouzid stated, "The power of cinema lies in its ability to convey at once what is on-screen and what is off-screen" (Bouzid and Barlet, "La Leçon de cinéma de Nouri Bouzid."

2. After studying psychology in Switzerland for a couple of years, Selma Baccar enrolled in 1968 in a two-year program at the IFC (Institut Français du Cinéma/ French Institute of Cinema) in Paris. When she returned to Tunisia, the situation of cinema in her own country was still tenuous, and she found work as a film director's assistant for the RTT (Radio Télévision Tunisienne, the Tunisian television state company). She thus acquired practical experiential training for the next five years. This launched her multifaceted career in cinema as assistant to several Tunisian directors (e.g., Nejia Ben Mabrouk,

H'mida Ben Ammar, Othman Ben Salem, Nouri Bouzid), as woman director of the documentary-style film *Fatma 75* (1976), as producer of films and TV shows in Tunisia. Her unorthodox itinerary led her to a filmography with long lapses in between her various feature films, due to the political vagaries of Tunisia and/or the difficulties in getting the funds necessary to secure the making of a film from its scenario to its completion.

3. See Martin, "Tunisia."

4. "Le rôle d'avant-garde joué par quelques cinéastes tunisiens amateurs était le produit d'un contexte politique et social galvanisant, d'une vie associative intense et de la foi en des causes et des idéaux, au cours de cette période des années 60 et 70 dominées par la répression de la contestation estudiantine, le démantèlement des groupuscules marxistes de gauche et les atteintes graves portées à l'autonomie de la centrale syndicale. Des cinéastes amateurs étaient là pour critiquer, souvent sur le mode de la dérision, le pouvoir personnel de Habiba Bourguiba . . . [qui] monopolisait tout le secteur audiovisuel à des fins d'oligarchie narcissique" (Khélil, *Abécédaire du cinéma tunisien*).

5. Ibid., 29–31.

6. French filmmaker Agnès Varda coined this term for her own documentaries spliced with historical or whimsical recreations. *Menteur* ("liar" in French) points to the unreliability of the pseudo-neutral distance of the filmmaker to her *documentaire*.

7. Adopted on August 13, 1956, this new legal code guaranteed women's rights, while respecting the spirit of Islamic law. For instance, it outlawed polygamy, abolished men's right to renounce their wives (replaced by judicial divorce with equal rights for men and women), and gave women the right to vote.

8. Ayari et al., "Entretien avec Selma Baccar," 164.

9. Chikhaoui, "Une Affaire de Femmes/Stories of Women."

10. "Elle a choisi sa vie. Elle l'a vécue à plein, c'est cette aspiration à la vie qui est importante.... La danse du feu est une danse de mort: le spectacle de danse préfigure sa mort. Elle est comme ce papillon qui sait qu'il va se brûler s'il s'approche trop de la lumière, mais qui ne peut s'en empêcher" (Baccar, interviewed by Tahar Chikhaoui, *Ecrans d'Afrique,* no. 8 [second quarter 1994]: 13).

11. Box, "Outrageous Behavior," 78.

12. Prix de l'Agence de Coopération Culturelle et Technique (ACCT), Namur International Francophone Film Festival (1996), and Prix Spécial du Jury, Montreal "Vues d'Afrique" Festival (1996).

13. Selma Baccar, interview with the author, Tunis, January 22, 2006.

14. In passing, let's note that Tunis is not the only place outside Asia in which women were administered opium on a regular basis to soothe their bodily pains and sexual frustrations; the recorded medicinal use of it in the American community of ninetenth-century Nantucket makes this clear. My thanks go to poetess Beth Spires, who signaled the custom to me. In his *Letters from an American Farmer,* Hector St. Jean de Crevecoeur noted that the wives of sailors at sea consumed opium every morning: "A singular custom prevails here among the women, at which I was greatly surprised; and am really at a loss how to account for the original cause that has introduced in this primitive society so remarkable a fashion, or rather so extraordinary a want. They have adopted these many years, the Asiatic custom of taking a dose of opium every morning; and so deeply rooted is it, that they would be at a loss how to live without this indulgence; they would rather be deprived of any necessary than forego their favorite luxury" (*Letters from an American Farmer* [New York: Duffield, 1904], 211–212).

Similarly, American babies were administered various "soothing syrups" to calm their teething or other pains: "Mrs Winslow's Soothing Syrup," marketed in 1849, contained morphine and was perhaps the most famous one; it was available for sale in the United States at least until 1910, and in the UK until 1930. I am indebted to Carol A. Kennedy for this information.

15. Selma Baccar, interview with the author, Tunis, January 22, 2006.

16. Barlet, "Fleur d'oubli (Khochkhach) de Selma Baccar."

17. "Le film se situe dans les années 1940 bien que l'histoire réelle se soit passée au début du siècle. J'ai choisi de le situer là pour trouver une osmose, un parallèle entre le drame personnel de Zakia et le drame de la Tunisie." (The film takes place in the 1940s although the real story occurred at the beginning of the century. I chose to situate it at this moment in order to find an osmosis, a parallel between Zakia's personal drama and the drama of Tunisia.) Baccar, quoted in Amarger, "La Tunisie cultive sa mémoire."

18. Foucault, *Discipline and Punish,* 198.

19. Ibid, 199.

20. Ibid., 201.

21. Ibid., 200.

22. Metz, *The Imaginary Signifier,* 94.

23. "The exchange of seeing and being seen will be fractured in its centre, and its two disjointed halves allocated to different moments in time: another split. I never see my partner, but only his photograph" (ibid.).

24. Foucault, *Discipline and Punish,* 201–202.

25. Novak, Marcos "Speciation, Transvergence, Allogenesis," 66.

26. Selma Baccar, interviewed by the author, Tunis, January 22, 2006.

27. Ibid.

28. Ibid.

29. Chebbi, Abou El Kacem (1909–1934).

"Lorsqu'un jour le peuple veut vivre,
Force est pour le Destin de répondre,
Force est pour les ténèbres de se dissiper,
Force est pour les chaînes de se briser.

"La Volonté de Vivre," in Cherait, *Abou El Kacem Chebbi*, 49.

30. Such was the case for lawyer Mohamed Abbou, for instance, who was arrested on March 1, 2005, for having written an online article in which he had compared the conditions of Tunisian jails to those of Abu Ghraib. He started a first hunger strike in October 2005 and then another one on March 11, 2006, for several weeks. He was finally freed on July 24, 2007.

31. Fakhfakh, "Le cinéma tunisien."

CODA

1. "So he sent at once for Dunyazad and she came and kissed the ground between his hands, when he permitted her to take her seat near the foot of the couch. Then the King arose and did away with his bride's maidenhead and the three fell asleep. But when it was midnight Shahrazad awoke and signalled to her sister Dunyazad who sat up and said, 'Allah upon thee, O my sister, recite to us some new story, delightsome and delectable, wherewith to while away the waking hours of our later night.'" Burton, *The Arabian Nights*, 22.

2. Gauch, *Liberating Shahrazad*, 81–82.

3. Hence, for instance, the shocked reactions that greeted Raja Amari's *Red*

Satin in Tunis in 2002; Narjiss Nejjar's *al 'Ayun al jaffa/Les Yeux secs/Dry Eyes* (about a village of women prostitutes in the mountains) in Casablanca in 2003; Laila Marrakchi's *Marock* (a teenage love story across the Muslim and the Jewish communities against the backdrop of Casablanca's spoiled bourgeois youth) in Casablanca in 2005; and more recently, Raja Amari's *Al dowaha/Les Secrets/Secrets* (on three marginal women united by the secret of incest) in Tunis in 2010.

4. "Documenter les résistances, faire sauter les verrous, oser de nouvelles représentations de soi, déjouer le contrôle grandissant des intégristes, appeler au respect des femmes seraient ainsi les tendances actuelles des cinémas du Maghreb." Barlet, "Cinémas du Maghreb: tendances contemporaines."

5. The notion of *Cinéma d'intervention* (a cinema of intervention) was developed by Nouri Bouzid. See Bouzid and Hurst, "'Poupées d'argile': Entretien avec Nouri Bouzid."

6. For instance, Selma Baccar's *Khochkhach* (2006) or Tlatli's *Silences of the Palace* (1994) and *Season of Men* (2000) or Yasmine Kassari's *L'Enfant endormi/The Sleeping Child* (2004).

7. "Le film ordonne la vie. Il ordonne mon regard par rapport au sien." Noureddine Saïl, Plenary Session, JCC Colloquium, Tunis, October 2010. Noureddine Saïl heads the Centre du Cinéma Marocain (CCM).

8. Ibid.

Bibliography

Accad, Evelyne, ed. *Sexuality and War: Literary Masks of the Middle East.* New York: New York University Press, 1992.

Alion, Yves, ed. *"Les Silences du palais:* Un film de Moufida Tlatli." *L'Avant-Scène Cinéma* 536 (November 2004).

Amarger, Michel. "La Tunisie cultive sa mémoire. Rencontre avec Selma Baccar, réalisatrice de *Fleur d'oubli* (2005), fiction." *Africiné* (October 7, 2007). http://www.africine.org/index .php?menu=art&no=6968.

Anderson, Benedict. *Imagined Communities: Reflections on the Origin and Spread of Nationalism.* Rev. ed. New York: Verso, 2006.

Apter, Emily. *Continental Drift: From National Characters to Virtual Subjects.* Chicago: University of Chicago Press, 1999.

Aresu, Bernard. "(D)écrire, entendre l'écran: *L'Amour, la fantasia.*" In *Littérature et Cinéma en Afrique Francophone: Ousmane Sembène et Assia Djebar,* ed. Sada Niang, 209–224. Paris: L'Harmattan, 1996.

Armes, Roy. *Postcolonial Images: Studies in North African Film.* Bloomington: Indiana University Press, 2005.

———. *African Filmmaking North and South of the Sahara.* Bloomington: Indiana University Press, 2006.

Ashcroft, Bill. *Post-colonial Transformation.* London: Routledge, 2001.

Ayari, Farida, et al. "Entretien avec Selma Baccar." In *"Cinémas du Maghreb,* ed. Guy Hennebelle, special issue, *CinémAction* 14 (1981): 162–166.

Baccar, Selma. Interview by Tahar Chikhaoui. *Ecrans d'Afrique,* no. 8 (2nd quarter 1994).

Bachy, Victor. *Le Cinéma du Tunisie.* Tunis: Société Tunisienne de Diffusion, 1978.

Badram, Margot, and Miriam Cooke, eds. *Opening the Gates: An Anthology of Arab Feminist Writing.* 2nd ed. Bloomington: Indiana University Press, 2004.

Bakrim, Mohamed. "Poétique hors-champ. *L'Enfant Endormi,* de Yasmine Kassari (Maroc)." *Africiné* (June 19, 2005). http://www.africine.org/?menu= art&no=6162.

Barlet, Olivier. *African Cinemas: Decolonizing the Gaze.* Trans. Chris Turner. London: Zed Books, 2000.

———. "A propos de *Bedwin Hacker* – Entretien avec Nadia El Fani." *Africultures*

(May 22, 2002). http://www.africultures
.com/index.asp?menu=revue_affiche_
article&no=2511.

———. "Cinémas du Maghreb: tendances
contemporaines."*Africultures* (April 29,
2009).
http://www.africultures.com/php/index
.php?nav=article&no=8622.

———. "*Enfant endormi* (L') Yasmine
Kassari." *Africultures 2005.* http://www
.africultures.com/php/index.php?nav=
film&no=970.

———. "Fleur d'oubli (Khochkhach) de
Selma Baccar." *Africultures* (June 1,
2006). http://www.africultures.com/
index.asp?menu=affiche_article&no=
4437.

Barthes, Roland. "L'Effet de réel." *Communications* 11 (1968): 84–89.

———. *La Chambre claire: Note sur la
photographie.* Paris: Éditions de l'Étoile,
1980.

Bedjaoui, Ahmed. "Assia Djebar,
l'immortelle." *El-Watan,* July 21, 2005.

Benali, Abdelkader. *Le Cinéma colonial
au Maghreb.* Paris: Éditions du Cerf,
1998.

Benasci-Lancou, Fatima. *Fille de Harki/
Daughter of a Harki.* Paris: Édition de
l'Atelier, 2003.

Benidir, Azîz. *Inititaion à la musique
arabo-musulmane.* Beyrouth: Les Editions Al-Bouraq, 1998.

Benlyazid, Farida. "The Gate of Heaven
Is Open" (excerpt of the script). Trans.
Miriam Cooke. In *Opening the Gates:
An Anthology of Arab Feminist Writ-
ing,* ed. Margot Badram and Miriam
Cooke, 296–303. 2nd ed. Bloomington:
Indiana University Press, 2004.

———. "Le Cinéma au féminin." *Quad-
erns de la Mediterrània* 7:221–224, 2006.

Benlyazid, Farida, Hamid Aïdouni, Igho-
dane, Bouchta Farqzaid, Fatim, Moulay
Driss Jaïdi, Suzanne Gauch. *L'Oeuvre
cinématographique de Farida Belyazid.*
Rabat: Publications de l'Association

Marocaine des Critiques de Cinéma,
2010.

Ben Miled, Emna. *Les Tunisiennes ont-elles
une histoire?* Tunis: Dar Ashraf, CERES
and Alif les éditions de la Méditerranée, 1998.

Ben Salama, Mohand, Maryse Léon, and
Monique Martineau. "Assia Djebar: J'ai
recherché un langage musical." Ed. Guy
Hennebelle. In "Cinémas du Maghreb,"
special issue, *CinémAction* 14 (1981):
105–109.

Bensmaïa, Reda. "La Nouba des femmes du
Mont Chenoua: Introduction à l'œuvre
fragmentale cinématographique." In
*Littérature et cinéma en Afrique fran-
cophone: Ousmane Sembène et Assia
Djebar,* ed. Sada Niang, 161–177. Paris:
L'Harmattan, 1996.

———. "Une rhétorique trop souvent
codée." In "Cinémas du Maghreb,"
special issue, *CinémAction* 14 (1981):
55–61.

Bhabha, Homi K. *The Location of Culture.*
New York: Routledge, 1993.

Bouchoucha, Dora. "Actes du Colloque
de Namur: 'La diffusion, promotion et
distribution des films francophones:
réalités et perspectives.'" *Cinemas-
francophones.org.* 2003. http://www
.cinemasfrancophones.org/upload/
actes_colloque_namur_2003.doc.

Bouhdiba, Abdelwahab. *La Sexualité en
Islam.* Paris: PUF, 2003 [1975].

Bourget, Carine. "Traditions orales et
littéraires dans *Une Porte sur le ciel* de
Farida Benlyazid." *French Review* 81,
no. 4 (2008): 752–763.

Bouzid, Nouri, and Olivier Barlet. "La
Leçon de cinéma de Nouri Bouzid."
Africultures (April 6, 2006). http://
www.africultures.com/php/index
.php?nav=article&no=4385.

Bouzid, Nouri, and Heike Hurst. "'Poupées d'argile': Entretien avec Nouri
Bouzid." *Le Monde Libertaire* (September 30–October 6, 2004). http://

ml.federation-anarchiste.org/ar ticle2984.html

Box, Laura Chakravarty. "Outrageous Behavior: Women's Public Performance in North Africa." *Meridians: Feminism, Race, Transnationalism* 6, no. 2 (2006): 78–92.

———. *Strategies of Resistance in the Dramatic Texts of North African Women: A Body of Works.* New York: Routledge, 2005.

Brahimi, Denise. *50 ans de cinéma maghrébin.* Paris: Minerve, 2009.

Braudel, Fernand. *Les Mémoires de la Méditerranée.* Paris: Editions de Fallois, 1998.

Bruzzi, Stella. *Undressing Cinema: Clothing and Identity in the Movies.* London: Routledge, 1997.

Burton, Richard F., trans. *The Arabian Nights: Tales from a Thousand and One Nights.* New York: Modern Library, 2001 [1885].

Caillé, Patricia. "Le Maroc, l'Algérie et la Tunisie des réalisatrices ou la construction du Maghreb dans un contexte postcolonial." In *Maghreb et Sciences Sociales,* ed. Pierre-Noël Denieuil, 261–277. Tunis: IRMC, 2010.

Calle-Gruber, Mireille. *Assia Djebar ou la résistance de l'écriture: Regards d'un écrivain algérien.* Paris: Maisonneuve & Larose, 2001.

Camps, Gabriel. *Des Rives de la Méditerranée aux marges méridionales du Sahara: Les Berbères.* Tunis: ÉdiSud, 1996.

Carrière, Christophe. "Pour l'honneur de l'Algérie." *L'Express,* January 2, 2003.

Carter, Sandra Gayle. "Farida Benlyazid's Moroccan Women." *Quarterly Review of Film and Video* 17, no. 4 (2000): 343–370.

———. *What Moroccan Cinema? A Historical and Critical Study, 1956–2006.* Lanham, Md.: Lexington Books, 2009.

Chamkhi, Sonia. *Cinéma tunisien nouveau – Parcours autres.* Tunis: Sud Éditions, 2002.

———. *Le Cinéma Tunisien à la lumière de la modernité: Études critiques de films tunisiens 1996–2006.* Tunis: Centre de Publication Universitaire La Manouba, 2009.

———. "Films de cinéastes femmes tunisiennes: Du discours social au discours de l'intime ou la démystification de la violence" [Films by Tunisian Women Filmmakers: From Social Discourse to the Discourse of the Private, or On the Demystification of Violence]. *Maghreb, des réalisatrices et leurs films* Colloquium, St. Denis, France, April 9, 2010.

Charpentier, Orianne. "'Dire la violence, toutes les violences . . .' Au-delà de la peur et de la douleur, *Rachida,* premier film de Yamina Bachir-Chouikh." *Le Monde,* January 8, 2003.

Chebel, Malek. *La Féminisation du monde: Essai sur les Mille et une nuits.* Paris: Payot, 1996.

———. *La Formation de l'identité politique.* Paris: Payot, 1998.

———. *Le Corps en Islam.* Paris: PUF, 1999 [1984].

———. *L'Esprit de sérail: Mythe et pratiques sexuels au Maghreb.* Edition revue et corrigée. Paris: Petite Bibliothèque Payot, 2003 [1988].

Chenchabi, Rachid. "Le Cinéma maghrébin, une dimension francophone?" *Französisch Heute* 15, no. 2 (1984): 224–232.

Cheniki, Ahmed. "Théâtre algérien, Itinéraires et tendances." Doctoral thesis, Sorbonne University, Paris IV, 1993. http://www.limag.refer.org/Theses/Cheniki.htm#_ftnref122.

Cherait, Abderrazak, ed. *Abou El Kacem Chebbi.* Tunis: Apollonia Éditions, 2002.

Chikhaoui, Tahar. "Maghreb: de l'épopée au regard intime." In *Au Sud du cinéma: Films d'Afrique, d'Asie et d'Amérique Latine,* ed. Jean-Michel Frodon, 22–39.

Paris: Cahiers du Cinéma/Arte Editions, 2004.

———. "Une Affaire de Femmes/Stories of Women." *Africultures* 8 (Summer 1994). http://www.africultures.com/revue_africultures/articles/ecrans_afrique/8/8_08.pdf.

Chion, Michel. *La Voix au cinéma.* Paris: Cahiers du Cinéma, Editions de l'Etoile, 1993.

Clerc, Jeanne-Marie. "La Guerre d'Algérie dans l'œuvre cinématographique et littéraire d'Assia Djebar." *L'Esprit Créateur* 41, no. 4 (2001): 89–100.

Deeb, Lara. *An Enchanted Modern: Gender and Public Piety in Shi'i Lebanon.* Princeton, N.J.: Princeton University Press, 2006.

De Franceschi, Leonardo. "Entre la maison et la ville, la lutte pour l'espace social." In "Cinémas du Maghreb," ed. Michel Serceau, special issue, *CinémAction* 111 (2004): 62–66.

Déjeux, Jean. *Assia Djebar: Romancière algérienne, cinéaste arabe.* Sherbrooke, Quebec: Editions Naaman, 1984.

De Lauretis, Teresa. *Technologies of Gender.* Bloomington: Indiana University Press, 1987.

Deleuze, Gilles, and Félix Guattari. *Capitalisme et Schizophrénie.* vol. 2: *Mille plateaux.* Paris: Editions de Minuit, 1980.

———. *A Thousand Plateaus: Capitalism and Schizophrenia.* Trans. Brian Massumi. Minneapolis: University of Minnesota Press, 1987 [1980].

Diawara, Mantha. *African Cinema: Politics and Culture.* Bloomington: Indiana University Press, 1992.

Djebar, Assia. *Femmes d'Alger dans leurs appartements.* Paris: Éditions des Femmes, 1980.

———. "Idiome de l'Exil et langue de l'irréductibilité" (speech given when she received the Peace Prize from German Publishers and Booksellers). Frankfurt, October 2000. http://remue.net/spip.php?article683.

———. *La femme sans sépulture.* Paris: Albin Michel, 2002.

———. *L'Amour, la fantasia.* Paris: Jean-Claude Lattès, 1985.

———. *Oran, Langue morte.* Arles, France: Actes Sud, 1997.

———. *The Tongue's Blood Never Runs Dry.* Trans. Tegan Raleigh. New York: Seven Stories Press, 2007.

Donadey, Anne. "Between Amnesia and Anamnesis: Re-Membering the Fractures of Colonial History." STCL 23, no. 1 (1999): 111–116.

———. *Recasting Postcolonialism: Women Writing between Worlds.* Portsmouth, N.H.: Heinemann, 2001.

Dönmez-Colin, Gönül. *The Cinema of North Africa and the Middle East.* London: Wallflower Press, 2007.

———. *Women, Islam and Cinema.* London: Reaktion Books, 2004.

Durand, Gilbert. *Les Structures anthropologiques de l'imaginaire.* 10th ed. Paris: Dunot, 1985.

Dwyer, Kevin. *Beyond Casablanca: M. A. Tazi and the Adventure of Moroccan Cinema.* Bloomington: Indiana University Press, 2004.

———. "Moroccan Cinema and the Promotion of Culture." *Journal of North African Studies* 12, no. 3 (September 2007): 277–286.

Dyer, Richard. *White: Essays on Race and Culture.* London: Routledge, 1997.

Elaji, Sanaa. "Société. Ragued, le mythe jamais endormi." *TelQuel Online,* no. 290 (September 28, 2007). http://www.telquel-online.com/290/maroc6_290.shtml.

Esposito, Maria. "Stay Close to Reality." *World Socialist Web Site* (June 9, 2004). http://www.wsws.org/articles/2004/jun2004/pont-jo9.shtml.

Fakhfakh, Abdelfatteh. "Le cinéma tunisien, un cinéma en renouvellement de génération. En marge de la 21ème session des Journées Cinématographiques de Carthage (11–18 novembre 2006)." *Le Cinéphile* (Tunis) – *Dossier JCC 2006* (June 1, 2007). http://www.africine.org/?menu=art&no=6607.

Fallaux, Émile, Malu Halasa, and Nupu Press, eds. *True Variety: Funding the Art of World Cinema.* Rotterdam: International Film Festival Rotterdam, 2003.

Fanon, Frantz. "Algeria Unveiled." In *A Dying Colonialism,* trans. Haakon Chevalier, 35–63. New York: Grove Press, 1965.

———. *L'an V de la révolution algérienne.* Paris: La Découverte, 2001 [1959].

Fischer, Lucy. *Cinematernity: Film, Motherhood, Genre.* Princeton, N.J.: Princeton University Press, 1996.

Foucault, Michel. *Discipline and Punish: The Birth of the Prison.* Trans. Alan Sheridan. New York: Random House, 1977 [1975].

———. "Discourse on Language." In *The Archaeology of Knowledge and the Discourse on Language,* 215–237. Trans. A. M. Sheridan-Smith. London: Pantheon, 1972.

Freud, Sigmund. "The 'Uncanny.'" In *The Complete Psychological Works of Sigmund Freud,* 17:217–256. Trans. and ed. James Strachey. London: Hogarth Press, 1964.

Gabous, Abdelkrim. *Silence, Elles tournent! Les femmes et le cinéma tunisien.* Tunis: Cérès Éditions, 1998.

Ganley, Elaine. "Algerians Transform Nation's Agony into Art." *LA Times,* March 21, 2003, E16.

Gates, Henry Louis, Jr. *The Signifying Monkey: A Theory of African-American Literary Criticism.* Oxford: Oxford University Press, 1988.

Gauch, Suzanne. *Liberating Shahrazad: Feminism, Postcolonialism, and Islam.* Minneapolis: University of Minnesota Press, 2007.

Gauvin, Lise. "Territoires des langues. Assia Djebar." In *L'Ecrivain francophone à la croisée des langues. Entretien,* 17–34. Paris: Karthala, 1997.

Geesey, Patricia. "Violent Days: Algerian Women Writers and the Civil Crisis." *International Fiction Review* 27, nos. 1–2 (2000): 48–59.

Givanni, June, ed. *Symbolic Narratives/African Cinema: Audiences, Theory and the Moving Image.* London: British Film Institute, 2000.

Gugler, Josef. *African Film: Re-imagining a Continent.* Bloomington: Indiana University Press, 2003.

———, ed. *Film in the Middle East and North Africa: Creative Dissidence.* Austin: University of Texas Press, 2011.

Guneratne, Anthony R., and Wimal Dissanayake, eds. *Rethinking Third Cinema.* New York: Routledge, 2003.

Hadda, Mohamed Hédi. *Bab el Web.* June 16, 2002. http://www.bab-el-web.com/archives/article.asp?ID=5214.

Hadj-Moussa, Ratiba. *Le Corps. L'histoire, le territoire: Les rapports de genre dans le cinéma algérien.* Paris: Publisud, 1994.

———. "Marginality and Ordinary Memory: Body Centrality and the Plea for Recognition in Recent Algerian Films." *Journal of North African Studies* 13, no. 2 (2008): 187–199.

Haggar, Nabil El, ed. *La Méditerranée des femmes.* Paris: L'Harmattan, 1998.

Halimi, Gisèle. *Djamila Boupacha.* Trans. Peter Green. London: Deutsch & Weidenfield & Nicolson, 1962.

Hibri, Azizah Al, ed. *Women and Islam.* Oxford: Pergamon Press, 1982.

Higbee, William. "Beyond the (Trans-) National: Towards a Cinema of Transvergence in Post-Colonial and Diasporic Francophone Cinema(S)." *Studies in French Cinema* 7, no. 2 (2007): 79–91.

Higbee, William, and Song Hwee Lim. "Concepts of Transnational Cinema: Towards a Critical Transnationalism in Film Studies." *Transnational Cinemas* 1, no. 1 (2010): 7–21.

Hillauer, Rebecca. *Encyclopedia of Arab Women Filmmakers*. Cairo: American University in Cairo Press, 2005.

Hochberg, Gil. "National Allegories and the Emergence of Female Voice in Moufida Tlatli's *Les Silences du palais*." *Third Text: Cinema in Muslim Societies* 14, no. 50 (2000): 33–44.

Jacquemond, Richard. *Conscience of the Nation: Writers, State and Society in Modern Egypt*. Cairo: American University in Cairo Press, 2008.

Kaplan, Caren, and Inderpal Grewal, eds. *Scattered Hegemonies: Postmodernity and Transnational Practices*. Minneapolis: University of Minnesota Press, 1994.

Kaplan, Caren, Norma Alarcón, and Minoo Moallem, eds. *Between Woman and Nation: Nationalisms, Transational Feminisms, and the State*. Durham, N.C.: Duke University Press, 1999.

Kassari, Yasmine. "Note de présentation avant tournage." In *Doc Diffusion France*. http://docdif.online.fr/qlh/note_pres_qlhp.htm.

Kateb, Kamel. "The Expansion of Access to Education and the Demography of Algeria." Background paper prepared for the Education for All Global Monitoring Report 2003/4, *Gender and Education for All: The Leap to Equality*. UNESCO, 2003. http://unesdoc.UNESCO.org/images/0014/001467/146791e.pdf.

Kéfi, Ridha. "Au Pays du dialogue interreligieux." *Jeune Afrique*, June 4, 2005.

Khabash, Wadi El. "Un cinéma soufi? Islam, ombres, modernité." *Écritures dans*

les cinémas d'Afrique noire,* ed. D'Béri Boulou Ebanda, special issue, *CiNéMAs* (Fall 2000).

Khannous, Touria. "Strategies of Representation and Postcolonial Identities in North African Women's Cinema." *Journal x: A Journal of Culture and Criticism* 1, no. 6 (2001): 49–61.

———. "The Subaltern Speaks: Assia Djebar's *La Nouba*." *Film Criticism* 26, no. 2 (2002): 41–61.

Khélil, Hédi. *Abécédaire du cinéma tunisien*. Tunis, 2006.

———. *Le Parcours et la trace: Témoignages et documents sur le cinéma tunisien*. Tunis: Médiacom, 2002.

Khlifi, Omar. *L'Histoire du cinéma en Tunisie*. Tunis: Société Tunisienne de Diffusion, 1970.

Knysh, Alexander D. *Islamic Mysticism: A Short History*. Leiden, Netherlands: Brill, 2000.

Lamrini, Rida. *Les Puissants de Casablanca*. Rabat: Editions Marsan, 1999.

Larguèche, Dalenda, and Abdelhamid Larguèche. *Marginales en terre d'Islam*. Tunis: Cérès Éditions, 2005 [1992].

Laviosa, Flavia, ed. *Visions of Struggle in Women's Filmmaking in the Mediterranean*. New York: Palgrave MacMillan, 2010.

Lazreg, Marnia. *The Eloquence of Silence: Algerian Women in Question*. New York: Routledge, 1994.

———. "Islamism and the Recolonization of Algeria." *Arab Studies Quarterly* 20, no. 2 (1998): 43–59.

Leclère, Thierry. "Elle filme la peur." *Télérama*, January 8, 2003.

Macleod, Arlene Elowe. *Accommodating Protest: Working Women, the New Veiling, and Change in Cairo*. New York: Columbia University Press, 1991.

Malkmus, Lizbeth, and Roy Armes. *Arab and African Filmmaking*. London: Zed Books, 1991.

Marciniak, Katarzyna, Anikó Imre, and Áine O'Healy, eds. *Transnational Feminism in Film and Media*. New York: Palgrave MacMillan, 2007.

Maréchaux, Cerise. "Portrait. Yasmine Kassari. Au-delà de la fiction." *Telquel Online*, no. 261 (March 23, 2007). http://www.telquel-online.com/261/arts1_261.shtml.

Marks, Laura. *The Skin of the Film: Intercultural Cinema, Embodiment, and the Senses*. Durham, N.C.: Duke University Press, 2000.

———. "Thinking Multisensory Culture." *Paragraph* 31, no. 2 (July 2008): 127–137.

———. *Touch: Sensuous Theory and Multisensory Media*. Minneapolis: University of Minnesota Press, 2002.

Martin, Florence. "*Bab al-Sama Maftouh/A Door to the Sky*, Farida Benlyazid, Morocco/Tunisia/France, 1988." In *The Cinema of North Africa and the Middle-East*, ed. Gönül Dönmez-Colin, 123–132. London: Wallflower Press, 2007.

———. "Cinéma and State in Tunisia." In *Film in the Middle East and North Africa: Creative Dissidence*, ed. Josef Gugler, 271–283. Austin: University of Texas Press, 2011.

———. "History 'Re-lit': The Poetics of Memory in Assia Djebar's *Une femme sans sépulture*." In *Memory, Empire, and Postcolonialism: Legacies of French Colonialism*, ed. Alec Hargreaves, 160–173. Lanham, Md.: Lexington Books, 2005.

———. "*Satin rouge* de Raja Amari: l'expression féminine sens dessus dessous." *Expressions Maghrébines* 5, no. 1 (2006): 53–65.

———. "Silence and Scream: Moufida Tlatli's Cinematic Suite." *Studies in French Cinema* 4, no. 3 (2004): 175–185.

———. "Transvergence and Cultural Detours: Nadia El Fani's *Bedwin Hacker* (2002)." *Studies in French Cinema* 7, no. 2 (2007): 119–129.

———. "Tunisia." In *Small National Cinema*, ed. Duncan Petrie and Mette Hjort, 213–228. Edinburgh: Edinburgh University Press, 2007.

———. "The Wiles of Maghrebi Women's Cinema." In *Visions of Struggle in Women's Filmmaking in the Mediterranean*, ed. Flavia Laviosa, 23–41. New York: Palgrave MacMillan, 2010.

Martin, Florence, and Mark Ingram. "Voices Unveiled: *Mémoires d'immigrés. L'héritage maghrébin*." In *Moving Pictures/Moving Cultures: Cinemas of Exile and Migration*, ed. Eva Rueschmann, 105–120. Jackson: University of Mississippi Press, 2003.

Méreuze, Didier. "Chronique algérienne des années de peur." *La Croix*, January 8, 2003.

Mernissi, Fatima. *Dreams of Trespass: Tales of a Harem Girlhood*. New York: Addison-Wesley, 1994.

———. *Women's Rebellion and Islamic Memory*. London: Zed Books, 1996.

Metz, Christian. *The Imaginary Signifier: Psychoanalysis and the Cinema*. Trans. Cecilia Britton et al. Bloomington: Indiana University Press, 1982 [1975].

Mohanty, Chandra Talpade. "Cartographies of Struggle: Feminist Scholarship and Colonial Discourses." In *Third World Women and the Politics of Feminism*, ed. Chandra Talpade Mohanty, Ann Russo, and Lourdes Torres, 1–50. Bloomington: Indiana University Press, 1991.

Mortimer, Mildred, ed. *Maghrebian Mosaic: A Literature in Transition*. Boulder, Colo.: Lynne Rienner Publishers, 2001.

Moura, Jean-Marc. "La Francophonie littéraire: quelle diversité et quelle cohérence?" *L'Année Francophone Internationale*, Actes du Colloque, 2001. http:// www.ulaval.ca/afi/colloques/colloque2001/actes/textes/moura.htm.

———. *Littératures francophones et théorie postcoloniale.* Paris: PUF, 1999.

Mulvey, Laura. "Moving Bodies: Interview with Moufida Tlatli." *Sight and Sound.* 5, no. 3 (1995): 18–20.

———. *Visual and Other Pleasures.* Bloomington: Indiana University Press, 1989.

Naef, Silvia. *Y a-t-il une 'question de l'image' en Islam?* Paris: Téraèdre, 2004.

Naficy, Hamid. *An Accented Cinema: Exilic and Diasporic Filmmaking.* Princeton, N.J.: Princeton University Press, 2001.

Niang, Sada, ed. *Littérature et cinéma en Afrique francophone: Ousmane Sembène et Assia Djebar.* Paris: L'Harmattan, 1996.

Nicosia, Aldo. *Il Cinema arabo.* Rome: Carocci editore, 2007.

Nietzsche, Friedrich. *Die Götzen-Dämmerung – Twilight of the Idols.* Trans. Walter Kaufmann and R.J. Hollingdale. 1968 [1895]. http://www.handprint .com/SC/NIE/GotDamer.html.

Nora, Pierre. *Les Lieux de mémoire.* Paris: Gallimard, 1997.

Novak, Marcos. "Speciation, Transvergence, Allogenesis: Notes on the Production of the Alien." *Architectural Design* 72, no. 3 (2002): 65–71. http:// www.mat.ucsb.edu/~marcos/trans vergence.pdf.

———. *The World Technology Network.* http://www.mat.ucsb.edu/~marcos/ transvergence.pdf.

———. "Trans Terra Form: Liquid Architectures and the Loss of Inscription." 1997. http://www.krcf.org/ krcfhome/PRINT/nonlocated/ nlonline/nonMarcos.html.

Omri, Mohamed-Salah. "History, Literature, and Settler Colonialism in North Africa." *Modern Language Quarterly 66,* no. 3 (2005): 273–298.

———. *Nationalism, Islam and World Literature: Sites of Confluence in the Writings of Mahmud al-Mas'adi.* London:

Routledge, 2006.

Orlando, Valérie K. *Francophone Voices of the "New" Morocco in Film and Print: (Re)presenting a Society in Transition.* New York: Palgrave McMillan, 2009.

Ovid. *Metamorphoses.* Trans. Frank Justus Miller. London: Putnam, 1925.

Pallister, Janis L., and Ruth A. Hottell. *Francophone Women Film Directors: A Guide.* Madison, N.J.: Fairleigh Dickinson University Press, 2005.

Pisters, Patricia. "Refusal of Reproduction: Paradoxes of Becoming-Woman in Transnational Moroccan Filmmaking." In *Transnational Feminism in Film and Media,* ed. Katarzyna Marciniak, Anikó Imre, and Áine O'Healy, ch. 4. New York: Palgrave MacMillan, 2007.

Ramanathan, Geetha. *Feminist Auteurs: Reading Women's Films.* London: Wallflower Press, 2006.

Renard, John. *Seven Doors to Islam: Spirituality and the Religious Life of Muslims.* Berkeley: University of California Press, 1996.

Rodríguez Magda, Rosa María. "Globalization as Transmodern Totality." In *Transmodernidad.* Barcelona: Anthropos, 2004. Also at http://transmodern theory.blogspot.com/.

Saïd, S. F. "New Cinema from the Islamic World." *Wasafiri* 43 (2004): 19–22.

Salhi, Kamal. "Assia Djebar Speaking: An Interview with Assia Djebar." *International Journal of Francophone Studies 2,* no. 3 (1999): 168–182.

Salhi, Zahia Smail. "Maghrebi Women Film-Makers and the Challenge of Modernity: Breaking Women's Silence." In *Women and Media in the Middle East: Power through Self-Expression,* ed. Naomi Sakr, 53–71. London: I. B. Tauris, 2004.

Schäfer, Isabel. "Le Dialogue des images entre l'Europe et la Méditerranée: *Entre "méditerranéisme et réalité." Eurorient,* no.10 (*Cinéma et Monde musulman: Cultures et interdits*) (2001): 91–112.

Schipper, Mineke. *Imagining Insiders: Africa and the Question of Belonging.* London: Cassell, 1999.

Serceau, Michel, ed. *Cinémas du Maghreb,* special issue, *CinémAction* 111 (2004).

Shafik, Viola. *Arab Cinema: History and Cultural Identity.* Cairo: American University in Cairo Press, 1998.

Sherzer, Dina, ed. *Cinema, Colonialism, Postcolonialism: Perspectives from the French and Francophone Worlds.* Austin: University of Texas Press, 1996.

———. "Remembrance of Things Past: *Les Silences du Palais* by Moufida Tlatli." *South Central Review* 17, no. 3 (2000): 50–59.

Shohat, Ella. "Framing Post-Third-Worldist Culture: Gender and Nation in Middle Eastern North African Film and Video." *Jouvert* 1, no. 1 (1997). http:// english.chass.ncsu.edu/jouvert/vii1/ SHOHAT.HTM.

———. *Taboo Memories: Diasporic Voices.* Durham, N.C.: Duke University Press, 2006.

Shohat, Ella, and Robert Stam, eds. *Multiculturalism, Postcoloniality, and Transnational Media.* New Brunswick, N.J.: Rutgers University Press, 2003.

Silverman, Kaja. *The Acoustic Mirror: The Female Voice in Psychoanalysis and Cinema.* Bloomington: Indiana University Press, 1988.

Simarksi, Lynn Teo. "North African Film through North African Eyes." *Saudi ARAMCO World* 43, no. 1 (January–February 1992): 30–35. http://www .saudiaramcoworld.com/issue/199201/ through.north.african.eyes.htm.

Sotinel, Thomas. "Productrice, réalisatice et actrice face aux préjugés." *Le Monde,* April 24, 2002.

Spaas, Lieve, ed. *Echoes of Narcissus.* New York: Bergham Books, 2000.

———. *The Francophone Film: A Struggle for Identity.* Manchester, UK: Manchester University Press, 2000.

Spivak, Gayatri. "Can the Subaltern Speak?" In *Marxism and the Interpretation of Culture,* ed. Cary Nelson and Larry Grossberg, 271–313. Chicago: University of Illinois Press, 1988.

———. "Echo." In *The Spivak Reader,* ed. Donna Landry and Gerald MacLean, 175–202. New York: Routledge, 1996.

Stam, Robert. "Fanon, Algeria, and the Cinema: The Politics of Identification." In *Multiculturalism, Postcoloniality, and Transnational Media,* ed. Ella Shohat and Robert Stam, 18–43. New Brunswick, N.J.: Rutgers University Press, 2003.

Stora, Benjamin. *Algeria: A Short History.* Trans. Jane Marie Todd. Ithaca: Cornell University Press, 2001.

———. "Constantine, la Jérusalem du Maghreb." Conference at the Museum of Judaïc Art and History, Paris, March 14, 2010. http://www.constantine-hier-aujourdhui.fr/images/divers/ conference_b_stora.pdf.

———. *La Gangrène et l'oubli: la mémoire de la guerre d'Algérie.* Paris: La Découverte, 1992.

———. *La Guerre invisible:* Algérie, années 1990. Paris: Presses de Sciences Po, 2001.

Suchoff, Benjamin, ed. *Béla Bartók Essays.* London: Faber & Faber, 1976.

Tarr, Carrie. *Reframing Difference: Beur and Banlieue Filmmaking in France.* Manchester, UK: Manchester University Press, 2005.

Tebib, Elias. "Panorama des cinémas maghrébins." *Notre Librairie* 149 (2002): 60–66.

Triki, Fethi. "Transculturalité et convivialité." In *La Presse* (Tunis), October 11, 2005. Cahiers Culturels I & II.

Vázquez, Angel. *La vida perra de Juanita Narboni.* Barcelona: Planeta, 1976.

Woodhull, Winnifred. "Postcolonial Thought and Culture in Francophone North Africa." In *Francophone Postcolonial Studies: A Critical Introduction,* ed. Charles Fordsick and David Murphy, 211–220. London: Arnold,2003.

Zahi, Farid Al. "'The Possessed' or the Symbolic Body in Moroccan Cinema." In "Arab Cinematics: Toward the New and the Alternative." Trans. Tahia Khaled Abdel Nasser. Special issue, *Alif: A Journal of Comparative Poetics,* no. 15 (1995): 267–271.

Zimra, Clarisse. "Sounding off the Absent Body: Intertextual Resonances in 'La femme qui pleure' and 'La femme en morceaux.'" *Research in African Literatures* 30, no. 3 (1999): 108–124.

Zuhur, Sherifa, ed. *Images of Enchantment: Visual and Performing Arts of the Middle East.* Cairo: American University in Cairo Press, 1998.

Index

FLORENCE MARTIN is Professor of French and Francophone Literature and Cinema at Goucher College in Baltimore and Associate Editor of *Studies in French Cinema.* She has published articles on cinema
internationally and is author of *Bessie Smith,* of *De la Guyane à la diaspora africaine* (with Isabelle Favre), and of *A vous de voir!* (with Maryse
Fauvel and Stéphanie Martin).

Lightning Source UK Ltd.
Milton Keynes UK
UKHW020428110119
335388UK00017B/736/P